THE CALL OF THE
WILD + FREE

THE CALL OF THE
WILD + FREE

Reclaiming Wonder in Your Child's Education

AINSLEY ARMENT

HarperOne

Photography:
Pages ii–iii: Rachel Kovac | @rachelstitchedtogether
Pages iv–v, 50: Kirsty Larmour | @kirstylarmour
Pages vi, 122, 132, 230: Bethany Douglass | @cloisteredaway
Pages viii–1, 106, 148, 226, 286: Naomi Ovando | @3bebesmama
Pages 2, 22: Michelle Garrels | @ellegarrels
Pages 10, 34, 62–63, 64, 92, 146–147, 188, 206, 224–225: Kristin Rogers | @kristinrogers
Pages 78, 270, 298: Hannah Mayo | @hmayophoto
Pages 156, 252: Rachael Alsbury | @fromfaye

Illustrations:
Recurring trees: pikolorante | Shutterstock
Pages 4, 41, 74 (paper and pen), 95, 98, 153, 161, 162, 166, 202, 217 (crayon): Paper Sphinx | Creative Market
Pages 7, 24, 31, 36, 53, 68, 73, 87, 101, 102, 108, 113, 119, 126, 141, 152, 154, 158, 165, 168, 172, 176, 183, 194, 197, 200, 208, 217 (camper and taxi), 228, 238, 246, 250, 255, 272, 285, 289, 295, 302: Graphic Box | Creative Market
Pages 18, 71, 74 (clipboard), 90, 125, 135, 151, 171, 180, 232, 280: Dainty Doll Art | Creative Market
Pages 56, 282: YesFoxy | Creative Market
Page 313: Janet Evans-Scanlon

FIRST EDITION

Designed by Janet Evans-Scanlon

Library of Congress Cataloging-in-Publication Data

Names: Arment, Ainsley, author.
Title: The call of the wild and free : reclaiming wonder in your child's education / Ainsley Arment.
Description: First edition. | San Francisco : HarperOne, 2019 | Includes bibliographical references. | Summary: "Speaking to the growing national trend, The Call of the Wild and Free equips families to provide quality homeschool education, and encourages all parents and caregivers to raise kids to experience the adventure, freedom, and wonder of childhood"—Provided by publisher.
Identifiers: LCCN 2019019923 | ISBN 9780062916518 (hardcover) | ISBN 9780062916532 (ebook)
Subjects: LCSH: Home schooling. | Education—Parent participation. | Child rearing.
Classification: LCC LC40 .A76 2019 | DDC 372.1042/42—dc23
LC record available at https://lccn.loc.gov/2019019923

19 20 21 22 23   WOR   10 9 8 7 6 5 4 3 2 1

To the one

who caught me reading

long after bedtime

and brought me a flashlight

instead of taking my book

who stepped aside

to make room for my wings

who saw my future

before I could dream it

who loved my wild

and let me be free

This is for you

Contents

THE MISSION

1 The Light Went Out in His Eyes

NINE YEARS AGO, I PUT MY FIVE-YEAR-OLD SON, Wyatt, on a bus for his first day of school and did what nearly every other mother does—I followed it.

I watched his little blond head bopping above the seat as the bus wound through the neighborhood. I drifted behind at every stop, watching the other kids get on and my son looking out the window. I hovered in the school parking lot as he walked into the building.

And then I proceeded to cry at the loss of his childhood.

I know, I know, this is what every red-blooded kid goes through in life. It's a rite of passage for growing up. Going to school is what kids do. It helps them become confident, independent, socialized, educated, and capable of thriving in the world.

I did it. You probably did it. So I went along with it. After all, I didn't know any different. And Wyatt thrived in school. He made friends. He got good grades. He impressed his teachers. He won Citizen of the Month, and we proudly displayed the banner in our front yard.

I joined the class for field trips, birthdays, and end-of-year celebrations. When he was home, we went on adventures, played outside, read lots of books, and made the most of our time together. He learned to read and sit in a circle, and at the end of the year, I felt proud of us both. He made it. I made it. I decided half-day kindergarten wasn't half bad. But then it was over.

The next year, we started all over again. This time for a full seven-hour day.

It wasn't long before I noticed some changes in my firstborn. His disposition toward us changed. He seemed more distant. He became more interested in what other kids thought of him. He was losing his childlike innocence.

I saw the light go out in his eyes.

My son had always cherished his childhood. He wasn't in a rush to grow up. He empathized with those who were hurting or suffering. He was troubled by coarse language. And he could easily discern the negative attitudes of other people.

By being thrust into the rushing stream of peers I couldn't filter, pressures I couldn't anticipate, and institutionalized learning with people who didn't know or love my son as much as I did, he was becoming someone other than who he was meant to be.

Also, I missed my boy. The bus arrived at eight o'clock in the morning and came home at nearly four in the afternoon. We had a little time for play before dinner, but then he had an hour of homework, and then it was time for bed.

It didn't seem right that strangers got to spend more time with my son than I did.

I wanted to give him a childhood. And I wanted to experience it with him.

THE LOSS OF CHILDHOOD

I'm just going to say it. Childhood has been lost. To video games, to sports leagues, to after-school programs, to day care, to mobile devices, to peer pressure, to Netflix, to "gifted" classes, to extracurricular activities, to homework, to being carted between split homes every other weekend, and to busy schedules, just like their parents.

Some say this is progress. That we've evolved as a species to the point where children are able to act like adults, carry the same responsibilities, and handle the same pressures.

And to a degree, this is true. Science has taught us so much about the young mind. We've learned there are billions of neurons making connections in a young child, that working memory is key to intelligence, and that the brain's ability to decipher the subtle sounds of foreign languages begins to diminish after the age of five.

We've learned that the immature brain is capable of extraordinary feats and that it is most flexible early in life to engage with a wide range of experiences, languages, and interactions.

We know this and much more. But the fact that a child is capable of so much doesn't mean she is meant to operate at full capacity all the time.

In fact, a 2014 study by the American Psychological Association revealed that the average reported stress in children during the school year exceeds that of adults.[1] Other studies reveal that children simply cannot learn under stress.

This isn't progress. It's preposterous.

All our knowledge about young minds has made us a bit neurotic. Rather than using it to supplement a natural learning environment and help us discern what is best for our families, we chase down every opportunity to make sure our kids don't miss out on getting into the best preschools and private schools, on being the first to read, on being three grade levels ahead in math, and on getting accepted into the gifted classes and honors programs.

These are all things that boost our pride as parents, to be sure. But our pursuit of them stems from something deeper and purer—a desire to give our children the best childhood possible. We want to give them what we didn't have, whether it's an advantage in life or unlimited options when they get older. And we want to give them the gift of having a "good" parent.

But in the interest of giving our children the very best of everything—education, experiences, safety, gadgets, clothing, and toys—we have traded their souls for a life in the rat race. We have forgotten that for everything gained, something is lost.

> ## "Remember when 'free range children' were just called children?"
>
> —ERIN KENNY

The "start them early" mentality has replaced the mind-set that "late is okay" on social development, relational connections, and stress-reducing environments for children to fully develop. Not just for their brains, but their whole beings— body, mind, and soul.

Homeschooling pioneer John Holt wrote, "There seems to be an unspoken idea, in instruction of the young, that the people who start the fastest will go the farthest. But that's not only an unproven theory; it's not even a tested theory. The assumption that the steeper the learning curve, the higher it will go, is also unfounded. If we did things a little differently, we might find out that people whose learning curves were much slower might later on go up just as high or higher."[2]

Our children need our time, not our intelligence. They bloom with love, not perfect language skills. They need mercy, not intellectual mastery. And they will learn—indeed, truly learn—when they are given time to explore ideas without constant fact-checking and examination.

Plutarch said that "education is not the filling of a pail, but the lighting of a fire." How have we come so far and yet failed to remember what the ancient scholars and teachers knew?

RECLAIMING THE WONDER OF CHILDHOOD

Childhood is not meant to be merely preparation for adulthood. It's a time to be cherished, protected, and preserved. Our kids will have many opportunities for careers, discipline, and hard work. But they get only one childhood. So let's make it magical.

A magical childhood isn't about having the best toys, gadgets, and vacations. It's actually the opposite. It's about simplicity. A magical childhood is about freedom. Freedom to explore, discover, and play.

Let's take them out to the rivers and forests, the mountains and the oceans. Let's let them daydream for hours at a time. Let's let them experience boredom and, in so doing, give them a fertile seedbed for imagination, play, and wonder. Let's let them swim in the creeks, run in the fields, get dirty, stay up late to see the stars, and catch bullfrogs with their bare hands.

Let's not force adulthood upon them just yet.

Educator, historian, and author Susan Wise Bauer wrote, "Children are not miniature adults. Requesting them to learn how to deal with adult levels of pressure is not good teaching—or parenting."[3]

All of us have things about our childhood we hope to redeem—how we were treated, what we missed out on, words that cut us down, or experiences that wounded us. We also have things we hope to reclaim for our own children. They're different for everyone. But I'm willing to bet they were moments of being wild + free.

I remember canoeing alone on the river behind my house when I was a girl. I remember running through the woods, pretending I was Pocahontas. I remember sledding down the hill behind our neighborhood. I remember the sun-drenched days of playing on the shores of Ocean City, New Jersey, during visits with my grandmother. I remember the hours I spent in the woods. It was up on the hill behind my house among the spruce and fir trees that I figured out who I was.

So much of a modern-day childhood is designed to assist parents as they work longer hours to pay the bills and to allay their fears that they're not doing everything possible to help their kids succeed in life. Every day there is a new app, toy, or curriculum to help our kids know more, do more, and be smarter. What used to exist abundantly in every childhood has now become a commodity, a product to be traded or sold for the sake of our technologically driven future or, worse, our own parental goals.

But we cannot give our children wonder, curiosity, or a desire to learn. Children are born with these things. Wonder is the birthright of every child. It's the natural tendency to look at the world and want to explore it. Wonder is triggered by beauty, by new discoveries, and by our imaginations. Children live in a constant state of wonder. They're always learning, exploring, and discovering new things.

Children are born with all the wonder they will ever need. Our job is not to take it away.

SAVING CHILDHOOD

It's been nearly a decade since I trailed behind the school bus watching my son's sweet blond head bobbing up and down. When I share this story with others, they probably think I simply had a hard time letting go of my little boy. Or they might assume I was a nervous parent. A worrier. A coddler.

And while I did have *all the feels* when he left for his first day of kindergarten, deep down I was immensely proud of him. As a parent, I never wanted to hold my children back from new experiences. In fact, Wyatt had attended a two-day preschool when he was just three years old and a full-day prekindergarten the previous year.

"Wonder is the beginning of wisdom."

—SOCRATES

No, letting go wasn't difficult. But stealing something precious from him was. In the interest of "maturity," I had inadvertently swept his childhood right out from under him.

And I knew I was the only one who could give it back to him.

2 Reclaiming Motherhood

A STIRRING IS HAPPENING IN MOTHERS ALL OVER the world, a desire for a simpler way of living and raising our children. We want to save their childhoods. We want to reclaim what's been lost over the past few decades.

Time in nature.

Time for childhood.

Time for exploration.

Time to learn at their own pace.

And time to pursue their own interests.

But in reclaiming childhood, we are reclaiming motherhood as well—trusting our instincts and doing what's best for our children, rather than what society says is normal or expected.[1]

When it comes to education, it can feel risky to diverge from societal norms. Without a standardized measuring stick, we have to tune in to our natural instincts as mothers. And that can be frightening when we've been trained to tune them out. We have to believe that our children are not products to be measured but souls to be set free. And we must trust that we have what it takes to teach our children at home.

In other words, we have to bring education in-house again.

You are your child's best teacher, not because you know everything about all the subjects. Not because you have an education degree or a PhD in physics. Not because you have the best ideas or make the most interesting lesson plans. Not because you're a great planner, conduct the best science experiments, or have it all together. Not because you're exceptionally creative or can set up a beautiful classroom or afford the best resources.

And certainly not because you have a limitless amount of patience.

You are your child's best teacher because you can lead by example. You can show them how to pursue knowledge by doing so yourself. You can join them on this learning journey as a guide through life and education, and sometimes the other way around.

You can show them how to push through hard subjects, how to navigate relationships, and how to interact with the real world every single day. You can offer hugs and kisses or a listening ear. You can talk with them about anything, no matter what else is going on. You can get them outside help when you need a hand or when they simply need a break from you and you from them (yes, that can happen, and yes, it's okay).

You can watch them, study them, learn their quirks and eccentricities. You can discover what makes them tick, what makes them frustrated, and what lights them up. And you can love them and believe in them like no one else ever could. Because you know them best.

A NOTE TO THE FATHERS

Without a doubt, fathers are also homeschoolers. Whether they take on this endeavor full-time or simply as a supporting spouse and parent, we applaud them. Homeschooling dads don't get nearly enough recognition or encouragement. When I think about the sacrifices—emotional, physical, and financial—my own husband has made over the years, not to mention his educational contributions to our children's lives, I am both humbled and grateful.

So no, this lifestyle isn't just for the women and mamas. The Wild + Free message is for all who take on this all-important work of raising and educating their children at home. But, as a mother, my heart has always been to create a space for women to become respected thought leaders.

Wild + Free operates from a deep passion to inspire mothers to tap into their natural gifts and follow their hearts in raising their children. The fact is that even though 97 percent of homeschoolers are women,[2] men still make up 68 percent of the speakers at most conferences.[3] While this doesn't determine where things are headed, it is the state of homeschooling today.

When Wild + Free began, I wanted to create a community that focused on the gifts women bring to their families and the strength of a sisterhood forged not by blood but by our stories. This is why Wild + Free, as an organization, has sought to turn this equation on its head—allowing everyday mothers, not simply educational "experts," to become respected voices in the homeschooling space.

If you're a dad reading this, thank you for all you do. For supporting us, for sacrificing so much, and for sharing your hearts with your children. You are making a world of difference for generations to come.

RELEASE YOURSELF
FROM EXPECTATIONS

I used to believe that being a good mom meant having a three-month-old who could sleep through the night in his own crib, take two naps a day, and drink from a bottle without any trouble. I thought my three-year-old should be able to sing his ABCs, count to twenty, solve puzzles, and not have separation anxiety when he was dropped off at preschool.

I remember reading all the baby books, from Dr. Sears to Dr. Spock and everything in between. One popular book proposed that children should conform to their parents' schedule, not the other way around, no matter how much it hurt your heart. It became the norm for moms to ask each other at play dates if their babies were sleeping through the night, what kind of nursing schedules they were on, and whether they fell asleep on their own.

Oh, the pressure.

I still remember lying outside my baby's door one night, curled up in a fetal position, listening to him cry himself to sleep with sobs that pierced my heart. I was doing everything my mothering instincts told me not to do because the books told me it was better this way.

It didn't start out this way. Those expectations crept into my consciousness over time, thanks to the experts, trends, and societal pressures. When I first became a mama, I believed that my love and mama instincts were all I needed, and I was right.

Well, that, and cute baby gear.

And oh, how I loved him. I loved him with my whole being. I loved him mind, body, and soul, and I would have died for him before I ever saw his face. I didn't need to be "educated" on how to love him well. I had never been a mother before, but it all came naturally to me.

Those first few weeks were both hard and beautiful. I nursed him until my nipples were cracked and bleeding. I cried with him at night as he writhed and screamed from colic. I slept with him when he slept. I held him despite the prevailing advice to let him go. Sometimes I would hold him so he could finally rest and, at other times, simply to stare into his face.

I followed my gut. I gave him my heart. And our souls were knitted together in an unbreakable bond. We were inseparable and perfectly content.

But then the questions came.

Is he sleeping through the night? How long does he nap? Does he fall asleep on his own? Oh, you nurse him to sleep? How many times does he wake up in the night?

I began to question what I was doing as well. I heard the voices when I was alone.

You're spoiling him.

He'll never learn to be on his own that way.

It's good for him to cry.

I was strong and independent, but over time, my confidence began to waver. I doubted my intuition. All I ever wanted was to be a mother, and I was failing.

You get questions at every stage. Mothers can't help themselves. Some want to judge, but I've come to see that mostly they just want to know they're not alone, that their baby is normal.

I have a pediatrician friend with two daughters. Neither of them was walking at seventeen months. She told herself not to worry. They were fine; nothing was abnormal. But she couldn't handle the stares from other moms at play groups. While all their toddlers were running around, her girls were still crawling. In spite of her own expertise, she began to doubt herself too.

Comparison is the thief of joy, but also of a mother's confidence.

If you think the pressures of motherhood are intense during babyhood, try educating your school-age children in an alternative way. There is nothing that will rattle you more than having friends and neighbors, let alone all of society, question your decisions.

And yet there is nothing more natural to a mother's heart than to look after the needs of her own children, to preserve their childhoods, and to give them the chance to be who they were made to be. We need only to keep the voices from convincing us otherwise.

For a mother who chooses to homeschool, it can feel as if she's defying cultural norms, social convention, and years of academic tradition when, in fact, she's simply trusting her instincts.

Raising children is hard, full of twists and turns, missteps and mistakes, regrets and trying new things. But even on its most challenging day, homeschooling is really just an extension of parenting. Rest assured, there is no perfect school, classroom, teacher, mother, or homeschool. But we can do the best we can, one day at a time. And that's good enough.

Let's stop striving to be good moms by other people's standards and start becoming the mothers our children need.

"Our children are children for such a small season of life. Let their laughter ring out, their imaginations soar, their feet stomp in puddles, their hands clap for joy. Too soon they will grow up and out of their youthful exuberance and zest and settle into the life and routine of adulthood."

—L. R. KNOST

BECOME YOUR CHILD'S EXPERT

The role of homeschooling mother is part teacher, part nurse, part mathematician, part naturalist, part scientist, part counselor, and part coach, and that's just getting started. For those of us who do it, homeschooling is not a "season of obscurity" or the fallback for what we really wanted to do in life. It's a calling, the most important thing we can do with our lives right now.

As author and homeschooling veteran Julie Bogart said, "You are not just washing dishes. You are not just keeping house for a man. You have chosen a career of education, just as worthy as all those schoolteachers who get up every morning and drive to a building. You're doing the same thing. It's a career."

So treat it like one. Don't just homeschool your kids. Become their expert.

No one knows your child better than you. You began to study your child from the time he was born, watching his mannerisms, how he acted and reacted, what made him tick. You brought him home from the hospital and immersed yourself in learning your baby, even when you had no idea what you were doing. You followed your instincts one day at a time.

Nothing could have prepared you for what was ahead. From birth and breastfeeding to colic and sleepless nights, the education comes quickly, and it comes in the form of experience.

You figured out what worked to calm your baby. You figured out the difference between a pain cry and a hunger cry. You figured out how to sneak in a nap. Maybe you figured out that holding your baby made you both happy, despite what the experts said. Or that nursing on demand felt right to you. Or that nursing didn't always help because it was sleep your baby wanted.

You figured out your baby because you were *with* your baby.

The same is true now. You are your child's greatest expert. In the past, you may have been silenced by the naysayers and the so-called experts. You may have doubted yourself when questioned by family and friends. But motherhood is yours to be reclaimed once again.

Trust your natural instincts, even when you don't know what to do, because if all else fails, you still know how to be a parent. You still know how to read books to your children. You still know how to spend time with them and share the wisdom of your years. And you still know how to love them and nurture them through the difficult and joyous seasons of life.

You had to become a parent for these insights to make sense. Experience was the most valuable education for you as the mother of a baby, and it still is today for your growing child.

Being your child's expert doesn't mean you won't make mistakes. It doesn't mean you won't need to seek out advice, help, or encouragement from time to time. But if we can trust moms to take their babies home from the hospital, to be responsible for their emotional and physical well-being, then we can certainly trust them to teach their children how to learn.

You are not perfect. Your child is not perfect. But you are enough.

Let's hold on to the grand vision of raising and educating our children according to their way. Let's not allow the noise and clutter of our culture to cast doubt on ourselves or let our insecurities get in the way of what we have been called to do.

KNOW YOUR WHY

I have been homeschooling for nearly ten years, and each year, something causes me to question my decision. This is familiar territory for any parent, but because of our close proximity with our kids, homeschool parents are set up to reevaluate their choices constantly.

The way we live and learn is so different from other people's ways that I used to have occasional moments of panic. But over the years, I have reminded myself that we brought our children home for a reason. We have nothing to prove and no one to prove it to. We have guidelines from the state, which I respect and follow because my children's education is at the top of my priorities. But a natural consequence of breaking the mold is being different. And I'm okay with different. At the end of the day, homeschooling is about relationships. It's why I do it, and it's why many other mothers do it. I want to savor every moment I have with my children. I know that one day, they'll go off and have adventures with their own families. But the time we spend together as a family will root them deeply in values that matter and dreams that inspire.

Everyone needs a "why" to make it through the difficult times, the seemingly unfruitful times, the times when you question your decision. And you will have those days more often than you think. Your "why" is your reason. Your "why" is the conviction that inspires you and fuels the passion within you. Your "why" gives you the strength to carry on when your will is wavering. Your "why" gives you the ability to inspire your children and guide them on this journey.

"Instead of raising children who turn out okay despite their childhood, let's raise children who turn out extraordinary because of their childhood."

—L. R. KNOST

Your "why" could be a vision for your children's futures, the quality of the time you have together, or any number of factors that motivate you to keep them at home. But by all means, have a purpose. Write it down, and remind yourself often. Because one day you'll need it.

My friend and fellow Wild + Free mama Jillian Ragsdale came up with a list of questions to define her "why" and to help others discover theirs:

- Why do you want to homeschool your children?
- Why do you think this is the best way to educate them?
- What is your main objective or focus in homeschooling?
- What goals do you want to achieve with your children at home?
- What do you want your children to achieve and do with their lives?
- What is your overall vision for this homeschooling life?
- How can you create the homeschool life you envision?

We all homeschool for different reasons. Some choose this path before their babies are born. Others vow they'll never homeschool but end up choosing homeschooling for one reason or another. Maybe you don't know yet what you'll do when your child reaches school age. Maybe your child is in the traditional school system but struggling with academics, peer pressure, bullying, or physical or mental illness, and you're leaning toward bringing her home.

No matter how you end up on this journey, your "why" gives you purpose and passion. Over time, your "why" may change, and that's okay. Revisit your vision often. Rewrite your "why" every few years. Sometimes our reason to start homeschooling isn't the reason we keep going.

> "'Stuff your eyes with wonder,' he said, 'live as if you'd drop dead in ten seconds. See the world. It's more fantastic than any dream made or paid for in factories.'"
>
> —RAY BRADBURY

I first brought my son home because I wanted more time with him, more time for him to be a six-year-old, and more time for him to rediscover the joy in learning. These are still goals I have for all my children. But today there are many more reasons on my list: learning at their own pace, discovering their individual passions, and traveling the world together, to name just a few.

If homeschooling is your second choice, or even a last resort, defining your "why" will be equally important. What might feel like a chore can bring so much joy if you allow your vision to guide you. What might start out feeling impossible can turn into something natural and beautiful. In the midst of a difficult time, you might find that the journey is the destination after all.

LET'S BE WILD + FREE

If we're going to raise wild + free children, we need to be wild + free mamas. In reclaiming motherhood, we are reclaiming a natural connection to our purpose, our calling, and our children. We are reclaiming the wildness and freedom that are our own birthright.

Without reclaiming motherhood, we have no chance at reclaiming their childhood.

Wild + Free mamas aren't worried about what others think of them. They're passionate about what they believe, how they want to live, and what they desire for their children. They embrace who they are, defy expectations, and raise children according to their natural bent.

Everything about this message clashes with the conventions of our society. We're conditioned to deny our instincts, outsource our expertise, and become numb to wonder.

It's time to find our way back. You weren't born to be status quo. You didn't become a mother to raise standardized children. You were born to live a life of adventure, to take risks, to live boldly, and to make mistakes. You were born to be wild + free.

I love what one Wild + Free mama shared: "Although I started homeschooling to give my children a wild and free childhood, I soon realized it was my husband and I who longed to be wild and free. We get to relive our own childhoods and make new memories as a family. I'm so grateful for how homeschooling has enriched every facet of our lives."[4]

Once you get a taste for living wild + free, it's impossible to go back to your old life. Taking risks, living with purpose, and writing your family's story together gets into your bones, and you won't be able to do it any other way. You'll be ruined for "normal."

3 The Call to Homeschooling

KEEPING THE INBORN WONDER ALIVE IN OUR children is a continual process. Preserving the curiosity and creativity of their youth requires intentionality. It takes time to let children grow and learn at their own pace, time to daydream, time to get lost in a good book or imaginative play.

It takes courage to homeschool, especially when society questions your every move. And then there are the long days, the lack of time for yourself, and the seasons when fatigue or discouragement get the better of you.

But the time we have with our children is a precious gift we get to unwrap each day. In the years to come when they are grown and on their own, we will remember the beautiful and rewarding, albeit difficult and often harrowing, journey we traveled together.

Homeschooling doesn't exist to replicate the classroom in the home. And if it did, we would never be able to compete. Homeschooling is about relationships, about individualized education, about freeing kids to learn what they want at their own pace—because we can.

Homeschooling isn't about keeping children in line with no disruptions. That's a classroom mentality. Our children are not living in a box. Life is messy, chaotic, and full of distractions, which means learning at home will be too at times. But it can still be rich and beautiful.

What if we stopped treating children like robots, capable only of inputting and outputting information, and instead treated them like human beings consisting of beautiful dreams, diverse intelligence, and natural talents? Our role would be more like gardening than aggregating.

Our children are gifts to treasure, not trophies to display. They may be little, but they are not small. They are real persons given to us to nurture and care for, not conform or control.

We are coming to a place in society where homeschooling is not an obscure lifestyle choice but a preferred one. Homeschooling is not a liability for a child but a leg up.

CONNECTING WITH YOUR KIDS

No one loves or understands your children as you do. You know their tendencies, their idiosyncrasies, their strengths, and their weaknesses. Other people and even remarkable teachers are doing their best by them. But they have to clock out at the end of each day for the sake of their own lives and families.

The most meaningful part of a child's upbringing is you. And yet studies show that the average family spends only thirty-six minutes together each day.[1] Homeschooling is a return to parent-child mentorship. It brings us closer than anything else ever will.

TAKING BACK YOUR SCHEDULE

There's something liberating but also unsettling about taking control of your own schedule. At first, you'll wonder if you're doing something wrong. Is it legal to let the kids wake up naturally without an alarm? What happens if you don't start your formal studies until eleven o'clock in the morning?

You might doubt yourself when you spot the school bus rattling through your neighborhood. Or when everyone else appears to be so busy with projects and science fairs and homework.

Surely the lack of activity is a sign of failing our children, right?

On the contrary, peaceful mornings are the reclamation of childhood. Diving deeper into subjects when things are getting interesting and changing course when things aren't going well are the best way to stoke a child's passion. There is no bell schedule. You have no academic week, let alone academic year.

Learning is life, and life is learning.

AVOIDING STIGMAS

Whenever I look at the face of my third son, Cody, or listen to one of his long and detailed stories, I can't help but think about his first four years of life, the ones when he didn't speak.

Cody was a beautiful and engaged baby, rolling over and tackling physical hurdles as if it were his job. He could run down our steep driveway without stumbling at ten months of age, and at fifteen months he could dribble a basketball with skills that rivaled those of our thirteen-year-old neighbor.

But at two years, he couldn't communicate verbally besides using a few words like *mom* or *ball*. And at three, he still struggled to put two words together. He performed daily concerts in which he played the guitar or drums and sang his little heart out. We just couldn't make out what he was saying.

Somewhere around the age of four, he started talking a bit more, and we could understand him better with each day. Now, at nine, he still pronounces quite a few sounds incorrectly, but he talks our ears off and we often laugh in disbelief.

If Cody had gone to traditional school, or even preschool, he would have encountered some wonderful people and even teachers who cared for him. But I also know from experience that he would have been forced to deal with something sooner than was necessary—becoming aware of his "disability" through discussions, testing, and schoolyard taunts.

The input Cody receives each day is how coordinated he is as he plays football with his older brothers. How mechanically minded he is as he builds kinetic Lego sets in record time. And how responsible he is as he looks after the safety of his little sisters.

The blessing of homeschooling is that we can be a constant source of encouragement to our children, infusing them with confidence and focusing on their strengths, while simultaneously addressing their weaknesses with the positive tools we have available.

THE DIFFERENCE BETWEEN INSTRUCTION AND LEARNING

Instruction is requiring our children to memorize facts and information. It comes from the outside in. Learning, on the other hand, is applying knowledge to their life in meaningful, life-changing ways. It happens from the inside out. Learning is the native method of a wild + free homeschool. A child can be excited about learning and not be ground down by a full day of classes, test taking, and then homework at night. If you can preserve your children's love of learning, you've given them everything.

Do some kids thrive in more structured environments?

Of course. I've got a few of them. I've learned to make charts and create schedules for my more organized children, and I've learned not to care if my other kids wake up late or read fewer books than assigned. My kids are not all going to learn or thrive at the same pace, and I trust the natural learning process.

PURSUING THEIR OWN INTERESTS

There's only so much time in the conventional classroom. Between the commute to school, discipline issues in class, and the lost hours between activities, students are in a race to learn all they can before the school bell rings. Then there's homework, extracurricular activities, sports programs, and parent-teacher conferences, leaving no time for their own interests.

Homeschooling clears the deck. Some states have requirements for homeschooling families, but for the most part, you get to decide how much time you spend on which subjects.

Our schoolwork doesn't span the entire day, so my children have hours in which they can pursue subjects that interest them. My eldest son, Wyatt, wrote two novels before his fourteenth birthday, spent the past year creating stop-motion animation projects that have garnered a respectable following on YouTube, and is currently teaching himself photography.

My middle son, Dylan, taught himself to play the piano by ear, composes his own songs on a laptop, and creates 3-D animations in a software application called Blender.

And my youngest son, Cody, builds bird feeders, toy hang gliders, and catapults out of wood, and he can fix just about anything in the house because he loves knowing how things work.

When you remove the stumbling blocks to education, you're left with the pull of passion. Each day becomes an opportunity to explore one's interests and curiosities.

Imagine education being driven by passion instead of pressure.

Educational advisor and author Ken Robinson wrote, "The fact is that given the challenges we face, education doesn't need to be reformed—it needs to be transformed. The key to this transformation is not to standardize education but to personalize it, to build achievement on discovering the individual talents of each child, to put students in an environment where they want to learn and where they can naturally discover their true passions."[2]

What if that place were home?

INDIVIDUALIZED ATTENTION

When I think about the varying strengths, tendencies, and weaknesses in my five children, I can't imagine how a systematic environment would allow them to thrive. I know they would adapt and learn the skills needed to do well, but no one stops to think about the toll it takes on their souls at such a young age.

There is a standard by which students are measured, and there's no honorable classification for those who don't fit in. Those who can't keep up with the standard become outcasts to those who are considered "normal." Teachers have so many students to consider, our children can't always be first.

No matter what student-teacher ratio a school might boast, you can't beat mama and child.

Childhood is not a time for enforced conformity but a time for freedom to learn and explore their interests at their own pace. Our kids have a pretty good idea of how they need to learn. We need only watch and follow their lead.

By giving our children an individualized education, we can move as quickly or as slowly through a subject as our children need. We can take time understanding their learning styles and passions. Think about how much more excited and engaged our children would be if we could take these things into account when planning lessons. Being able to give our children

individualized attention, even for a brief time each day, allows us to put the joy back into learning. And joy in learning, my friend, leads to success.

"As teachers, parents, and caregivers, we become not scientists with microscope and laboratory, but naturalists who observe life and nature within its element—plein air (outdoors)—like the modern-day ethnographer observing children in real life to see how and why they learn as they do."
— JACK BECKMAN

LEARNING AT THEIR OWN PACE

We all know that every child is unique, and yet, for some reason, we still assume this doesn't apply to learning. Especially when it comes to our own children.

My son Cody may have some learning challenges ahead of him, but I am so grateful he is about to turn ten and is a confident, happy boy. His speech challenges don't prevent him from getting up in front of his peers at our homeschool co-op to give a presentation. In fact, it's one of his favorite things to do.

Still, Cody doesn't fit the mold. He can't write a paragraph or read a book. But he creates books, tells stories, can identify the violin in any musical number, and can reverse engineer a kitchen appliance like nobody's business. Even more, no one puts him in a box. Of course, he knows his shortcomings, but he doesn't have to dwell on them. He's allowed to learn at his own pace.

Sandra K. Cook, author of *Overcome Your Fear of Homeschooling with Insider Information*, wrote, "Notice the difference: a child's disability is the focus in traditional classroom settings, but his abilities are the focus in the homeschool environment."

But allowing children to learn at their own pace isn't beneficial only for kids with learning disabilities. My six-year-old daughter, Annie, has been wanting to write and read since she could identify a book's usefulness.

I would hear her alone at night "reading" stories in her room, trying to recall the plotlines and making up new twists as she went along. She would scrawl lines of gibberish on a piece of paper, bring it to me, and ask, "What does this say?" as if the very marks carried meaning.

Now she's mastering each letter by copying it onto a personal chalkboard I bought her. She's stringing wooden letters together to make words and arranging words together to make sentences. And I've never asked her to do it. The words and stories are her own creation.

All along, I've never doubted that Annie would learn to read when she was ready. I've seen firsthand how it's her passion that drives her to learn, not the drills and exercises.

All children deserve the right to discover things for themselves in their own time. Developmental psychologist Jean Piaget wrote, "Every time we teach a child something, we keep him from inventing it himself."[3]

Children want to experiment, explore, and do their own research. Of course, that doesn't mean we should sit back and do nothing. Piaget urges us to guide children "by providing appropriate materials, but the essential thing is that in order for a child to understand something, he must construct it himself, he must re-invent it."[4]

When children play with math, they engage in what psychologist and author Peter Gray calls "pure math." This, he observed, is "what real mathematicians do, and it is also what 4-year-olds do. Playful math is to numbers what poetry is to words, or what music is to sounds, or what art is to visual perception."[5]

I am not concerned at all about the varying paces of learning in my children, nor am I willing to rush them to do things before they are ready. Henry David Thoreau, who coined the phrase *wild and free*, also wrote, "The more slowly trees grow at first, the sounder they are at the core, and I think the same is true of human beings."

THE WHISPER OF HOMESCHOOLING

Sometimes you don't know what your heart desires until you experience it. That's how it was for me.

"My children *will* go to school," I said. "No weird, unsocialized children in this house." I was certain of it. When my eldest was three years old, we began thinking about preschool.

Wyatt had speech difficulties and more food allergies than we could count, but I didn't want him to miss out. No matter how hard it was for me to let go, I decided he would go to preschool.

I enrolled him in a two-day cooperative preschool that was a beautiful blend of Montessori- and Waldorf-inspired philosophies. Long before I knew the origins of these methods or what they meant, I was drawn to the small classrooms of eight or fewer and the focus on child-centered independence, free play, dramatic play, and artistic experimentation.

The fact that it was a co-op meant that I had to be in the classroom every other week as the teacher's assistant. It was the perfect environment for both Wyatt and me.

There was a brief circle time in which the children gathered for a song or two, a beautiful storybook reading, and gentle movement such as yoga or stretching. Afterward, they took turns changing the month, the day of the week, and the weather picture on a beautiful cloth tapestry.

But otherwise, there was never a moment when the children were forced to sit at a table doing exactly the same thing as everyone else.

They did art projects, took turns with the sensory tables, worked puzzles, built structures with wooden blocks, dressed up in costumes, served meals to one another with hand-sewn fabric food, and went outside to play every single day, no matter the weather.

I was fortunate to stumble upon this gem of a preschool back when homeschooling was not yet a whisper in my heart. The school was tucked away on a lone, forgotten country road. It wasn't flashy or boasting of its academic prowess, and I almost dismissed it.

But now I can see how my heart was searching for a different way of learning all along. A way for my children to have the freedom to explore and discover through play, nature, music, and books. A way for them to be children while growing in independence, interdependence, and imagination at the same time. And a way for them to have beautiful opportunities to learn at their own pace. They were treated as individuals, free to grow and go about in their own way.

That tiny preschool ruined me for traditional education forever.

We moved to another state the following year, and I was forced to find a new school for my son. This time, there weren't as many options, and he ended up in a four-day-a-week program.

It felt like a corporation for toddlers. There was a dress code, and there were rules for the playground, systematic lessons by professional educators, and strict rules for drop-off and pickup. I had to practically push my four-year-old out our sliding van door with his sack lunch. No time for a proper goodbye. It was quite traumatic for both of us.

All the while, there was a tug at my heart. A voice gently calling. A whisper. Something telling me that this wasn't the way. I didn't heed it, but I didn't stifle it either. I let it settle into the quiet spaces of my heart. My son went to school. Made friends. Got good grades. And our days became captive to the schedule and system assigned to us.

The whisper grew louder and louder until I could no longer ignore it. Passion began to well up inside me. And one day, I awakened to find that the voice within me had become my own.

THE ONES WHO ANSWER THE CALL

Most of us who do this are unlikely homeschoolers. We didn't plan to do it this way. We didn't know if we *could* do it or even if we should.

We know the drill. Kids go to school. That's what they do. And their lives become an endless race—to the bus stop, to the next reading level, to Christmas break, to the finish line.

But there's a quiet voice calling out to us. Nudging us to see our children for who they really are. Inviting us to give them the freedom they truly desire. The freedom to learn and grow at their own pace, to follow their passions and see where they go, to explore the world without an agenda.

We might not have all the answers. Doubt will creep in at times. But we know our children. And we know the right path—for us.

I know you've heard it too. You wouldn't be reading this book if you hadn't.

It's the call of the outdoors. The call of childhood. The call of more time as a family. The call of wonder and adventure. A stirring inside you—to do something different, be someone different.

So here we are. The ones who have answered the call.

The call of the wild + free.

4 Preparing for Your Journey

OVER THE PAST FEW YEARS, I HAVE RECEIVED thousands of messages from people wanting to know how to get started in homeschooling. These are everyday modern mothers, who know very little about homeschooling and never dreamed they would be considering it. They are drawn to the beauty, freedom, and organic way of learning this lifestyle provides. They want more for their children's futures, and they desperately want more for their childhoods.

There will always be people who misunderstand what it means to be wild + free. They assume it means letting kids run amok without any structure at all. There are certainly homeschools that are less structured than others, but you can be wild + free *and* organized.

Some contend that homeschooling isn't rigorous enough to turn out successful adults. On the contrary, homeschooling is driven by a child's innate desire and capacity to learn, which is often inhibited by the conventional school system. Homeschooling can actually provide a more rigorous education than any other. Imagine not being held back by the pace of an entire class.

Some people need systems and programs to feel secure. They want prescriptions to follow so they can feel that they've accomplished something. This is why families come away from homeschool conventions with arms full of boxed curriculums. This fear of missing out (FOMO, as we call it) drives an entire industry of educational products, and it's all completely needless.

An entire world of advanced learning lies at your fingertips. As a homeschooler, you don't have to merely read about the Revolutionary War; you can visit the actual sites and relive history in the places where it happened. No school bell beckons you back by three o'clock. You don't have to calculate how many gallons of theoretical milk a herd of cows can produce, you can actually milk them yourself and ask the farmer about sustainable farming while you're at it.

There are internet search engines, Wikipedia, the Khan Academy, virtual tours of art museums, online courses, and, best of all, books. There is nothing you cannot learn, no information you cannot access.

Your children's education is not made possible by standardized systems and programs but rather is limited by them. Every education has learning gaps, even the best private schools and colleges. But somehow, we feel better about those gaps because they're committed by experts with credentials. In homeschooling, the only gaps are in your curiosity and desire to learn.

Let's look at how to get started.

REGULATIONS AND REPORTING

Yes, you are allowed to do this. There are some countries, such as Germany and Denmark, where homeschooling is illegal, but it is perfectly acceptable in the United States and Canada, and it is a relatively new but fast-growing phenomenon in the United Kingdom. According to the BBC, the number of children being homeschooled has risen by 40 percent in the past three years.[1]

States vary in the degree of requirements that parents are required to meet. For example, California requires parents to check in with their local school district and keep a record of their activities, but it also offers charter school programs in which funds are available for resources.

In Virginia, where I live, we're free to homeschool without much day-to-day accountability, but we must submit a letter of intent each August and complete standardized testing unless we opt out with a religious exemption.

You can contact your local school district to find out what conditions must be met. It could be as simple as emailing their office to let them know you're doing it or making a phone call to find out the procedure. While city and state requirements differ, I've found that our local school district is more than willing to help homeschoolers navigate the process.

Additionally, most states have homeschooling associations that try to help families understand their local requirements. You can contact your local association or talk to other homeschooling families in your area to find out what they do.

The Homeschool Legal Defense Association is a nonprofit organization that was established in 1983 to "defend and advance the constitutional right of parents to direct the upbringing and education of their children and to protect family freedoms." HSLDA.org is a great resource for getting legal advice, staying informed, and finding necessary forms and requirements for each of the fifty states. Don't let all the legal talk intimidate you. The organization exists to protect the rights of homeschooling families but also to keep us informed.

When I first started homeschooling, I felt twinges of guilt when taking my kids out in public during the school day. I worried that strangers would accuse my kids of truancy. But homeschooling has become a cultural norm, and most people are aware of it.

In fact, I've found that most people are genuinely curious when they ask questions, while the naysayers have learned not to say anything at all because what they get from us in return is a motivational speech about the merits of homeschooling.

It's like asking a multilevel marketer how he's managed to create a life of financial freedom with an online business. No one really wants to go there.

And if confrontation isn't in your DNA, please know that you are not accountable to strangers or even disgruntled family members. I recommend composing an answer that you can pull out of your back pocket whenever you're stuck in an awkward conversation. Keep it short and succinct, and then change the subject. Something like this: "Homeschooling isn't for everyone, but it's working for us. Can you please pass the potatoes?"

TEACHING ALL AGES

Most homeschool moms find teaching different ages one of the biggest hurdles to overcome. It doesn't have to be. Subjects such as language arts, science, and history can become a family affair. There is nothing a fifth grader is learning that a third grader cannot or would not be interested in, whether it's about robots or the rain forests in Brazil. When you're a one-room schoolhouse, gathering together for a time of reading books, memorizing poetry, and studying history is a beautiful way to combine ages and subjects.

A great example of how all ages can work together is a practice called morning time, when everyone comes together to read aloud, play games, recite passages, learn a handicraft, or even sing songs. It can last from ten minutes to two hours and is a practical way to build relationships and get in the daily reading for language arts, history, or other subjects.

Many families have a basket of books and materials they can pull out for morning time. It may hold the books you are currently reading, handicraft supplies, puzzles, games, paper, crayons, and anything else you want to include.

If your young children's attention spans are shorter, let them draw or play while you read aloud. Even the older kids often enjoy doing something with their hands. It's not a sign of immaturity if they can't sit still. Moving could actually be their brain's way of learning.

I think our fear as parents is that by engaging their hands, we might be disengaging their minds. But research says the opposite is true. Studies show that retention is greater and anxiety is reduced when a person's hands are engaged or one's body is moving.

My two older boys don't mind settling in for a read-aloud, but my nine-year-old son, Cody, has to be tinkering, building, and moving around the entire time. He will even leave the room and come back minutes later, acting like nothing's the matter.

There are times when I want to make him sit still, stop playing, and pay attention. But he's actually quite aware of what I'm reading. He's taking it all in, even if he doesn't look like he is. When I ask my boys to tell me what they remember about the story, Cody is often the first one to respond, recalling details that the other two boys can't remember.

Tackling other subjects, such as writing and math, can also be a family affair. By sitting around the table together and focusing on one subject at a time, older children are able to work on their own, and they always have you nearby if they need support. You can help the younger ones play with numbers, complete worksheets in context, or work out problems with manipulatives.

Having multiple ages together is a blessing for the home-school mom and children alike, so don't let it intimidate you. Make the most of your environment, and find ways to bring everyone together as much as possible. Toddlers are the most challenging to keep engaged. Your days will have interruptions, and you'll have to get used to it. But there are a few things you can try.

First, help your older children become self-directed in certain subjects, such as math, keyboarding, or specific online programs. Work together to create manageable expectations. Ask them if they're ready to do more on their own—with your support, of course. If you're working through a curriculum, figure out what assignments they need to complete each day. Depending on their age and your personal style, you can either give them a game to play together when they're finished or let them move on to their own pursuits. This way, if you're tending to the little ones, the older kids will know exactly what to do with their time. If allowed the freedom, children won't need much guidance before they're off to their own creative endeavors.

Of course, some kids are more capable of this than others. You can't expect a nine-year-old to have the same self-directing capabilities as a thirteen-year-old. Plus, experience shows that children learn better with a partner. It keeps learning exciting and engaging. And this, after all, is why we're homeschooling. The idea of self-directed learning sounds wonderful and is at times necessary, but our goal shouldn't be to push children toward complete removal of partnership. That isn't always fun for them, and it can diminish their desire to learn.

Second, find similar activities that can help the younger ones feel that they're participating with the older ones. If the older kids are reading independently, give the younger ones a picture book to flip through. If the older ones are doing math, help the younger ones count with objects.

Finally, make the most of those concentrated times when you can pour into the older ones without any distractions, such as when the little ones are napping, engrossed in imaginative play, or spending time with Grandma. And don't forget evenings and weekends. No one said school has to be completed Monday through Friday.

This is a short season of life and won't last for long. You can do school where and when it works best for you. Being wild + free is about creating a family culture of living and learning.

FAVORITE ACTIVITIES DURING READ-ALOUDS

- Easy handicrafts like finger knitting
- Clay or modeling beeswax for sculpting
- Wooden blocks, letters, and peg people
- Puzzles, magnetic tiles, or sorting games
- Small bin of Legos (small because the sound of kids sorting through big bins is stressful when you're trying to read and may make you want to hurl the Legos; trust me on this)
- Colored pencils and paper
- Play dough with various natural items, such as shells, rocks, and flowers
- Water beads with measuring cups and small animal figurines
- Watercolor paints

CHOOSING A CURRICULUM

Before you ask about curriculum, it's better to discover your unique approach to homeschooling. Both parents and children approach the world differently. Some children thrive in a structured environment, while others need less organization in their day. Some parents are better teachers through physical activities, such as hiking and nature journaling, while others are better at reading literature and hosting book clubs.

There's no sense in shoehorning an approach that doesn't fit your family. You'll get frustrated, your kids will check out, and homeschooling won't work for either of you. If you need permission to quit something that isn't working, you've got it. If you're wondering whether it's okay to try another approach, consider this permission granted.

My third-born son, Cody, has wanted to play the violin for as long as I can remember. He has dyslexia, and I've heard the violin is a great instrument for dyslexic kids to exercise their extraordinary minds. But with his propensity to roughhouse his instruments and subsequently break them, we chose to wait until he was a bit older. Cody's desire never went away, so earlier this year, we decided to surprise him. On a rainy Tuesday morning, we took him to a quaint little violin shop where a brilliant craftsman named Yordan Popov matched him with the perfect one. We just happen to live in the same town as our favorite family band, The Hunts, and their violinist, Jenni Dowling, took him on as a student.

The lessons went well for a few weeks, and then Cody suddenly stopped practicing. He loved cleaning his instrument and taking it in and out of its case, but he wouldn't play it. My husband, Ben, suspected that Cody needed more structure than our other children, so he worked up a practice chart in Microsoft Excel and printed it out for Cody to follow.

Sure enough, Cody loved checking practice times off the list. He even started practicing two and three times a day so he could keep marking boxes. Turns out, his sweet little mind couldn't handle a schedule with no accountability. To-do lists feel like a prison to me, but to a structured child, they represent freedom and fulfillment. Go figure.

When it comes to homeschooling approaches, there are many styles to consider. You can combine these approaches and incorporate a little of each. It may take some time to figure out your style, but by understanding your unique approach, you'll create a rich environment for learning. But remember, it isn't just about you.

Many parents think about how they personally, not their children, are wired. While it's important to feel passionate about our teaching style, it's equally important to consider how our children learn. When you understand how your child learns, you can create lessons that are project based, literature driven, hands-on, visual, or a combination of approaches.

1. Do I prefer a more structured or less structured learning environment? How about my kids?

2. Do my children learn better in more natural places or walled ones?

3. Do I value literature as a source of all education?

4. Do I believe in the value of play as a tool of education?

5. Do I think screens are a good or bad idea for kids?

6. Do my children learn better if they are using their hands, working on a project?

7. Or do they prefer to work quietly, book and pen in hand?

8. Do my children reject all formal learning, or are work-books okay on occasion?

These questions will help you as you consider the various styles and curriculums, but for most of us the real answers will come with hours spent in the trenches, figuring it out as we go. In time, you'll discover which homeschooling approach works best for your family, the curriculum will fall into place, and you'll be on your way to a healthier, happier homeschool.

ESTABLISHING A ROUTINE

If you are thinking about homeschooling while your children are still little, before they have "gone to school," establishing a routine won't be an issue for you. Homeschooling from the start is an organic process that grows out of your relationship with your young child.

As you introduce a daily rhythm that includes activities you value, such as making meals, taking nature walks, doing art projects, and reading books together, you will establish a basis for your involvement in their learning journey. Sure, you'll run into struggles, just as in any parent-child relationship, but you'll work through them as you would with any other issue.

Taking your child out of traditional schooling to bring them home poses a different dynamic that can be intimidating to a lot of parents. Most kids need a period of time called "deschooling."

This isn't when you let them sit around and play video games or do whatever they want; rather, it's an intentional time to forgo any formal studies and give your child time to rediscover the love of learning, as they did when they were little. Through having outdoor adventures, visiting museums, working on art projects, and diving into good books, together you will discover what passions lie dormant in your child's heart and mind. Your child will begin to come alive again.

Homeschooling is essentially parenting amplified. It brings out the best in your kids, but it can also bring out the worst. That's simply the downside to living under the same roof. The good news is that kids are highly moldable and will exhibit the fruit of your relationship with them.

If you have a time of formal studies, you'll need an effective system for helping them settle into a routine. Not every tactic works with every child. Some kids just need some verbal guidance, while others might need a ritual, such as a song or a saying, to start the learning time and focus their attention. Some might enjoy having a personal timer to help them stay focused on a task for ten-minute sessions. If you're just starting out with an older child or a teenager, invite him or her to help you create the daily schedule. Work together to find a rhythm that works for both of you.

We homeschool not to do school at home but to do life together.

FIND YOUR TRIBE

No one can do this alone. Homeschooling will expose your children to new worlds and provide unlimited possibilities for their education. You'll grow closer as a family and become each other's best friends. At first, you'll love the simplified schedule, the unhurried pace, and the lack of obligations. But keeping everyone home all the time creates a sense of isolation that can discourage the best of us on difficult days. All of us need a community of friends to share this journey with. Mothers need mama friends, and our kids need peers who understand them.

I've involved our family in co-ops, nature groups, paid classes, and even moms' nights out. And there have been months when I've skipped all of them for a season of rest and solitude. But I treasure the relationships that have brought such richness and joy to our homeschooling life.

I love that I can call my friend Hannah and meet at one of our homes to make soup and bake sourdough bread together while our children play in the backyard. I love that my friend Katie and her family will join us at the beach on weekday nights to enjoy a picnic dinner and play football. I love that my friend Paula will invite us to her home on the lake for a day of water sports. And I love that our Wild + Free Group hosts nature hikes, book clubs, and handicraft fairs throughout the year.

Whether it's a weekly gathering or a quarterly outing, finding your tribe can be the difference between a joyful homeschooling experience and one that feels like drudgery.

I'll confess that I don't resonate with every homeschooling family. Sometimes their values greatly differ from mine or I can't relate to the approach they take, which is why Wild + Free has been such a blessing to me personally. It provides a common language for the values we hold dear and knits together those of us who believe this lifestyle can be so much more than "schooling at home."

There were a few years when we didn't have much in the way of a local community, but because of Wild + Free I now have dear friends all over the country I can call or text and even visit on occasion. Some of my dearest homeschooling friends live hundreds of miles away.

I love the story Wild + Free mama Nikki Moore shared in a recent Instagram post. "A couple of years back, we started to have conversations about what our kids' education was going to look like. The idea of homeschooling my kids filled me with overwhelm and drudgery and resentment, but we could see that Silas wasn't going to thrive in a traditional school environment. So we made the decision to keep him at home. We figured we could homeschool for the upcoming year, then reevaluate. I looked into a few different homeschool 'styles' and local groups and couldn't see them being a good fit for Silas' needs. Even though I was homeschooled myself, I didn't have a strong vision for what homeschooling could be for my own family. Sometime in that year, I discovered the Wild + Free homeschooling community. And it was like a revolution in my heart. I read and listened to everything from W + F I could get my hands on, and sparks started to fly in my imagination. I began to envision what an education could be, and it didn't feel like drudgery. My mental picture of homeschooling shifted from 'replicating school at home' to something deeper and wider. A high quality education—and along with it, wonder and adventure and freedom. And for the first time, I felt the confidence to be the teacher my kids needed. I found 'my people.'"[2]

BE BRAVE

I don't know anyone starting out in homeschooling who thinks they know what they are doing. For that matter, I don't know anyone who has homeschooled an entire houseful of children—and is on the other side—who thinks they got it all right.

Anyone who takes on this all-important endeavor of educating their own children does so holding their breath, crossing their fingers, and praying for a miracle.

It takes bravery to do what we do.

There are moments when the pain of it is greater than our passion for it.

At some point, we all ask ourselves, "Why the heck am I doing this?" The times when strangers quiz our children in grocery stores. The times when parents or grandparents remind us that it's never too late to put them in school. The times when we threaten our kids with putting them on a bus when they drive us crazy or won't stop bickering. Or those times when we feel like we're failing them because of our own inadequacies.

But there is a reason we do this that defies explanation. There is a quiet whisper calling out to us, beckoning us to give our children a different way, inviting us to preserve their childhood, to give them (and us) the gift of more time together.

Many of you may not be homeschooling in five years or even one year from now. Your goal is to give your children the gift of a childhood, a slower, more intentional start. And you might choose a different path later on, and that's more than okay. We must always follow our heart and do what we think is best for our families, especially our children. And that takes bravery too.

But the rest of you will keep on going. In time, you will realize that this path isn't just for childhood but for a lifetime of our kids' exploring their own interests; responding to life, not bells; pursuing their passions; and building a life based on purpose, not perfection.

No matter the reason, you are reading this book because you have heard the call, and you have answered it. You too believe that childhood is a time to foster wonder, creativity, and discovery through play and exploration. You believe children learn because they want to, not because they're forced to. And you believe in letting them learn at their own pace.

Your knees might be knocking. Your voice might be quaking. You might feel scared or on the verge of giving up. But you are not alone. All over the world, in your state, down the street from where you live, unbeknownst to you, there is a mama, just like you, going the distance, day in and day out, attempting to change the course of history by investing in her children.

And in case no one's told you lately, you're doing an amazing job. All those hours of training hearts, making meals, reading books, teaching math, nursing babies, conducting science experiments, going on adventures, inspiring minds—they're not being wasted. Whenever you have a moment of doubt, remember this: extraordinary lives are formed in the ordinary moments of a relationship-rich childhood.

When I was a child, I was highly introverted. I barely spoke at all. I just wanted to hide in the crowd. Standing in front of people would have made me vomit. And I still want to.

But in third grade, I had a teacher who noticed me and told me the meaning of my name, Ainsley. She said it meant Bold One. I hated the sound of it. Or what it implied.

Every day, I went to school mortified that I had to answer roll call by standing up and saying, "Bold One." I would think, "Why couldn't my name be Sarah, which means Princess, or Jenny, which means Gift of God?"

Years later, I discovered that my name actually means My Own Meadow. I scoured name books from every generation looking for one that said my name meant Bold One, and it wasn't to be found.

My teacher lied to me.

But it did the trick. I went my whole life thinking I was supposed to be brave. And today, even when it's painful, I choose boldness over comfort.

I want to take a moment and tell you the meaning of your name.

It means Brave One.

(Just do me a favor and don't look it up.)

The next time you look in the mirror, remember these words: Brave One.

And when you hit a wall with homeschooling a month or a year from now and wonder if you can go on, you're going to hear a whisper. Brave One. You might try to ignore it, even laugh it off, but trust me, these words will haunt you.

From this day forward, your name means Brave One.

Courage, dear heart.

You are brave. And don't ever forget it.

5 Becoming Wild + Free

WILD + FREE STARTED AS AN INSTAGRAM ACCOUNT in 2014. Before this, every time I shared posts about homeschooling on my personal account, I saw an unusually high response—more than you would expect from a homeschooling mother of five with subpar photography skills.

There was a disturbance in the force, you might say.

These weren't funny or embarrassing posts, mind you. Just average-looking photos from our backyard, where I had prepared a blanket and hot tea for an afternoon reading time. Or photos from a nature hike at the nearby state park. But something in these posts resonated with lots of other mamas out there.

At the suggestion of a friend, I started the official Wild + Free Instagram feed, and the rest is history. The account grew faster than I ever could have imagined, and it's still growing at a surprising rate each week. I couldn't be more grateful for the community that's come around it. Together, we are a group of parents and caregivers who believe that we can reclaim childhood for our kids, that education can look different from the cultural norm.

Have you heard the story of the woman who prepared a Christmas ham each year by first cutting off the end and throwing it away? Year after year, her husband and children watched her repeat this ritual until, finally, they asked her why she did it. She said her mother had taught her to do it. Why, she had no idea. They asked Grandma why she did it, but she couldn't tell them either. Her own mother had done it for years. Finally, they asked Great-Grandma, the originator of the practice, and she provided a simple answer—the ham was too big for the pot she owned.

Generation after generation, we've been conditioned to believe that education must be carried out in a certain way, so we refuse to give homeschooling a try, even though we have no reason why. The Industrial Revolution is over. An assembly-line education has been proven to be ineffective, and yet we can't stop educating in the same way. We fear repercussions that no longer exist and feel pressured to conform to systems that were made for uninformed times.

Homeschooling is not the second-rate version of education. It's not plan B for people who dislike public school. And it's not a commune for families seeking ideological asylum. It is an enlightened choice for parents who desire a slower, more intentional way and want their children to thrive as lifelong, passionate learners.

We don't homeschool in order to replicate the classroom at home. We homeschool in order to make the world our classroom, to do more than what the classroom can provide, to go beyond what the conventional institutions of education can offer us.

Homeschooling is like manure. Keep it in one place and it stinks up the room. But spread it around the neighborhood, the forests, and the fields, and it enriches the world.

RETURNING TO THE WILD PLACES

When I think about growing up, I recall endless summer days, the freedom to roam the neighborhood and nearby parks, playing in the mud, riding my bike, and staying out late to catch lightning bugs. Don't you? Of course, I have memories of sleepovers, pizza parlors, and school projects, but the most indelible moments, the ones that marked me for life, came from being outside.

What happened to childhood?

We brought it indoors to air-conditioned, safety-inspected, supervised environments, free of bug bites, skinned knees, sunburns, and sweat-drenched brows. We traded adventures for video games and imagination for virtual reality. Long gone are the days of exploring alone.

On a recent Saturday, my husband and I headed out for a quiet morning with the kids. We took our children to the park as we used to do when the boys were little. We sat on a bench drinking our coffee and solving the world's problems while our children played. They explored a natural rocky area near a pond filled with lily pads and bullfrogs rather than playing on the manufactured playground equipment. I was careful to make sure no signs forbade it, but the other parents murmured their displeasure and cast disapproving looks in our direction.

Since when has childhood become an indoor activity?

Since when have we had to manufacture the environments for childhood?

The call of the wild + free is the call of nature, beckoning us back into its wild places. Children come alive by being outdoors. It awakens their minds, centers their hearts, and gives them depth of soul. It's not an abandonment of academic work but rather a help to it.

Nature is where children learn to learn.

At first, our children might balk at this strange new environment. They might decry the boredom of nature hikes or complain about the banality of forest exploration, mosquito bites, and dirty shoes. I think of Chunk in the classic 1980s coming-of-age film *The Goonies*. He's all alone in the dark, crawling through the woods. He talks to himself to bolster courage: "I'm not all alone in the dark. I like the dark. I love the dark. But I hate nature. I HATE nature!"

But give it time. The wild places will reward you for your devotion. They will show you things only after they're convinced that you're not merely a passerby, an uninterested pedestrian eager to get back to civilization. Nature will not cast its pearls before swine.

A friend and fellow Wild + Free mama, Jodi Mockabee, shared an eye-opening experience with her children in nature: "I remember a situation at the tide pools months ago," Jodi said. "When we arrived, it should have been prime time to discover life, yet we were having a hard time finding anything. My son Everett suggested that we sit and wait, and he mentioned that perhaps our feet were vibrating their homes, causing the sea life to hide and find cover.

"Sure enough, within a few minutes of quiet, crabs began to come out, anemones opened, and the pool took on various vivid colors. It looked completely different than three minutes prior. Letting children go outside for long periods of time allows them to build up a tolerance for the creative process, which requires slow and methodical decision-making and results in a higher level of peace. In our household, if the children are restless or struggling with their work, I release them outdoors. Hours later, they return refreshed and ready to focus. Nature brings out peace and patience in us, which can then encourage us to be more effective in our daily tasks."

Real play happens in the forests, streams, and meadows and on the sandy shores—not in the designated play areas. Inspiring places, filled with real adventure, interesting wildlife, and a chance of danger. Children learn from these experiences by creating their own challenges, making up their own games, and taking responsibility for their own actions. In nature, they learn something that could never be taught in a classroom—they learn how to live.

THE NEED FOR FREEDOM

Learning is a meritocracy. You are justified by the results that you get. And when your child needs something different from what the establishment prescribes, you should have the freedom to pursue it. I understand that the sheer number of children in our communities necessitates that education be standardized. But if you prefer to look at your child as an individual with unique gifts, skills, and tendencies, you should be able to customize their education accordingly.

The good news is that you *do* have the freedom to choose your child's education, at least in the United States and most of the world, with the exception of Germany, Greece, and Denmark.

You have the freedom to use a curriculum. The freedom not to use a curriculum. The freedom to travel full-time. The freedom to replicate the classroom. The freedom to homeschool the way you choose. The freedom to homeschool like no method done before. The freedom to homeschool in the first place. And the freedom to put your kids back in school if it doesn't work out. This freedom doesn't diminish our educational opportunities; it expands them.

And what about freedom for our children? Gone are the days when kids could roam the neighborhoods on bikes, explore the woods behind their houses without fear, or get lost in their imagination in the backyard. I don't believe my independence is simply a personality trait; rather, it's the result of having an abundance of freedom as a young child. Children today are given so little freedom to play, explore, pursue their own interests, and learn at their own pace. It's not only hindering their ability to learn but also detrimental to their development.

Peter Gray, a research professor at Boston College and author of the college textbook *Psychology*, has been researching the biological foundations of education. In his book *Free to Learn*, he stated, "Lack of free play may not kill the physical body, as would lack of food, air, or water, but it kills the spirit and stunts mental growth. Free play is the means by which children learn to make friends, overcome their fears, solve their own problems, and generally take control of their own lives. It is also the primary means by which children practice and acquire the physical and intellectual skills that are essential for success in the culture in which they are growing."[1]

Gray has seen this occur in his own children as well as in the families he has studied over the years. He goes on to say, "Nothing that we do, no amount of toys we buy or 'quality time' or special training we give our children, can compensate for the freedom we take away. The things that children learn through their own initiatives, in free play, cannot be taught in other ways."

Free play not only leads to independence but also produces creative adults. Creativity doesn't result from structured lessons and artist studies. These inspire it, yes, but as British educator Charlotte Mason professed, "Education is an atmosphere, a discipline, a life."

Children need freedom to try out what they've learned, to make it their own, and to present their own interpretations. Whether it's engaging in a creative art or reading literature or simply coming to understand a historical event, time to process without judgment is crucial. Children also need freedom to experiment and work with materials without any instruction.

In Susan Schaeffer Macaulay's timeless book *For the Children's Sake*, she observed, "Free time is necessary for the fruit of creativity. It grows out of [a rich life]. All children respond to this abundance with ideas, plans, imagination,

THE CALL OF THE WILD + FREE

playing. They solve problems, think, grow. Children respond to life by living. They need this time to grow."[2]

We may not always see the fruit of what they are learning, but make no mistake, our children are growing deep roots. You must trust the process, embrace this journey for the long haul, and hold on to your hat, because the beauty is going to blow you away someday soon.

RECLAIMING CHILDHOOD

Those of us who attended traditional schools are used to early mornings, long days, inefficient bus commutes, and stalled classes due to disciplinary problems. With the rise of dual-income families, school serves not only as an educational system but also a daycare program.

A typical day for most elementary-age kids is filled with waiting for long times, taking group bathroom breaks, standing in line, waiting for the teacher to handle unruly kids, and doing busywork that doesn't necessarily contribute to their education. It adds up to a six- or eight-hour day that's topped off with homework because there wasn't enough time to fit in the real learning.

But this is not a childhood. Maybe the way forward is rethinking why we are doing what we are doing. In the words of Jim Henson, "The way forward is sometimes the way back."[3]

Homeschooling is a big commitment, to be sure. It takes an incredible amount of emotional engagement. Educating our children is both a great privilege and a responsibility. But doing regular subject studies doesn't take as long as you might think.

Many homeschool families finish their "book work" within a few hours, leaving afternoons free for creative pursuits. In some cases, they don't schedule formal studies every day of the week. With this extra time, they're able to spend more time exploring, reading, and going on exciting field trips. There's nothing missing from their education. In fact, there's more time for it.

OH CHILDHOOD, WHERE DID YOU GO?

Oh childhood, where did you go?
We sped up the process, thinking that's how you'd grow.
Gave up fort building and climbing trees.
To avoid muddy hands and skinned-up knees.
Enrolled you in things you were expected to do.
Not stopping to realize it was for us more than you.
Remind me—giving up daydreams was better for who?
When did we quit dreaming, to notice or care?
Stop looking at stars or remembering they're there?
We put you on buses and shipped you away.
To preschools and programs and preceptors for pay.
Who said the experts know better than us, anyway?
You were made for summers that go on forever.
Getting lost in good books in inclement weather.
Making up stories and writing new songs.
Until long past your bedtime and the porch light comes on.
No need to rush childhood; it goes by too fast.
What you need is the time to make it all last.
You belong out in nature, staring up at the sky.
Blowing dandelion puffs and watching them fly.
Turning clouds into shapes that you want them to be.
Fending off dragons if that's what you see.
If only there were a way to be wild + free.
We read the great books but ignore their wisdom.
Go our own way instead of trusting what's in them.
Childhood is a treasure, a gift to behold.
I'm sorry to say you've been traded and sold.
Oh childhood, where did you go?
Oh childhood, say it ain't so.
We'll bring you back home if it's the last thing we do.
We'll reclaim the wonder; that's my promise to you.

Homeschooling should never be about what we are keeping from our children; rather, it should be about what we are giving to them. The net result is a reclamation of childhood.

The beauty of homeschooling is that it gives our children something no other school can offer. It gives them time. Time to explore, play, experiment, think their own thoughts, and pursue their own passions. It gives them more time to go more deeply into subjects, to study topics for longer times, and to be bored by inactivity, which leads to creative ideas. When children go from one class to the next, followed by extracurricular activities, sports, and then homework all evening, when do they get to experience the wonder of childhood?

We are all natural learners. We can learn anywhere and anytime. Whether you choose to have formal studies or give

"Once in a while it really hits people that they don't have to experience the world in the way they have been told to."

—ALAN KEIGHTLEY

your children the freedom to study and explore interests on their own, shake free the chains of convention and give your children a life of learning and adventure.

We all desire to give our children the best advantages in life, to prepare them to be responsible adults. But sometimes we forget that before we can be adults, we must be children. If you want to give your kids the best chance at being healthy adults, give them a childhood.

Dear friend, don't let a bustling culture determine the needs of your own children. You get to choose how they grow up. You can protect their time, energy, and imagination. You are the gatekeeper of the garden of their childhood.

A NEW KIND OF HOMESCHOOL

Most objections to homeschooling come from adults who cite the impossible challenge of replicating the classroom at home.

But that is neither necessary nor valuable. Break the mold. Let the world become your classroom. Fling open the windows. Swing wide the doors. Let your curiosities spill out into the streets, the fields and forests, where your children can pursue their passions and make the most of their one wild and precious life.

Choose not to isolate but to liberate your children.

Chuck the chalkboard. Ditch the desks. Gather around the table each morning to become a family once again. Throw the puzzles on the floor and play games together. Read great books not within four walls but upon a blanket spread across a meadow or a mountain, where their authors probably imagined their stories in the first place. Let them play, pretend, and imagine. Give them opportunities to build, create, and take things apart.

Everything you've heard about homeschooling is wrong. It is not only for the strange, eccentric, and socially awkward. It is the future of education. Just as Uber and Lyft put ride sharing in the hands of drivers and Airbnb put lodging in the hands of homeowners, homeschooling is putting education back in the hands of parents and changing the face of education as we know it.

Self-directed learning is not only the best way to maximize a child's gifts—just look at what the Khan Academy has accomplished by making free education available worldwide— it is also dismantling the hierarchy of education. It no longer matters which college accepts your child when the highest level of learning is accessible to all.

All your child needs is a guide. Not a professional teacher. Not an academic expert. Not a docent with a doctorate. Your child needs you, a companion with whom to traverse the mountain.

You can't go wrong. There may be times when you'll need to put down the work, call it quits for the day, for the week. But you are no longer bound by the constraints of an eight-to-three education. Your children are always learning. You don't have to instill the desire to learn in them. They are born to learn. Let's release them back into their natural habitat and watch them thrive.

THE MYTHS

GASTROPODS ARE HUGELY DIVERSE IN SIZE, COLOR, AND SHAPE

SEASHELLS OF THE WORLD

A GUIDE TO THE BETTER-KNOWN SPECIES

$1.50

HAWK-WING CONCH

ATLANTIC YELLOW COWRY

STRIATE MARGARITE

GIANT PACIFIC OYSTER

HOOKED MUSSEL

LIMPET

JACKKNIFE CLAM

YELLOW COCKLE

213

6 Objections to Homeschooling

AFTER NINE YEARS OF HOMESCHOOLING MY KIDS and nearly five years of running Wild + Free, I've heard every conceivable objection to homeschooling. Public teachers who object that we're belittling their profession. Traditionalists who say that homeschooling is insufficient without test taking and textbooks. Podcasters who protest that there's nothing wrong with replicating the classroom at home. The list goes on and on.

But many meaningful questions come up for parents who are trying to sort out the realities of homeschooling and can't get past some of the larger objections. It reminds me of Tom Hanks in the movie *Castaway*, when he's trying to escape the island but can't get beyond the crashing waves that keep holding him back.

Think of this book as your Wilson.

Homeschooling isn't for everyone, it's true. But many of the concerns are based on the misconceptions of homeschooling rather than on what it can be. Let's walk through some of the common objections and see if we can't get your raft out into the open sea.

#1 I CAN'T DO THIS

Occasionally, mothers will tell me, "I can't homeschool my children. We're too much alike. We would butt heads. My kids need to learn from other people. It's just better that way."

The thinking here is that some parents are suited for it and some are not. They assume that homeschooling families must have a higher threshold for chaos, noise, and messes.

They're right about one thing—parenting is fraught with distractions, chaos, and tension. But it's not accurate to say that homeschooling is an especially worsened case of it. Those emotions and tensions are all happening between a child and a parent whether you're there for it or not. As homeschoolers, we have the ability to work through it with them and grow in our relationships.

This tension can come from any number of sources. Sometimes it's a disciplinary issue. I don't mean discipline in the sense of punishing a child but rather in providing a framework for living under the same roof. Guidance, if you will. Children need healthy rhythms to help them know what to expect. Of course, we still have skirmishes. There are days when I want to pull my hair out. But know this—you were made for your children. You were equipped to handle them.

Sometimes this tension comes from inborn neurological, nutritional, or emotional issues. I have a child who often resists doing everyday tasks, such as making his bed or tying his shoes. He throws a fit when we speak to him in a stern voice because he can't handle the conflict.

It's taken my intuition and several years of consultations to discover that he's battling some neurological issues and his brain is in a constant state of fight or flight. We're getting him the therapy he needs to restore those brain synapses, and his behavior is starting to turn around.

I have another child who was slow to develop his speech and processing skills. In consultation with several medical specialists, we overhauled his diet to eliminate several foods. Over the next several months, his brain became less foggy, his speech took off, and his face stopped appearing puffy and swollen.

As a parent, I could have easily thrown in the towel when addressing those issues. At first, I didn't have any idea what the problem could be. There were days when I lost hope and their outbursts got the better of me. But what was the alternative? To send them to a school where they would be relegated to the remedial program or thrown into detention for behavioral issues?

I'm so grateful that I get to walk alongside my children, assume the best of them, and find the individualized attention they need to overcome life's challenges.

This is not to say that conventional schools can't help your child. But you're gambling on the hope that someone will work with and care as much about your child as you do. If you're waiting for someone to step in and give your child what she needs, it just might be you, Mama.

Not only *can* you do this, but the greatest act of love you can bestow upon your child is to work through the difficult times together—to help her, nurture her, and find solutions.

You can do this. You are exactly the parent your child needs. And you can be exactly the teacher she needs as well.

OBJECTION

#2 I'M NOT QUALIFIED

There is another aspect to feeling incapable, which is the academic side. Plenty of mothers hated school growing up, didn't go to college, and can't fathom being responsible for their children's education. Others are just the opposite. They loved school, have multiple degrees, and still think education is best left in the hands of professionals.

When starting out, I fell somewhere in the middle, and what I lacked in abilities I made up for in passion and confidence.

But that doesn't mean I haven't had my fair share of days feeling inadequate.

The beauty of homeschooling is that you are not the almighty teacher who needs to have all the answers long before your children do. You get to learn and experience this information along with them, even if it's the first time for both of you.

My dear friend and Wild + Free mama Alisha Miller refers to it as "climbing the mountain with our children." The picture of education is not standing at the top of the mountain calling our children to climb up to us, but rather grabbing a pickax and climbing along with them.

I love the story of Helen Keller, who was born blind and deaf. She was paired with a remarkable teacher named Anne Sullivan, who not only taught her how to read Braille and learn multiplication tables but also accompanied her for thirteen years throughout her education.

When Helen attended Radcliffe College in Cambridge, Massachusetts, Anne went along with her to every class, spelling out the lectures into her hand. When Helen graduated from college four years later, Anne had also gained an incredible education right along with her.

You are the Anne Sullivan of your child's education.

If that doesn't convince you, know this: homeschooling is legal in the United States and many other countries, and no teacher certificate, accreditation, or doctorate is required.

In other words, even the government believes you can do this.

You just have to decide if you have the heart for it.

#3 I DON'T HAVE THE TIME

I've heard mothers say, "I don't have time to homeschool my children. I need time for myself. How would I be able to work, go to the gym, or have coffee with a friend?"

It's true, homeschool mothers don't get a lot of time for themselves. We can't just run out for coffee or brunch with friends, not to mention read a book in peace or, heaven forbid, go to the bathroom alone. I understand the concern. I'm a desperate introvert who needs time alone to recharge my energy and collect my thoughts.

And I crave peaceful environments. Cluttered surfaces, dirty bathrooms, and messy rooms stress me out. When my two older boys were in school, it was easier to keep the house clean, laundry folded, groceries stocked, and dinner prepped on a consistent basis.

Some things don't get done or look the way I'd prefer. But homeschooling gives us the opportunity to involve our kids in these daily household chores. It teaches them how to work and learn housekeeping skills, and it reminds them that we're all in this together. Homeschooling is a team effort. We are not doing this *to* them but *with* them.

All my kids have simple daily chores, such as keeping their bedrooms tidy, making their beds, and emptying the dishwasher or taking out the trash. Things like doing laundry, cleaning toilets, decluttering, and mopping often take a back seat to more important things, like story tea time, math work, or playing outdoors, but everyone pitches in when needed.

If nothing else, we spend a few hours once a week (usually Fridays) doing a more thorough cleaning so I can breathe a little easier and our home feels more like a haven than a hovel.

I'm not eager for my kids to leave the house. This time with my children is such a short season. There will be plenty of time for pedicures, Pilates, and pinochle when they're grown up. And I don't see this as sacrificing my best years by devoting time to them. *These* are my best years. I can't imagine anything more rewarding than shaping another human's life and building a legacy.

Besides, I've found that with a little bit of creativity, there's still room for the important things, like quality time with my husband, doing meaningful work, feeding my soul, and pursuing my passions. Our families benefit greatly when we care for our own mental, spiritual, and physical well-being. But I'm not missing out on a preferable life. Right now, I'm savoring every moment I have with my kids. The greatest commodity we have in life is time, and I want to invest it in my kids, not just me.

OBJECTION
#4 I CAN'T AFFORD IT

For many, homeschooling poses a threat to the family's bottom line. I understand that the decision to homeschool has real financial ramifications. It makes having two incomes nearly impossible. Someone either has to quit their job, find one that has flexible hours, increase their income, or find a creative way to work from home. But if you determine to give your child an educational experience at home, there is a way. It may be challenging. It may stretch you beyond what you think you can handle. But there is always a way.

In my family, we decided to reorient our lives around the decision to homeschool. We knew it would mean making sacrifices. We've chosen to prioritize this lifestyle over all other options. My husband and I have created income opportunities outside of conventional employment to make this choice possible. As a result, my husband and I trade off homeschooling duties. My husband has his days to work on the business, and I have mine.

I realize this arrangement isn't possible for everyone. Not everyone is an entrepreneur or has a flexible work schedule. But if you decide to homeschool, you can sit down with your spouse and work out a plan to make it happen. It'll take sacrifice, hard work, and creativity, but the value you'll gain from homeschooling will pay off.

Stephanie Newcomb is a real estate agent who homeschools her children. She knew homeschooling would be tough, but she and her husband weighed their options and felt it was the right decision for their family. "Craig and I made a bold decision to pull our daughter out of public school and homeschool her. She was getting lost in the crowd and we could see that learning was not enjoyable. The spark had started to die, and we needed to do something."

The challenge was to make it work with their schedule as busy professionals.

"When our kids were young," she continued, "I left corporate America and dipped my toes into the world of real estate. The schedule had proven flexible, but there were situations when I needed to be kid-free. We didn't know how we'd make it work, but we took the plunge. Our schedules force everyone to play their part, but this makes sense right now, so we press on."

According to a report by the US Department of Agriculture, the cost for a middle-income family to raise a child born in 2015 through the age of seventeen is $233,610.[1] I'm willing to bet that much of that cost is for school clothing, designer backpacks, lunch money, and PTA and student activity fees. Homeschooling is a sustainable form of parenthood. It's free-range child-rearing.

Sometimes the financial barrier lies in the misconception that you need to purchase expensive materials in order to homeschool your kids. When resources are limited, it can be difficult to shell out additional money for the numerous homeschooling resources that are available today.

Hear me on this. You don't need a big-box curriculum to homeschool your kids, any more than you need a blackboard and a framed teaching certificate. If you have a good pair of walking shoes and a library card, you've got all you need. Everything else is icing.

MY SPOUSE IS NOT ON BOARD

Here's the hard truth: if your spouse is not on board, home-schooling is probably not the best fit for your family in this season. Homeschooling is hard enough to do on your own, let alone with a spouse who is opposed. You're going to need the support of your spouse to make this work.

I understand there are many single parents who homeschool their children and work extremely hard to make this life possible. These parents have my utmost respect and admiration. I love seeing how they make it work with a tremendous amount of creativity and dedication. And if they also work a full-time job, they deserve a special medal of honor.

Wild + Free mama Jennifer Schuh described her decision to homeschool her children even after divorce: "I was a new single mom with a two-year-old and an eleven-month-old clinging to me," Jen said. "I ran the textbook cycle of emotions and grieved the losses. Would we ever have joy? Or would the tough times taint all of my children's memories? Would we always be broken?

"Through time, counseling, family support, and lots and lots of mistakes, the answers became clearer. I can do this, even if I can't do it all. I decided that continuing to be present at home most of the time would be best for our family.

"Since my expenses were low, I began working part-time, three evenings a week, at a fine dining restaurant. While I worked, a member of my family spent quality time with my kids. What a beautiful school we've made! It was all birthed from the desire for stability and hope for a healthy family."

When I first proposed the idea of homeschooling to my husband, Ben, he was opposed. We both came from homes where higher education was valued above all else, and he assumed that homeschooling our kids would mean producing adults with limited career options available to them. And, honestly, he didn't want them to be weird.

This wasn't a topic we had ever discussed before, so I didn't try to convince him in the same conversation. I simply shared the results of my research and tried to answer his questions, just as I was seeking answers to my own. I didn't want to hinder our kids either.

I had always imagined my kids going to school and my cheering them on as they ran for student body president or played on the soccer team. I wanted to give my kids a leg up, both academically and socially. I was dedicated to giving them the best education, and I was committed to helping them become socially well adjusted.

So I understood all of Ben's concerns, and I gave him time to process this unconventional idea. Over the next few months, I shared my feelings, as well as the facts that I had been collecting that covered academic to social aspects.

Eventually, after a lot of research and discussion, Ben agreed that this seemed like a good idea for our son. I don't know what it will take in your situation. If your spouse isn't there yet, have patience. Keep sharing your findings. Keep pointing out the accomplishments of other homeschooled kids. Find answers to the hard questions. When the time is right, you'll both be on the same page, and you'll be grateful you waited.

6 I CAN'T DO THIS ALONE

Homeschooling has been legal in all fifty states only since 1993, but hundreds of homeschooling pioneers paved the way before that. For every trailblazer, I imagine there was a great amount of fear and loneliness. But I'm so glad they didn't quit.

At our Wild + Free conferences, I run into quite a few grandmothers who confess to have been wild + free before the term existed. These women have creases around their eyes, have shocks of gray and white hair pulled back in a topknot, and are the most beautiful women you'll ever meet, both inside and out. They walk around beaming with joy.

One such woman, Gaye Keough, homeschooled all six of her children in Nebraska before it was popular. "Our six children span sixteen years," Gaye said. "We had only two years of having all six kids at home. The days were full and long, but, looking back, the years seem short."

There weren't a lot of homeschooling resources or communities at the time, but Gaye became resourceful with what she had.

"We had no extra money for buying books or other ready-made curriculums," she said. "We got piles of books from the library. We walked all over our little town, visiting everything

it had to offer. Really, we just lived. And we loved it. It was beautiful and simple."

Gaye is still homeschooling two teenagers and now helping out with her grandchildren, and her approach to education hasn't changed all that much.

"Our homeschool style remained true through the years. We read a lot of great stories, talked to each other, laughed and sang together. We wrote about what we read, things that happened, and what we were thinking about. We often acted out the stories we read. We learned history and science along with literature by searching for answers to our questions.

"There was very little focus on workbooks or long assignments unless that was the personal bent of a particular kid. We spent a lot of time playing, doing household chores, and pursuing creative activities that appealed to the kids. We traveled to interesting places, visited the elderly, spent time at the library, and found outside social activities that motived the kids (4-H, drama club, and the like). They each took music lessons, and some took Spanish lessons from my mother."

Each of these women, like Gaye, has shared one common confession with me at our events. They wish this community had existed when they were getting started decades ago.

In 2016, the US Department of Education reported that 1.69 million students were homeschooled, which represents 3.3 percent of school-aged children.[2] This may not seem like a large percentage, but there are scores of homeschooling families all around you. We are fortunate to be a part of a global movement of like-minded, like-hearted families.

You are not alone.

WE ARE ALL WEIRD— AND WEIRD IS WONDERFUL

When I was five years old, I lived on the campus of the US Military Academy at West Point, where my father was a lieutenant colonel and professor. I spent countless hours outdoors, and for some reason my mother trusted the place enough to let me roam unsupervised.

Even as a five-year-old, I would spend the afternoons exploring the woods behind my house, playing in the alley with friends, or riding my bike around my neighborhood.

One day when I was five, I was walking home from a friend's house and must have looked a little lost. A young cadet saw me—the cadets often rode mules around campus—and ended up giving me a ride back home. I pretended I was Sacagawea returning to camp. Call me weird, but it was the highlight of my childhood.

There was a giant boulder situated on the hill behind my home—not six feet up from the street. Sometimes when my mother called me in for dinner, I ignored her frantic calls.

I hid behind the rock and pretended I was an orphan lost in the woods.

I was a weird child.

Eventually I grew up, got married, had children, and began homeschooling.

And guess what? I'm still weird.

I ditched the classroom to take my children for hikes in the woods. I piled them into the car to watch the sun rise over the ocean and search for sea glass before anyone else got to the beach. I visited museums and spent days just talking with my kids. I collected interesting nature finds and, just as I did as a child, tried to save all the worms on the sidewalk after the rain.

In our schoolroom, instead of following a textbook and sitting at desks, my children enjoyed freshly made scones and hot tea as we read books on a picnic blanket in the backyard. At the edge of the shore, I created math problems in the sand and we acted out our favorite books.

When Instagram came along, I started posting some of my weirdness for all to see. Many of my friends didn't understand. They would ask, "What curriculum do you use?" or "How do you have time to do this?" and "When do you do school?"

It was hard to explain that this *was* school.

But then there were others who chimed in and said, "Me too," or "That's my favorite way to spend a school day." Slowly but surely, one weird mama after another came out of the woodwork and connected. We came together at gatherings and started telling our stories. We were inspired and encouraged by each other and shared the best (and worst) things we did. We met in Virginia and Oregon and Long Beach and Texas and Nashville and Portland. And the number of Wild + Free mamas is growing by the day.

I am weird. You are weird. Our children are weird. And we wouldn't have it any other way because weirdness births dreamers and artists, authors and poets, mathematicians and scientists, and those who see the world through a different lens.

Weird, as it turns out, is wonderful.

7 The Socialization Myth

ONE OF THE BIGGEST MYTHS ABOUT HOMESCHOOLING IS that the children turn out "socially awkward." The stereotype has been firmly established in the way some homeschooled children look—unfashionable high-water pants, tousled hair, blank stares, a lack of conversational skills. People laugh at the thought of them piling into the family van wearing matching denim.

Oh, so much denim.

There's a difference, however, between unsocialized and weird. *Unsocialized* means lacking the ability to adjust to societal norms. *Weird*, on the other hand, isn't quite so bad. While many parents would be offended by the idea of their kids being weird, we embrace it. The truth is, we don't want our kids to be like everyone else. We want them to discover what they love and have the freedom to pursue it, even if it's unusual, different, or misunderstood.

But there is a real fear among parents that their children won't turn out normal. This feeling is rooted in a genuine love for their children and a desire to give them every advantage in life.

All of us are new to this parenting thing. We get one shot to do it right, and we don't want to screw it up. If you've ever felt the pain of watching your child go ignored in a group of kids, it's enough to scare you onto the conventional path. We don't want to take any chance of their being bullied, cast out, or ostracized. If you're anything like my husband, when coming up with names for your newborn baby, you ran through every conceivable nickname that your child could be labeled with on the basis of rhyming, cultural references, or any sort of demeaning alliteration.

If there's any chance that homeschooling will produce unsocialized kids who will be rejected by society, we want nothing to do with it. But I think you'll find the opposite to be true.

"Doing something so different can scare people, because it questions the assumptions on which they have built their lives. And when people get scared, they stereotype. Thus, the ever-present stereotype of the unsocialized and unworldly homeschooler."

—BLAKE BOLES

WHAT IS NORMAL?

Let's be clear about one thing. What we fear is not weirdness but our children's lack of ability to interact in society. That is the textbook definition of being unsocialized.

But if there is any species of child that is least susceptible to being unsocialized, it is a homeschooled kid. There is too much self-awareness, too much independence, too much strength of identity to make them incapable of navigating society in a successful, healthy way.

There are outliers, to be sure. I remember reading about a homeschool family who refused to engage in academic studies because they were certain the rapture was about to happen.[1] But those are the exceptions to the rule. Studies show that homeschooled children are more likely to have higher self-esteem and be less susceptible to peer pressure.[2]

In other words, homeschooling produces socially competent kids.

Not only is there no proof that children who are not in traditional school have a disadvantage in social interactions, I would argue that being homeschooled gives them the upper hand.

I have three homeschooled boys, and some of their friends happen to be three homeschooled girls who are the same ages. They hang out, conduct science experiments, make movies, and take music lessons from the same instructor. In any other context, this friendship would seem strange. When the six of them hang out in public places, other kids don't know what to make of them. But this is because society separates the boys from the girls, and kids have been conditioned to think it's the norm.

Other kids don't know what to make of it and occasionally will tease my sons, saying, "You must love each other!" or "You've got the hots for them!" Let me ask you—who is the "normal" one in this situation?

What good comes from our children being so "socialized" that their identities, preferences, mannerisms, and ambitions become indistinguishable from everyone else's? What good comes from their running with a pack of influencers who determine their sense of self? What good can come from normality being defined by other kids who are still forming their own identities?

CHILDREN NEED A CHILDHOOD

Even though my husband is only in his mid-forties, he grew up watching *The Andy Griffith Show* in black and white. Not only has he seen every episode; I think he believes he's an actual citizen of Mayberry.

His one wish as a father has been for his children to fall in love with the show, just as he did. I told him not to get his hopes up. "Times have changed," I told him. "They might not go for the outdated production quality . . . or the boredom," I said, as he shot me a menacing glare.

So it was with great trepidation that he introduced the series to them one fall evening a few years ago. He stood in the back of the room biting his nails as the kids gathered around the TV set with their blankets and popcorn. It took a few minutes of Ben coaxing them to "keep watching" until they fell hook, line, and sinker for Opie, Barney, Aunt Bea, and the rest of the characters.

Since that momentous night, my children not only have become fans of the show but also have devoured every episode of *I Love Lucy*, *Bonanza*, and *Leave It to Beaver*. Even more, Ben has dragged, er . . . treated us to the annual Mayberry Days fan festival in Mount Airy, North Carolina (Andy's hometown) for the past three years in a row. (And yes, he announced the first road trip to our family in his best Gomer Pyle voice: "Surprise, surprise, surprise!")

The interesting thing about my children's newfound love of black-and-white TV shows is watching them introduce these relics to their friends, only to be met with confused looks and murmurs of "Are you serious?" It's rare that my kids find a friend who shares this interest, and they are still okay with it. I'm okay with it. And Ben is definitely okay with it.

What children need is a childhood, in order to discover themselves, awaken their passions, and explore their interests— no matter how long it takes. Unfortunately, far too often, social pressure takes it away.

FINDING FRIENDS

We want our children to have the freedom to be themselves, but we don't want to strip them of a healthy community to which they can belong. On the contrary, friendship is a vital part of their childhood journey, and homeschooling can offer them a rich community.

No matter how we choose to educate our children, we all want them to have friends, to be liked, and to find their tribe. Much as with adults, this comes easier for some kids simply because of their natural temperaments. We all know the fun-loving few who don't know a stranger, have thirty best friends, and can't wait for the next party. But not every child—or adult, for that matter—is built that way.

As homeschoolers, it might take some time and we might have to try a little harder, but we can help our children find their people. Whether it's a small group of friends who get together every week or a single kindred spirit with whom they can share long chats and swap books every month, we will discover what our children need to thrive on this journey.

There are co-ops, charter schools, associations, and community classes that all exist to serve homeschooling families. In fact, at Wild + Free, we created a map to allow mothers in our community to form and post groups. Within one year, we had over a thousand groups all over the world. All it takes is a few mentions on social media and these groups quickly fill up. One Wild + Free group leader in California, Maria Gervase, saw her group grow to 250 families before she turned her focus toward raising up and training new group leaders.

Wild + Free groups are a wonderful way for parents to connect with other like-minded families, as well as for kids to meet friends who are on the same journey.

For me, it started with hosting a book club the year after I brought my son Wyatt home from school. We had been reading *Little House on the Prairie* and decided to host a party to celebrate the book. We invited a few other homeschool families to join us in discussing and living out this beloved story of Laura Ingalls and her family. The twenty-plus children ate sandwiches wrapped in brown Kraft paper, searched for beads in the dusty earth, as Laura and Mary did at the abandoned Native American camp, and strung them together into necklaces and bracelets.

As parting gifts, we gave each child a tiny heart-shaped cake, a peppermint stick, and an old-fashioned penny, just like the ones Laura and Mary received from Mr. Edwards at Christmas.

The children threw themselves into the experience, dressing up like their favorite characters and answering questions about the story. Before the gathering was over, they pleaded with their mothers to finish reading the series when they got home so they could come back for more.

Book clubs have become a wonderful way to bring literature and stories to life. And celebrating books with friends has proved to be a significant part of their learning journey.

I also learned that our communities are replete with opportunities for homeschooled kids. They can join sports teams in their school districts, sign up for college courses while in high school, and get special access to state parks, local farms, museums, theaters, and amusement parks.

In fact, a *USA Today* article from 2012 cited research revealing that "on average home-schooled students routinely participate in eight social activities outside of the home, and typically consume considerably less television than do traditionally-educated students."[3]

Homeschooled kids are no longer the outcasts of society but are surrounded by bright, talented, and well-adjusted friends. They tend not to be insecure about their status, and they even have their own proms, graduation ceremonies, yearbooks, and special nights at the roller rink.

These days, being homeschooled means becoming part of an extraordinary community.

BEHAVIORAL ISSUES

It probably takes twenty informative experiences for a parent who isn't already on board to decide to homeschool her child. One of those happened for me while I was visiting my son's first-grade class in public school. I don't have anything against the child, but a girl named Lenae had singlehandedly commandeered the entire classroom.[4] The teacher gave it her best shot, but she was no match for Lenae.

Lenae lying on the floor.

Lenae making fart noises.

Lenae running in place.

Lenae speaking out of turn.

Lenae cracking her knuckles.

And Lenae getting out of her seat.

The teacher tried all of her best tactics, but she fought Lenae, and Lenae won.

Now, Lenae was funny and kept the kids laughing. But the class had to wait until order was restored before they could move on to other productive activities. I kept an eye on the clock and wondered how much shorter the school day could have been if it weren't for these kinds of interruptions.

I realize some parents would say, "The world is filled with Lenaes. I want my kid to be socialized enough to interact with all the Lenaes out there." Or they might even suggest, "If my kids aren't around Lenaes, they won't know how to function in society."

But I'm not convinced that's true.

The Discovery Institute, a Seattle-based think tank, published an extensive report on homeschooling written by senior fellow Dr. Patricia Lines. She described several controlled studies comparing the social skills of homeschoolers with those of non-homeschoolers.

In one study, trained counselors viewed videotapes of mixed groups of homeschooled and non-homeschooled children at play. The counselors didn't know the school status of each child.

The result? Homeschooled kids demonstrated fewer behavioral problems.

Dr. Lines concluded that "there is no basis to question the social development of homeschooled children" and that "the homeschoolers scored as 'well adjusted.'"[5]

Homeschoolers have their characters, to be sure. I have one or two myself. But one of the unintended outcomes of educating our children at home is the formation of character. There are no lines to wait in, fewer cliques, and less activity for activity's sake—the breeding ground for behavioral aberrations.

Show me a child who has been homeschooled, and I'll show you a kid who has learned how to shop for groceries while his mother nurses a baby in the car. Show me a homeschooled kid, and I'll show you someone who knows how to sit quietly in a waiting room. Someone who knows how to look you in the eye. Someone who knows how to finish his work on his own. Someone who can read a novel in one sitting or create a comic book series in his spare time.

They may not all start out this way, but homeschooling grows a child's character.

THE ONE-ROOM SCHOOLHOUSE

I know what you're thinking. Homeschooling puts all your children in one room, which means their only friends are siblings. How do we reconcile the lack of same-aged peers?

We've gone through seasons without community when my children's only friends were each other, and I've been grateful for the gift of family during those times. My kids often butt heads, but we still gather around the dinner table each night, spend lots of time together as a family, and, late at night, I can hear them laughing and telling stories to each other from their beds. My children are a lot closer to each other than my siblings and I were because they spend so much time together.

This closeness isn't to be viewed as a deficit but rather as an advantage in life. Time will tell, but I have a feeling that my kids will grow up and still be each other's best friends.

As for their education, our little one-room schoolhouse has tended to pull everyone up to the same level. When my eldest son was seven years old, I read Susan Wise Bauer's Story of the World series on history to him each day and asked him to read portions to me as well. One day, his five-year-old brother announced that he'd like to have a turn. I was secretly in a hurry, trying to finish up with Wyatt before my toddler woke up from his nap. Taking time to humor my brand-new reader was the last thing I needed.

But, surprisingly, Dylan read the next passage.

And I didn't even know he could read full sentences.

Typically, when kids are bored in school, it's because they need something more challenging to engage them. But they have to wait for the rest of the class to catch up before they can move on. Their poor performance can actually be an indicator of intelligence.

Homeschooling removes all the barriers to learning. You decide the pace. Your child can go as far as she likes, without the limitations that are placed on curriculums by grade level.

Peter Gray spent many years interacting with and studying the educational model of Sudbury Valley School in Massachusetts.[6] The school doesn't have grades or even required classes. Rather, the children are free to attend the classes of their choice, interact with students of all ages, and engage in various activities such as art, writing, and drama throughout the day.

Gray asserts the positive benefits of younger children interacting with older students and also the organic ways in which older students are helped by the younger ones.

He wrote, "The advantages of age mixing go in both directions. By interacting with younger children, older ones practice leadership and nurturance, and they gain the experience of being the mature one in the relationships (which is especially important for children without younger siblings). Older children also gain deeper understandings of concepts by teaching younger ones, which forces them to think about what they do or do not know."[7]

He shares several ways he's observed the older ones adapting their games to include younger students, showing younger ones how to treat others, and gaining understanding by teaching concepts to a younger child.

For most homeschooling families, learning and interacting with siblings is a naturally built-in benefit. Co-ops, charter schools, weekly classes, and nature groups also provide this, especially for single-child families. But the advantages aren't just one-way.

Gray continues, "And just as older children inspire younger ones to engage in more complex or sophisticated activities than they otherwise would, younger children inspire older ones to engage in more creative activities than they otherwise would."[8]

From artistic endeavors, such as painting and building, to imaginative games like chase or make-believe, the older students are drawn to the younger children's activities.

"Even when they weren't playing directly with them," Gray wrote, "the mere presence of younger children and their playthings seemed to inspire the older students to play more creatively than they otherwise would."[9]

I have witnessed this with my own children and their group of friends.

I'll never forget the times over the years when I'd thought my eldest had outgrown certain things, only to see him fall back into them at the prompting of his siblings. From playing with Lego sets to dressing up in full battle regalia for an epic sword fight in the backyard, his ability to play like a child was reawakened in the presence of younger children. And while he prefers time alone to nurture his introverted, bookish interests, he can't resist stopping to touch a warm ball of homemade play dough or a fresh bin of water beads on the table.

What others may see as regression I see as reclamation. A reclamation of childlike wonder, a reclamation of imagination, and a reclamation of spirit, free from peer and academic pressure.

What Peter Gray saw at Sudbury was telling.

> "It is only in the presence of loving, respectful, trusting adults that children will learn all they are capable of learning, or reveal to us what they are learning."
>
> —JOHN HOLT

"Through such continued play, many students at the school become excellent artists, builders, storytellers, and creative thinkers," Gray wrote. "Many of the graduates go onto careers that require a high degree of creativity, and I suspect that their age-mixed play experiences are part of the reason."[10]

ADULT INTERACTION

The belief that children's socialization happens best when they are surrounded by children of the same age is simply unfounded. Think about it. Outside of the classroom, where else do people associate with each other solely on the basis of age? Segregation of children by age is not healthy for social development, any more than it is for culturally diverse backgrounds.

In fact, socializing with adults is a far better preparation for life, especially when those adults have something exciting to offer by way of ideas and accomplishments. As Thomas Armstrong wrote in his book *Awakening Genius*, "When children are surrounded by curious and creative adults, they have their own inner genius sparked into action."

Whenever someone mentions socialization in their objection to homeschooling, I want to ask them, "Have you ever talked to my kids? I mean, really talked to them?" Because my kids will engage you just as well as any adult. And so will their homeschooled friends. They've got real opinions, hobbies, passions, and interests. And they'll be happy to talk to you about yours.

My kids are better off spending time with their parents, who start businesses, write books, and launch creative projects. Or our homeschooling friends Gregg and Katie, who have opened a chain of certified organic vegan restaurants throughout the country. Or our homeschooling friends Steven and Hannah, who are gifted gardeners and cooks. The list goes on.

Much like schools, the family predates the factory. Prior to the industrial age, children played, learned, and worked right alongside their siblings, mothers, and fathers. From working on the farm, playing at Mama's feet, or sitting down for dinner at the end of the day, the table was their classroom. It's where both a child's education and his socialization took place.

Interacting with kids and adults of different ages and experiences is not harmful to a child's social development but a benefit that traditional schools simply cannot offer.

GIVE YOUR CHILD THE WORLD

Socialization isn't a valid factor for most homeschoolers today because we aren't looking to socialize our kids according to the contemporary interpretation of the word. Since when did socialization equate to homogenization? Creating cookie-cutter kids who all act and interact the same is not our goal.

Our children were meant to bloom in their own time and at their own pace. If your child is introverted, hangs back in social situations, or prefers to observe rather than engage, respect her. Give her space. Continue showering her with love, and allow her to emerge when she's comfortable. After all, as Rumi said, "It is rain that grows flowers, not thunder."

When our shier children act sheepishly around strangers, we can be quick to wonder what others must be thinking about their sociability. It behooves us to remember that no matter how they are schooled, personalities and friendliness vary from child to child. And we must let neither desire for praise nor fear of embarrassment guide our decisions in parenting. Our children are not personal projects to prove our competence to outsiders. They are unique individuals, beautiful souls, who need our support both privately and publicly.

"The idea that children need to be around many other youngsters in order to be 'socialized' is perhaps the most dangerous and extravagant myth in education and child rearing today."

—DR. RAYMOND MOORE

I work hard every day to teach my kids not to let others look down on them because of their youth. Our society may put them in age-based groups because it's an efficient way, but that doesn't mean it's the best way. In fact, I believe it undermines their potential.

We also don't want to hide our children away from culture or shut out the world. Quite the opposite. We want to give our children the world and make it approachable and explorable.

We're not concerned with socialization because we desire to give them something better—the ability to learn, grow, and make meaningful connections with people of all ages.

8 The Qualification Myth

THERE ARE TWO REASONS WHY YOU SHOULD NEVER homeschool. One is if you don't have even an inkling of desire. The other is if you don't like your children. But your ability to homeschool has nothing to do with having a teaching degree or feeling qualified to teach your own kids.

We all want the best education for our children. So why wouldn't we want them in the hands of professional teachers who have spent years learning the best ways to help children learn? For some parents, that is the best route. But if you've been considering homeschooling and think you aren't qualified because you don't have a degree in education, think again.

In fact, you might discover that you enjoy learning, creating, and discovering things too. Wild + Free mama Kelly Hardee said that she started homeschooling because she thought it was the best path for her kids. She expected them to thrive in the simplicity of this kind of life. What she didn't expect was how much *she* would thrive.

"A whole new world awakened within me," she said. "Like a part of me that was stolen has been given back to me, and I didn't even know it was gone. Here I am, reliving years past and growing up right alongside of them. Thirty-one years old and yet I feel, in many ways, like I'm only five inside, giddy about my new love for watercolor painting and learning to read (I mean, really read) for the first time in my life. It's been the sweetest discovery and unexpected joy for me in this journey thus far."

"Education is thought of as an affair for teachers, something to major in in college, something that requires a large amount of brains and has very little to do with ordinary people."
—KAREN ANDREOLA

HOMESCHOOLING REQUIREMENTS BY STATE

Let's start with the basic legal requirements. In the United States, thirty-nine of the fifty states have absolutely zero requirements for homeschooling parent qualifications. That means you can homeschool with a college degree, a PhD, or not even as much as a high school diploma.

That leaves only eleven states—Georgia, New Mexico, North Carolina, North Dakota, Ohio, Pennsylvania, South Carolina, Tennessee, Virginia, Washington, and West Virginia—that require parents to have some form of educational qualification, such as a GED or high school diploma. None require a college diploma, and some offer supervision in lieu of a high school education. Homeschooling is not only legal but also requires little to no educational qualifications.

This can feel both liberating and scary at the same time. I mean, does the government really entrust the education of future generations to any uneducated parent? The answer is yes;

yes, it does. Freedom is an inherent right of every American, and, for good or for bad, parents are able to choose how and where their children are educated.

Homeschooling isn't for everyone, but it's accessible to anyone.

Homeschooling is not only a right but also a responsibility. It takes intention and commitment to giving our children an individualized, quality education. And this is a responsibility that homeschoolers don't take lightly. Don't be intimidated by the notion of it. As a parent, you already hold the highest form of responsibility.

If you can parent, you can homeschool.

FEELING INADEQUATE

My gut says that most parents don't feel paralyzed by whether they are *legally* allowed to homeschool but rather by their own feelings of inadequacy.

I get it. We don't want to hold our kids back.

It's why we read parenting books before they're even born, enroll them in preschools before they turn two, and take them to the pediatrician every year to make sure they're growing and developing in all the right ways.

It's why we see programs that teach our kids to read in preschool and wonder if we're missing something. It's why we trust the "experts" who say that kindergarten is no longer a time to learn through play and social interactions but a time to prepare for the rigor of first grade. It's why we doubt our own intuition about how to raise and care for another human being.

What I'm asking you to do is have a little faith in yourself.

LEARN ALONGSIDE YOUR CHILD

Take any stay-at-home mother whose days are spent managing the household, planning meals, changing diapers, and contributing to society with her marketplace skills in the gig economy—all with a nursling attached to her bosom around the clock—and ask her to take responsibility for the education of her children on top of everything else. No matter how many or few degrees she has or corporate positions she has held, she's never going to feel qualified.

Parenting is hard stuff. It builds us up, then beats us down. Swells our pride, then wounds our ego. Fills us up, then exposes our flaws. It defines our future and breaks our bodies. All within the same twenty-four-hour day. But we wouldn't have it any other way.

Parenting is the greatest privilege, and there are times when we cannot fathom that these beautiful little creatures have actually been entrusted to us. But we are determined, despite our flaws and mistakes, to do everything we can to raise them well and honor who they are.

Homeschooling is no different.

You won't have all the answers. You won't know what you're doing most of the time. You won't meet all your expectations (or the expectations of other people, for that matter). You won't get everything done. You won't get it all right. But you will not fail your children.

You will doubt yourself on more than one occasion. You will be misunderstood by friends and strangers alike. You will make mistakes. You will let your children down. You will let yourself down. You will grow in character. You will learn alongside your child. You will learn to walk by faith. You will love them. And you will witness beauty, growth, and miracles.

FIGURING IT OUT AS YOU GO

I meet a lot of new homeschoolers who think they need to have it all figured out before they begin. And while it's wise to research and weigh this decision heavily, homeschooling is something you figure out as you go. It takes time to find your way, to discover your tendencies as a parent, to discover your child's strengths, personality, and learning style.

"I learned most not from those who taught me but from those who talked with me."

—SAINT AUGUSTINE

The year I brought Wyatt home from school, I purchased a big-box curriculum, which is what I thought all homeschoolers were supposed to do. Rich literature was important to me, so I chose one that included lots of living books for reading aloud and language arts assignments.

A few weeks in, he was working on a simple assignment that required reading a short passage and then answering questions about it. Reading Comprehension 101.

Wyatt was a great reader. But for some reason, he struggled to answer the questions. They seemed so easy to me. I couldn't understand why he was getting them wrong. I grew frustrated that he wouldn't try harder. After a few more weeks of exasperating sessions, I took a closer look at Wyatt and realized that he wasn't being lazy or rebellious. It had to be something else.

I decided to try an experiment by reading a passage aloud and then asking him questions about it. Suddenly, he had no trouble comprehending what he heard. Apparently, Wyatt is an auditory learner. And thankfully, I could adjust our learning environment to accommodate him.

This was the first of many discoveries I have made by observing my children and discovering how they learn, what they need from me, and what they don't. Nothing could have prepared me to homeschool my children more than actually teaching my children.

Homeschooling isn't something you do when you have all the answers. It's a continual process of learning, unlearning, and relearning. It is an opportunity to invest in your children's passions, interests, and relationships. It may take you five months or five years just to discover what makes your kids tick or how you work best together. And that's okay.

Wild + Free mama Jessica Telian shared how it took her one full year of homeschooling to figure out the best approach for their family. "There is an incorrect assumption among homeschoolers that there is a 'best way' to homeschool their children," Jessica said.

"It's a scenario I've seen too often. A new homeschooling mama is completely gung-ho about this exciting educational journey that she's begun with her children. She researches and researches and researches some more. She talks with seasoned homeschoolers and gets all the best tips and tricks. After much deliberation, she chooses the approach and curriculum that seems like the best fit, and they are ready to start.

"The first weeks go well, especially as everyone thrives on the novelty of it all. But as the school year wears on, things don't always go so well. Somebody cries over their math. Another child can't seem to take off in reading. And the day's read-aloud time ends with the toddler making yet another huge mess while Mama tries to read and settle a sibling squabble at the same time. Mama gets discouraged and wonders what she's doing wrong.

"She sees and hears of other homeschooling families who always seem to be enjoying their schoolwork and decides that she must not have picked out 'the best' educational approach.

"After more research (which is more stressful this time because she's discouraged and pressured), Mama buys a different curriculum. The abrupt changes are disorienting for everyone, and the cycle continues. Though the specifics vary, we've all been there.

"Homeschooling is hard," Jessica pointed out. "And many times, we mistake that difficulty as an indicator that we're somehow doing it wrong. Floundering feels a lot like failing, but they're actually very different. No matter how much you know about homeschooling beforehand, educating your children at home is something you have to learn by doing. And only by doing it over and over again will you learn what works for your family.

"So we must give ourselves grace and accept that we may not find our homeschooling groove for a while. It might take a year, or even two. Even after figuring out what works for us, the start of each new school year can bring its own challenges. And each season can throw its own curve balls. As such, giving ourselves grace needs to happen continually."

Whether we're just starting out in homeschooling or embarking on another year, the vision we have in our minds rarely plays out in reality as well as it does in our imaginations. But that's okay. The beautiful part of homeschooling is that we get to keep reimagining the journey for our families and, more often than not, discover a better way.

TEACHERS ARE TRAINED FOR THE CLASSROOM

Of course you need a teaching degree for the classroom. Of course you need special training to wrangle twenty-five diverse children at a time for seven hours a day and have them score above a certain threshold each year or risk losing your funding. And of course you need preparation to handle the behavioral issues, threats, learning disabilities, and social challenges of the modern classroom.

Teachers have an incredibly difficult and important job, and the advocacy of homeschooling doesn't diminish their role in the lives of children who need them.

> "A teaching degree is to homeschooling as a culinary degree is to grandma's cooking. It just can't touch the care and personal standard that only she can stir in."
>
> —DAWN SHELTON

But homeschooling doesn't require the same training. To assert that homeschooling parents are not qualified to teach their own children is a fallacy of comparison. It's not the same thing. When you change the mode of learning, the expertise required for the other one goes out the window.

In fact, we have many former teachers in the Wild + Free community, and many of them feel that their background is a hindrance to their new course. They say they have to unlearn much of what they have been trained to do, in order to teach their own children. Children are natural learners. They don't need trained teachers to learn. They simply need a caring guide to walk the path with them, allowing them to explore, investigate, and pursue what's before them.

We mean no disrespect to teachers, but upending the establishment in our own households doesn't make us many friends in the traditional establishment. By taking hold of our freedom to educate our children however we choose, we unwittingly bring an indictment upon those who do it the conventional way.

John Holt understood this tension when he wrote, "Anyone who makes it his life work to help other people may come to believe that they cannot get along without him and may not want to hear evidence that they can, all too often, stand on their own feet. Many people seem to have built their lives around the notion that they are in some way indispensable to children, and to question that is to attack the very center of their being."[1]

QUALIFY YOURSELF

I want to let you in on a little secret. There are no home-schooling experts. Don't get me wrong. There are people who possess a particular combination of knowledge, experience, discernment, and clarity to guide others on this journey. But they can never replace you.

You are the expert on your own children.

When we feel insecure about our homeschooling abilities, we often reach out for the validation of a curriculum, a convention, or a consultant. While all these things can be valuable at different points in our journey, nothing beats a mother's intuition and her own natural abilities to love, nurture, and create an environment of learning for her children.

In his book *Outliers*, Malcolm Gladwell made famous the concept of spending 10,000 hours on any one thing in order to become an expert in that field. According to Gladwell, hockey players, psychologists, artists, orators, and criminal investigators must hit this threshold to become experts. Well, if you spend five hours a day with your child before they turn five, you will in effect have spent 10,000 hours on becoming an expert on your child, just in time for their formal education to begin.

The beautiful part about homeschooling is that it qualifies us for the task as we go. In other words, homeschooling teaches us to become teachers. It's a gentle instructor in that it allows us to start with young minds that don't yet need to study calculus or biology. We can wade into the pool with simple subjects by the very nature of our children's ages. We grow as they do.

Susan Wise Bauer advises us not to become overwhelmed by homeschooling when we're first starting out. "When you're just moving into homeschooling, even if they haven't been in

school, you start with your grammar and your math," she said. "And that's all you do, until you figure that out. Then you add another subject, and then you add another subject."

In other words, take the pressure off yourself during the first year and figure out what works, what you and your children enjoy doing, and how you enjoy doing it.

Study the core subjects and, if you add anything, do so only when you have your daily rhythm in place. This is especially true if you are bringing a child home from school.

"The first year needs to be about pulling the kid out of school," Bauer said. "It's about establishing a learning routine. . . . The focus has to be on being at home."[2]

The same goes for co-ops and learning communities. When you're starting out, you might be tempted to fill your day with organized classes provided by others. But don't fall for it. Take the first year to simplify your life rather than complicate it. By all means, have playdates and meet-ups for the sake of community, but take some time to figure out your own preferences. Most of us don't yet know how our children learn, let alone how we will learn together.

A Wild + Free mama who is now raising teenagers, Bethany Douglass, said, "Every home will have different goals and reasons for homeschooling. I have learned over the years to glean and appreciate the varied terrain in homeschool communities, using it more as a wealth of resources as opposed to a litmus as to whether I am headed in the right direction."

Your approach to homeschooling will reflect the strengths, skills, and passions you have as a mother, and that's okay. Just as there are magnet schools, agricultural tracks, and vocational programs in public education, the learning environment you create will reflect your unique gifts as an individual. You may have much to learn, but you also have much to teach your children.

Bethany said, "While I spent much of my first years of homeschooling worrying whether my children would receive everything academically they needed, I've realized in more recent years that the real gift of homeschooling is time—relational attention and space to explore interests and curiosities. Of course, academics are an important, vital aspect of homeschooling, but the foundational gift of this journey is knowing your children and being known by them."

Much like anything that's worth doing, homeschooling is hard. You will have doubts and think you've failed a thousand times along the way. And you will have to start over more than once. But remember this: you cannot ruin your children any more than you can perfect them. They will find their way. You will find yours. And little by little, you'll figure out this crazy, beautiful thing together until it feels like you've been doing it your whole life. Until it feels like, well, home.

Rest, dear mama, in the grace of homeschooling. What you are reclaiming for your children is worth more than any test could tell you.

YOU ARE THE EXPERT

You don't need anything or anyone to qualify you as a home-schooler. But know this—time will qualify you. Experience will give you the confidence to press forward without fear or doubt. It might seem hard to believe right now, but eventually, you will become an expert in your field.

The first four years of the elementary years will be like getting a bachelor's degree in homeschooling. Another two years, a master's degree. Another two years, a doctorate.

After all, what is expertise but time, intentionality, and practice?

"You've always had the power, dear; you just had to learn it for yourself."

—GLINDA THE GOOD WITCH

Wild + Free mama Toni Weber has homeschooled five children and graduated four of them. She reflected on her more than twenty-five years of homeschooling: "All of the perfectly laid out systems, programs and curriculum cannot replace the power of a loving, joy-filled, and encouraging home," she wrote. "This is the magic of homeschooling. An environment where our children are loved, protected and nurtured by the two people who care most for them in all the world.

"With this as the foundation, you can build an atmosphere that will support any style of learning and carry you through hard times when you feel like nothing is getting accomplished. The truth is—there are so many more important things to think about than biology or algebra."

As you come into your own as a parent-teacher-guide, you will trust your instincts more and more. You will know exactly what your children need to thrive. You'll figure out your rhythms, what works, and what doesn't. There is nothing that will limit your ability to help your children.

And there is no one more qualified to do this than you.

The Governor Albert D. Rosellini Bridge at Evergreen Point is the longest floating bridge in the world. The bridge connects Seattle and Medina across Lake Washington.

Washington

The Evergreen State
Rains and floods and storms
Population 6,753,369

Washington state has more glaciers than the other 47 contiguous states combined.

of the Olympic Peninsula are among the rainiest world and the only rainforests (such as the est) in the continental United States.

High Ra

The rainforest
like Bilbo Bags
beautiful. The
and it was
raining, and
touch.

9 The Learning Myth

HOMESCHOOLING IS CONTROVERSIAL BECAUSE it raises the question of how children learn. And it's an important one. All parents want their kids to receive a quality education. So, is home the best place for learning? The conventional educational model insists that learning happens in groups with one standardized system for everybody. Because of classroom restraints, there's a lack of individualized attention. Every child is taught the same information and tested on the basis of their ability to retain and comprehend that data. Any failure to comply ends with that child being demoralized with a poor GPA at best and labeled as having a learning disability at worst.

The homeschooling model says that children learn differently and thrive in an environment where they can go at their own pace, pursue subjects that interest them, and have the time and space to experience the wonder of childhood. It asserts that learning is a natural process for children and that if we only guide and encourage them, they can fully become who they were meant to be.

This might sound like a revolutionary concept, but children were educated this way until school got swept into the Industrial Revolution and learning was relegated to the assembly line with the likes of automobiles, railroad ties, and machine parts. Kids became viewed as products to manufacture rather than individuals to nurture, cultivate, and grow.

In 1906, the US Commissioner of Education, William Torrey Harris, who instituted many of these changes, made the troubling remark that "ninety-nine [students] out of a hundred are automata, careful to walk in prescribed paths, careful to follow the prescribed custom. This is not an accident," he said, "but the result of substantial education, which, scientifically defined, is the subsumption of the individual."

In other words, modern education is designed to suppress a child's individuality.

Harris's vision for school was equally disturbing: "The great purpose of school can be realized better in dark, airless, ugly places. . . . It is to master the physical self, to transcend the beauty of nature. School should develop the power to withdraw from the external world."[1]

Clearly, Harris was operating at a time when children were viewed and treated much differently from the way they are today. Our educational system has improved, reforms are constantly in the works, but many of the pitfalls of the industrial model of education still remain. While the conventional model of education is convenient, it hardly allows children to flourish as individuals. We no longer want to constrain our kids for long periods of time and shut out the natural world. We long to give them more than short recesses and instead allow them to experience the beauty of nature as an integral part of how they grow up and learn.

American author Henry Beston wrote, "If there is one thing clear about the centuries dominated by the factory and the wheel, it is that although the machine can make everything from a spoon to a landing-craft, a natural joy in earthly living is something it never has and never will be able to manufacture."[2]

Like the farm-to-table movement in food, homeschooling is a return to an organic model of education. It's not about how much information we can cram into our kids but rather how much they love learning. Because if they do, they'll keep learning beyond the bounds of school.

> "Like winds and sunsets, wild things were taken for granted until progress began to do away with them. Now we face the question whether a still higher 'standard of living' is worth its cost in things natural, wild and free."
>
> —ALDO LEOPOLD

It's not about how quickly our kids can memorize data or reach certain milestones because all children learn at different rates. Albert Einstein, for example, didn't speak until he was three years old. In fact, he credited his incredible achievements to his slow early development.

He said, "The ordinary adult never gives a thought to space-time problems. . . . I, on the contrary, developed so slowly that I did not begin to wonder about space and time until I was an adult. I then delved more deeply into the problem than any other adult or child would have done."

In other words, delayed learning isn't always a setback but can be an advantage. Children, as it turns out, do better with a prolonged childhood.

LEARNING RIGHT ON TIME

I sat at the classroom table and stared at a pile of reports that Wyatt's preschool teacher had been compiling all year. After going through his work, she looked at me with empathetic eyes and said, "I have to tell you that I don't think Wyatt is ready for kindergarten."

I was flabbergasted. What child isn't ready for kindergarten? Play dough? Hopscotch? She assured me he was doing great, made friends easily, and was a diligent worker, and she thoroughly enjoyed having him in class. "I just don't think he's ready for the rigor of kindergarten," she said.

She went on to describe what kindergarten was like these days—the requirements, the homework, the intensity of the long days. She didn't want to see him rushed off to the next stage before he was ready. Kindergarten, it seemed, was no longer for the faint of heart.

I wonder what Friedrich Froebel, the eighteenth-century German inventor of kindergarten, would think of what we've done to our five-year-olds. He wrote, "The child, the boy, the man should know no other endeavor, but to be at every stage of development, what that stage calls for."[3] We may not be able to change the school system, but we can choose to let our children live at every stage of development they are in. We can hurry up and slow down.

If you talk to other parents, you'll discover pretty quickly that no one really believes in hurrying our children. And yet, no one wants their child to be left behind, left out, or left wanting. From soccer teams to kindergarten, parents are forced to prepare their children for these rigors earlier and earlier. It's not that these things are bad, but in an effort to squeeze in as much as possible so they don't miss out on something, we end up skipping past childhood altogether.

David Elkind, a psychologist and author of *The Hurried Child: Growing Up Too Fast Too Soon*, said that parents need to slow down the process of rushing our kids into adulthood:

No parent, educator, or legislator I ever spoke to believes in pressuring children to do things well beyond what they are capable of doing. "I don't believe in hurrying children but," and there is always a but. A parent says, "I don't believe in hurrying but if I don't put my child in soccer, he will have no one to play with and won't make the team." And the educator says, "I don't believe in hurrying but the curriculum says I have to teach reading in kindergarten." The legislator says she does not believe in hurrying but that is what her constituents want. If we want healthy, happy children who can compete in an increasingly global economy we have to get beyond the but. We have to use what we know about healthy childrearing and education.[4]

Because we delight in our children so much, we will do anything to conceal their deficiencies—enroll them in extra classes, sign them up for remediation, push for advanced placement, load up their proverbial plates, and otherwise rush them through childhood.

Childhood, with all its shortcomings, inadequacies, and "issues," has become something to move beyond as quickly as possible. We rush kids into adulthood so they'll become competent and well-adjusted. But in an effort to cover a multitude of sins, we commit an even greater one.

Every childhood "issue" doesn't need to be "taught out of them" as soon as possible. We can let our kids be free in who they are and allow some of the development to come later. There's a time for learning, and there's a time for simply letting them be kids. We can delight in their childhood without constantly worrying about whether we should be advancing our children to the next stage.

Wild + Free mama Erin Armijo explained why she decided to homeschool her kids: "I longed to be with my children, learning alongside them," Erin said. "It felt unnatural being apart from my children all day, even if by society's standards they were old enough."

Erin said she always viewed homeschooling as a sacred kind of freedom that was otherwise not an option. Isn't that the way breakthroughs happen? We go the way of society, enduring its pressures, until we finally trust our mothering instincts and do what's right for our children.

When Erin finally made the leap, her goal was simple—to reclaim their childhood.

"My initial plan was to get to know my children again," Erin said. "Maybe that sounds silly. We'd always been a close family, but school had changed my boys, and I was making it my aim to get them back."

"I have no special talent. I am only passionately curious."

—ALBERT EINSTEIN

We aren't holding our children back by delighting in their childhood. We're giving them a foundation for all future learning.

In retrospect, I realize that Wyatt's preschool teacher was offering him another year of childhood. She saw his childlike heart, his eyes full of wonder, and his delight in play and didn't want to see him stripped of it. This is the same child who at fourteen has written two novels and who disciplines himself daily to accomplish all that he intends. But he truly loves being a kid.

As parents, we can choose to set the boundaries for our own children, learn to say no, and be the guardians of their childhood, which exists for only a brief moment in time. We must guard their hearts, protect their play, and give them the freedom to focus on being kids. Their futures depend on it.

RIDE THE WAVES

I love books. When I was a teenager, I spent many a Friday night reading in my room rather than going out with friends. I can disappear for hours in used book stores. I even commissioned my husband to build a book nook in our living room. I love how books feel in my hands, how they feed my introverted soul on a rainy day, and what they mean to me as collector's items. Books are the souvenirs of great stories and ideas.

But an education isn't based solely on books.

In fact, sometimes it's better to put down the books and set aside the curriculum. Kids learn by doing, exploring, and living life. It keeps their education from growing stale. Kids are so good at learning that we don't want to snuff it out. We want them to keep coming back for more.

As homeschoolers, we get to ride the waves of interests and passions in our children—and us. We get to make the most of natural learning and fall back into our schedules, courses, and books in due time. This not only keeps their education alive and vibrant, but it's also part of human nature to learn and tackle projects in short bursts.

John Holt said, "How much children can learn at any moment depends on how they feel at that moment about the task and their ability to do the task. When we feel powerful and competent, we leap at difficult tasks. The difficulty does not discourage us. . . . Part of the art of teaching is being able to sense which of these moods learners are in."[5]

Our role as educators is to foster the right environments for learning, to seize upon moments when our children are eager to learn, and to pull back when they've had too much. The admonition to "look busy" does not apply to authentic learning, for if a child is either bored or bothered, she will retain nothing at all.

"Education," as Einstein said, "is what remains after one has forgotten what one has learned in school." There is certainly a time for applied studies and rigor, but it is wise to remember that only the things that stick truly matter.

This permission to pull back is a boon to every homeschooling mother who believes her job is to press on regardless of how her children are feeling. The tick of the checkbox and tasks of the curriculum become her master. What a gift to be able to put down the books and say, "Let's try again later." A pot of tea and honey, some warm scones, and a good read-aloud just might do the trick. Or a hike in nature. Or an art project on the back porch. But certainly not a school bell.

Holt went on to say that when our children are down, "it's useless to push them or urge them on; that just frightens and discourages them more. What we have to do is draw back, take off the pressure, reassure them, console them, give them time to regain—as in time they will—enough energy and courage to go back to the task."[6]

What a capacity for learning our children have when they're ready. One idea can trigger a wildfire of curiosity and intrigue that will carry them through multiple subjects and interests.

My friend Jodi Mockabee shared a story of how this happened to her children one day:

"They were engrossed in paper airplanes," Jodi said. "They had been making dozens of them, comparing flight distance, weight, shape, and style. Carter was charting times and distances. Everett was recreating different shapes and experimenting with weight. Scarlett learned how to make various styles from a paper airplane book, as well as her brothers' direction, and the twins enjoyed coloring their airplanes and taking part in the competition.

"Later in the afternoon, we sat down for a snack and discussed flight. I introduced them to the concept of aerodynamics and suggested comparing 'weight vs. lift' and 'drag vs. thrust.' We applied the scientific method to multiple flight tests and the children recorded their own hypothesis, variations, and results in their notebooks the following day."

Jodi intended to talk to her kids about bird observation and flight history, but before she could do it, the children came running up from the woodpile shouting, "Rattlesnake, rattlesnake!"

"After discovering it was not a rattlesnake, but a gopher snake," Jodi said, "we looked up the differences in our nature books, rehearsed them, and quizzed each other, as, in this area, it's imperative to know what's what. The next day, Everett chose to illustrate and write about the differences of the snakes, rather than document the scientific method of flight analysis."

By riding these waves, we may not complete the required curriculum for the day, but one unforgettable lesson will lead to another, and our children will never grow bored of it.

"Traditional education focuses on teaching, not learning. It incorrectly assumes that for every ounce of teaching there is an ounce of learning by those who are taught. However, most of what we learn before, during, and after attending schools is learned without being taught to us. . . . Most of what is taught in classroom settings is forgotten, and much of what is remembered is irrelevant."

—RUSSELL ACKOFF

Children are natural learners. It's hardwired into their DNA. They cannot help but learn when the conditions are right. To make the most of this extraordinary capability, we have to ride the waves of interest, learn to spot teachable moments, and pull back when it's too much.

What if, rather than trying to fill all of their time, we choose to savor it? What if, rather than filling our children's day with tasks, we choose to give them time to discover what they love?

If we can keep the natural love of learning alive in our children, we will have succeeded as their mothers and teachers. Einstein said, "Education is only a ladder to gather fruit from the tree of knowledge, not the fruit itself." We are showing them how to learn for a lifetime.

Imagine your children learning independently, eagerly devouring every book they can find on a subject, or researching a question on their own rather than waiting for you. If you haven't experienced this yet, just wait. There's no feeling quite like it for the homeschooling mama.

"The more we want our children to (1) be lifelong learners, genuinely excited about words and numbers and ideas, (2) avoid sticking with what's easy and safe, and (3) become sophisticated thinkers, the more we should do everything possible to help them forget about grades."

—ALFIE KOHN

THE TROUBLE WITH TEST TAKING

The age-old question of whether a tree makes a sound if it falls in the forest has an educational equivalent: If students aren't tested in school, have they actually learned anything?

Of course they have. But the idea of school without testing is inconceivable to most people. I've heard mothers say they enjoy seeing test scores because that way they know exactly where their child stands. This is all well and good for kids who are proficient at test taking. But what about those who are gifted in other ways or know different things from what tests can show us?

The truth is, tests are not only poor indicators of what children are actually learning, but they can also damage their self-esteem and force them into identities that hinder them.

In her book *Rethinking School*, Susan Wise Bauer described the problem: "Our current standardized exams encourage schools to teach test preparation instead of history, science, music, art, and foreign languages, none of which are typically tested. They are unfair to students with immature fine-motor skills, and they have repeatedly been show to unfairly lowball poor and minority students who don't share the same cultural references as their white middle-class classmates, as well as gifted students—who can always think of reasons why more than one multiple-choice answer might be considered correct."[7]

Tests can measure only certain facets of a child's education. If all the square pegs are evaluated by their ability to fit into round holes, is the test really measuring anything at all?

Einstein said, "Everybody is a genius. But if you judge a fish by its ability to climb a tree, it will live its whole life believing it is stupid."

In 2014, veteran educator Marion Brady wrote, in reference to standardized testing, that "no machine can measure the quality of complex, emotion-filtered, experience-based learning. . . . If you're testing the wrong thing, there's no reason to keep score."[8]

The ability to retain information is a talent, to be sure. But wouldn't it be better to channel that gift into something more meaningful than merely taking tests? What of the other billion things a child knows, like how a robin makes its nest or why the stars twinkle at night?

My children have taught me more than I ever could have imagined, from circuits and robots to anacondas and aerodynamics. But hardly any of those things appear on tests.

Bauer acknowledged that tests can be useful "when they're given in a non-pressured individualized setting, tailored to the student's learning and expression styles, and treated as only one of many ways to find out how to meet the child's education needs."

If you find tests useful for your kids, you can incorporate healthy methods of testing into your schooling. But those kinds of tests don't exist in traditional school systems. Instead, they function like an academic version of Russian roulette, where one wrong answer in a highly pressured environment can have serious repercussions for that child's identity and future.

It's survival of the fittest for test taking.

"What we all want, as parents, is to find the educational situation that matches our child's particular blend of passions, abilities, and talents; meshes with our vision for our kids; and teaches to our child's strengths while gently improving on weaknesses."

—SUSAN WISE BAUER

A BETTER WAY TO ASSESS CHILDREN

How we assess our children reveals what we value. If we remove testing altogether, we are forced to allow our values about education to guide the learning, and this can open up a whole new world of possibilities.

If you want to know what a child is actually learning, just listen. What lights them up? What do they talk about? What do they wonder aloud about? What do they want to know? What do they reveal when you ask them to repeat back to you something they've read or heard? Learning in relationship provides a rich environment in which to both learn and express what is learned.

In the twentieth century, Charlotte Mason implemented the practice of narration in dozens of schools across Great Britain. Narration, or the art of telling, has been used as an educational tool since ancient times, but Mason was integral in helping this become a regular practice of many homeschoolers today.

When we engage our children in conversation and have them repeat back to us—verbally or in writing—what they're learning, they can better communicate what they actually know.

Not only that, but the simple act of narration has profound effects on a child's ability to retain, understand, and think at a higher level.

This practice isn't solely a verbal exercise. Over time, children learn to pay attention and connect with what they're learning. Eventually, natural narrations begin taking place throughout the course of the day. Our children will chat about a bird they saw in the backyard, a story they read during lunch, or a Lego creation they're working on. Or perhaps their narration will come in the form of play, acting out a story with props, creating a comic book, or—in the case of my six-year-old Annie—illustrating storybooks. It's a beautiful thing to behold.

LEARNING WITHOUT REALIZING IT

When I was in college, I pursued a teaching degree in hopes of one day becoming an English professor. On the first day of class, I entered the room to find a beautiful, dignified woman named Hephzipah standing in front of us with untamed hair and a gracious smile.

She sat down on the edge of her desk and began talking about a book she had read. I was mesmerized by the way she recounted the tale, regaling us with the characters, setting, and cultural applications. She conversed with us throughout the hour, and I wrote down the name of the book and vowed to read it, in spite of my already-miles-long required reading list.

I enjoyed every second, but when the class ended, I thought, "The poor woman. She just wasted the entire class telling us about that book."

The next class came along, and once again, Hephzipah told us about another book, equally as riveting in its storyline. Again, I added it to my list of must-read novels.

It happened again in the next class and again in the following ones. I finally realized that what she was doing was helping us fall in love with books rather than fill in blanks, recite rote facts, or create lifeless lists on how to teach English to high schoolers. She was demonstrating that it was more important to love what we were teaching than to train to be teachers. She was showing us, not telling us, how to help kids fall in love with learning.

It was a pivotal moment for me.

After that semester, I not only changed my major from education to English, so I could devour all the great works in literature, but also vowed to name my first daughter Hephzipah. It was voted down by a narrow margin after I married, but she still holds a dear place in my heart.

> "The natural learning process works because learning is an activity as natural as breathing."
>
> —ELLEN CRISS

Why do we assume that education shouldn't be enjoyable and that a better measure of learning is difficulty? Julie Bogart, author of *A Gracious Space*, wrote, "We doubt success when we should doubt struggle—we overvalue struggle as evidence of learning, when if we really think about it—joy and pleasure are much better signs of learning and growth."[9]

Children's brains are sponges and capable of absorbing so much. But information does not equal education, and cramming more and more into a child's head does not make the child any better off.

The classroom model of education was intended for large numbers, and tests are an efficient way of evaluating everyone at once. But as Julie Bogart said, "We need to get over this idea that volume equals learning."[10]

As homeschoolers, we have the opportunity to tailor our children's education according to their unique learning styles, interests, gifts, and needs. We can observe their work and appreciate their insights by using tools such as narration and meaningful projects. Using that kind of evidence can give us a much better understanding of the scope and depth of their learning.

Our children are not living or learning in a box. Life is messy, chaotic, and full of disruptions, and, at times, learning will be too. But it's also rich and beautiful and presents its share of peaceful, quiet moments. There will be times when everyone is working happily and productively—not because they were forced by coercion, bribery, or sticker charts—but because the desire is there inside them. Homeschooling is about relationship. It's about individualized education. It's about freeing kids to learn about the things that interest them at their own pace.

Because we can.

10 The Rigor Myth

SOME PEOPLE AVOID HOMESCHOOLING FOR THE same reason I avoid dentists who work out of their garage— the appearance of illegitimacy. I get it. I've asked all the same questions of my own homeschooling efforts: How does this count as school? How are we fulfilling the academic requirements? Am I sabotaging my child's future?

For some, school is a matter of family honor that gets passed down from generation to generation. I know how they feel. I once kept a Citizen of the Month sign in my yard for three months, and my child was only in kindergarten.

I've met desperate mothers at Wild + Free events who had told their husbands they were going to a women's conference to avoid the mention of homeschooling. They introduced themselves to me in hushed tones, saying, "I want this so badly, but my husband is opposed. How can I get him on board? He's convinced that homeschooling is for hippies."

There's a palpable sense of joy, freedom, and excitement when I walk into our conferences, as these mothers experience sheer elation at being in the midst of such kindred spirits. It's the one place we don't have to defend ourselves or our decision to homeschool. We can put down our guard and celebrate this lifestyle without apology.

I understand the questions about the legitimacy of home-schooling because I've asked them all myself at one point, and I've had to answer them as well.

It all boils down to rigor.

We've come to believe the myth that school must be busy, boring, or brutal to be effective.

Even members of the homeschool community have bought the lie by turning their dining rooms into schoolrooms complete with desks, chalkboards, organizational charts, and textbooks. By trying to replicate the classroom in our homes, we're attempting to placate the guilt in our hearts.

But the perception of legitimacy doesn't mean that something is true.

For decades, mothers have used those brown bottles of hydrogen peroxide to clean their children's wounds, and each time the stinging pain convinces them that it must be working.

Not only are there less painful ways to clean a wound, but one notable doctor claims that hydrogen peroxide "should never be used on your cuts and wounds" because it "disrupts healthy tissue and prolongs healing."[1] Several companies have created painless cleaning solutions as an alternative. The trouble is, none of them sell. People like their cleansers to hurt. They've been conditioned to believe that's how you know it's working.

The same question is applied to homeschooling. If children are given all this time to play, explore, and learn at their own pace, how could they possibly be getting a legitimate, rigorous education?

The answer lies with how learning actually occurs and whether we have the courage to embrace it, in spite of social pressure, in spite of what the "experts" say, in spite of our fears.

MEANINGFUL WORK

Young children love to work. Take any toddler playing at his mama's feet while she sweeps the floor or mixes cookie dough. They want to help and often won't take no for an answer.

My three-year-old, Millie, is the hardest worker in our house. She is the first to clean up spills, push a chair over to the kitchen counter to stir the ingredients, or even run outside to retrieve groceries from the car. Often buck naked, I might add.

Sadly, we often turn our little helpers away, wanting to get the job done quickly—or, worse, right. We buy them the toy versions of mops and vacuum cleaners and relegate them to pretending to work rather than enjoying the real thing. But they don't want a shallow alternative. They want to participate in real-life activities. They were born to engage in meaningful work.

Our children need us to give them space—more than what we're giving them—but they also crave our intentionality, time, and creativity. Here are some favorite activities my younger kids enjoy as both play and work:

- Washing things like the windows or the car
- Folding the laundry and putting items in separate piles
- Organizing the kitchen junk drawer
- Making the beds with special touches
- Watering the plants and naming them
- Raking the leaves into a jumping pile
- Shoveling snow with buckets to create a castle

Providing a rich childhood doesn't mean keeping children from real work. In Susan Schaeffer Macaulay's book *For the Children's Sake*, she commented, "In trying to give a child a carefree existence, we often leave him stranded with meaningless tasks. A sensitive balance must be established so that the routine of a child's life is not burdened with work responsibilities that rob him of a childhood growing time. Yet, they love to participate in the work just as others do."[2]

As children get older, they begin to apply this work ethic to the things they love. Whether it's skateboarding, cooking, playing the piano, or woodworking, kids will do the hard work it takes to learn about their passions. Researching. Practicing. Pushing through the learning curve.

If you walked into my home on a typical afternoon, you might find my fourteen-year-old typing away in our book nook on his latest manuscript, my twelve-year-old hunched over his laptop refining a video in iMovie, and my nine-year-old fashioning a ninja warrior course in the backyard. My six-year-old daughter would be making a village out of peg people on the fireplace hearth, and my three-year-old would be building a castle out of blocks that are color coordinated by levels.

I didn't teach my kids any of this. I simply gave them the freedom to explore their interests. And they surprise me every day with new projects that require hard work, from learning complex arrangements on the piano to building woodland hideouts and fixing old record players.

When we assume that children will work only for rewards, we do them a disservice. The same goes for assuming that children are lazy. Once they experience the pride and joy that come from completing meaningful projects, they have all the motivation they need to work hard.

As parents, we can channel this natural affinity into their education. In her book *Project-Based Homeschooling*, Lori Pickert wrote that children both need and benefit from work on something that matters to them with the help of a dedicated mentor:

Allowing children to learn about what interests them is good, but helping them do it in a meaningful, rigorous way is better. Freedom and choice are good, but a life steeped in thinking, learning, and doing is better. It's not enough to say, "Go, do whatever you like." To help children become skilled thinkers and learners, to help them become people who make and do, we need a life centered around those experiences. We need to show them how to accomplish the things they want to do. We need to prepare them to make the life they want.[3]

> "Child-centeredness does not mean lack of rigor or standards; it does mean finding the right match between children's developing interests and abilities."
>
> —DAVID ELKIND

By working on self-directed projects, kids can dive deep into a subject, learning the necessary skills to research, make things, and communicate intelligently about it. Giving children meaningful things to do—things that interest them—is a great way to instill a work ethic and prepare them not only for college but also for life beyond their formal educational years.

This is often missing in the traditional school setting. While some students excel at academia, others are left behind, and it simply isn't possible for every child to have a dedicated mentor assigned to them. But personal apprenticeship is the essence of homeschooling.

RIGOR AS A STANDARD

We could apply the question of rigor to conventional schools as well. Sure, there are students who vie for the honor of becoming valedictorians, and I'm sure the advanced placement classes are filled with earnest students. But, as you probably know, mere attendance at a conventional institution or even a private preparatory school doesn't equate to a rigorous education.

Schools are evaluated on the basis of test scores and receive funding on the basis of students' performance, so of course *rigor* is a buzzword that gets tossed around a lot. But what is rigor?

In her book *Teaching from Rest*, Sarah Mackenzie observed:

We have this desire to give our kids what we call an academically "rigorous" education. . . . The word "rigor" comes from the Latin rigor, rigoris, *which means "numbness, stiffness, hardness, firmness, roughness, rudeness."* Rigor mortis *literally means "the stiffness of death," which I think we can all agree is not the goal of homeschooling our children! . . . Work toward "diligence" instead. "Diligence" comes from the Latin* diligere, *which means to "single-out, value highly, esteem, prize, love; aspire to, take delight in, appreciate."*[4]

"If we are aiming to order our children's affections, learn to love what is lovely, join in the great conversation, and cultivate a soul so that the person is ready in every sense of the word to take on the challenges around the corner and on the other side of the college entrance exams."

—SARAH MACKENZIE

In the Wild + Free community, we call this intentionality. Most homeschooling mothers I know are extremely intentional about raising thoughtful, caring, and diligent human beings. In the early days, I described Wild + Free as "a community for homeschoolers and intentional parents." We are parents who are passionate about giving our children a quality education without sacrificing their freedom or failing to honor their natural desire to discover new things.

Certainly, not all homeschoolers are created alike. But homeschooling in itself does not equate to lazy students who don't know how to work hard. Quite the opposite, I've found.

Dan Cumberland was homeschooled while growing up and became an entrepreneur, starting an organization called the Meaning Movement, which helps people find their calling in life.

"One of the biggest gifts of my homeschool experience was the ability to learn on my own," Dan said. "In many ways, I was self-taught under my parent's supervision. Because of that, I'm very willing to pick up something and try it out—an essential skill for an entrepreneur and running a business today. Every week, I have to figure out how to solve the next challenge. I'm used to doing it myself, so I'm going to find a way to get it done.

"Similarly, I'm also accustomed to being self-motivated and a self-starter. I always did my lessons first thing, and I didn't have to wait for a bell to ring or class to start. I started on my own and finished early so I could go outside. I learned to get stuff done and take initiative. My livelihood depends on my ability to make stuff happen—and I know that no one is going to do it for me. I think homeschooling helped build that work ethic in me."

HARD AT PLAY

Early in my efforts to serve the homeschool community, I discovered that mothers didn't need permission to find a better curriculum, double down on their textbooks, or finish their math lessons each day. They needed permission *not* to do those things.

Hear me out.

For generations, the human race has combined life with learning and play with productivity. Children didn't attend lectures on Shakespeare followed by algebra and shop class followed by homework at night. Life was the laboratory in which hands-on learning occurred every day.

Families worked together as farmers, blacksmiths, bakers, or shopkeepers. They got up early for chores, followed by breakfast, writing, and arithmetic. They told stories, played music, and read poetry in the evenings by the hearth. Kids took every opportunity to play in the hours between, whether it was climbing trees, swimming in the creek, or running through the woods.

"Once upon a time, all children were homeschooled. They were not sent away from home each day to a place just for children but lived, learned, worked, and played in the real world, alongside adults and other children of all ages."

—RACHEL GATHERCOLE

Work, play, and education were woven together into one beautiful tapestry. In today's society, it's inevitable that the segregated schedules of children fall perfectly in line with the hours in which working parents need their children to be supervised and occupied. And while this is certainly nothing to belittle and is necessary for some, we can't assume that a system of scheduled after-school activities is beneficial just because it exists.

Play for the sake of play has become an endangered species. It's now restricted to assigned areas where children must be "so tall" to enter. Playground floors have been replaced with rubber surfaces—because God forbid a grass stain. And heaven help our children if they play at the wrong scheduled time. Thanks to homeschoolers everywhere, play is making a comeback.

Play is part of the rigor of learning.

When we weave play, work, and learning all together in one endeavor, the result is a productive and happy homeschool life.

My friend and fellow Wild + Free mama Nichole Holze recently shared an experience of how she was able to streamline all three for her children. She and her children were studying the works of Michelangelo, particularly his paintings on the Sistine Chapel ceiling.

"I looked outside and realized that our climbing dome was the perfect shape to allow them to paint while standing. I raced outside and began madly taping paper across the inside ceiling of our climbing dome. I filled up my children's paint trays, and they ran outside to see what I had constructed. The experience was exactly what I had hoped it would be for our culminating art project. Sometimes the best experiences we can give our children are the ones that we pull together out of sheer, in the moment, inspiration."

Preserving childhood and giving our kids time to learn and grow at their own pace doesn't equate to a poor education. You can create a family culture that esteems both childhood and education—understanding that learning is a natural outgrowth of an enriching environment.

Our biggest fear is that our children won't be prepared for adulthood, for "work life." But what if we created a new future in which our children lead the way? Kids take their time because they're taking it all in. They get excited about the things we take for granted. What if we looked at their dawdling as savoring?

Kids play hard at what they love to do, and that play looks an awful lot like work. They're not just building things; they're learning the fundamentals of engineering and architecture. They're not just playing restaurant; they're dabbling in the basics of running a small business. And don't think that an afternoon spent outside is wasted time. Our children are discovering themselves and gaining identities that will set their futures into motion.

Consider this your permission to put the books down for a day, for a while even. When we create an atmosphere of living, playing, working, and learning, we inspire a desire to wonder, explore, and investigate. A life-giving environment is the spark that lights a fire within our children's hearts and minds, inspiring them to create, think, and—yes—do hard work.

11 The College Myth

THE PROSPECT OF ATTENDING COLLEGE IS probably one of the top reasons why families don't consider homeschooling their children. Most of the materials that prepare kids for college are aimed at traditional school students. And skeptical friends and family members can strike more fear in our hearts with their concerns about this one aspect of homeschooling.

Simply put, many people believe college is not possible for homeschooled students or, at the least, that it hinders their chance of getting into a good college. I get messages all the time from mothers who fear that they won't be able to provide the kind of formal structure or preparation needed for their kids to attend college. They don't mind homeschooling their little ones during the elementary years, but as soon as their kids approach high school, they're quick to pull the rip cord for fear of ruining their children's lives.

But nothing could be further from the truth. Not only do homeschooled children typically score slightly above the national average on both SATs and ACTs, but they also make exceptional college students if they decide to follow that path.

As parents, it's important to have a solid grasp on the college application process and what it takes to qualify, so we can help our children get there if they decide to go that route.

SETTING KIDS UP FOR SUCCESS OF ALL KINDS

For many homeschooling families, college is not the ultimate goal. Their goal is for their child to lead a fulfilling and productive life, able to make a living in creative and entrepreneurial ways. It's no coincidence that some of the most enterprising people I know homeschool their kids or were homeschooled themselves.

Homeschooling is compelling because it gives children the ability to discover what they love and go after it without waiting for a high school diploma. Teens are finding they don't need a college degree to have a career in their desired field, and many are launching creative start-up businesses.

Alex McGrath was homeschooled and grew up to form and play in several bands, one of which has toured extensively and produced musical soundtracks for films.

"The most obvious benefit of my homeschooling experience was having the ability to learn at my own pace," Alex said. "For me, that meant moving more quickly through some subjects so I could spend more time focusing on the ones I was most interested in, such as music and art. What got me through algebra was knowing I could play the drums when I was finished."

It's fair to say that without homeschooling, Alex couldn't have spent the time needed to grow his skills and pour his talents into his passion.

"Hours and hours were spent practicing drums and guitar, and whenever I wasn't exploring something musical, I was outdoors using my imagination or building something. Free time is so necessary for kids to develop creativity, and I'm so grateful for that time."

Once students get a taste for creating their own tailored education and finding purpose and passion in their everyday lives, it's likely that, unless they aspire to neurosurgery, law, dentistry, or another field with specialized knowledge, they won't see the benefit of a four-year degree. The cost, inconvenience, and inevitable debt just don't seem worth the end result, not when they can continue on the path of self-education.

Blake Boles, author of several books including *College Without High School* and *Better than College*, is a self-directed learning advocate who works with teens outside the traditional high school environment. He talks extensively about the merits of college, as well as the drawbacks. He acknowledges that for several licensed professions some amount of traditional college is necessary, but he reminds us not to confuse college with higher education. "In our oft-heralded 'modern age'—with its global competition and ever-shifting technological landscape— higher education is unquestionably important. It gives you the perspective and tools to deal with rapid change. But assuming that higher education only comes from college is like assuming that all delicious meals only come from restaurants."[1]

If you've ever watched an episode of *Top Chef*, you know that many skilled chefs are self-taught through hard work, dedication, and mentorship. And the number of people in temporary jobs such as Starbucks baristas and Uber drivers who hold college degrees is more than you'd expect. A college degree, it seems, no longer equates to a secure financial future.

As parents, we all want what's best for our children—to be happy, healthy, and financially stable—and none of us want to shortchange their potential. But don't believe the lie that a college degree is guaranteed to lead to all, if any, of those outcomes. Consider Bill Gates, Steve Jobs, Oprah Winfrey, and Mark

Zuckerberg—all college dropouts who used their passion and grit to get where they are today.

For many homeschool graduates, entrepreneurship may prove the path to a more fulfilling life. If your child decides to skip college, don't think for a minute that she is sacrificing a higher education. For most homeschool students, this is only the beginning.

GOING TO COLLEGE

For those whose children do desire to go to college, know that homeschooled kids not only can attend college but can thrive there. They can get into the best schools, graduate at the top of their class, pursue graduate degrees, and go on to become practitioners and professors who teach the teachers. Statistically, homeschooled kids are about as likely to go to college as their traditionally schooled peers, and they often graduate from college at a higher rate than their peers— 66.7 percent, compared with 57.5 percent.[2]

The homeschool environment breeds a culture of discovery, so students are more adept at self-education, which gives them an advantage at the university level. Author and admissions counselor Marjorie Hansen Shaevitz has coached thousands of students through the college admissions process, including homeschool students. She said, "The possibilities of showing all the kinds of things that colleges are looking for—curiosity, confidence, resourcefulness, ability to deal with challenges— you name it. That's a part of being a home-schooled student."[3] In short, homeschooling is a help, not a handicap, when it comes to pursuing higher education.

Wild + Free is a new movement and made up of mostly young families, but many of the forerunners in our community have graduated children who are thriving in college. For example, the daughter of our podcast host Jennifer Pepito is attending law school in Ireland, and the son of a beloved Wild + Free presenter, Terri Woods, is studying to become a mechanical engineer. Pioneering homeschoolers who are part of this movement, such as Julie Bogart and Sally Clarkson, have children attending graduate schools in the United States and England.

"The secret of Education lies in respecting the pupil. It is not for you to choose what he shall know, what he shall do. It is chosen and foreordained, and he only holds the key to his own secret."

—RALPH WALDO EMERSON

But the evidence isn't just anecdotal. In 2012, *USA Today* reported that homeschooled students "generally score slightly above the national average on both the SAT and the ACT and often enter college with more college credits" than traditionally schooled students. "On average home-schooled students have higher grade point averages in their freshman years and have higher graduation rates than their peers."[4]

In other words, homeschooled kids can and do excel in college.

The best colleges and universities in America know this, as 83 percent of them now have formal admissions policies for evaluating homeschooled applicants. In lieu of standardized transcripts, they're often asked to submit letters of recommendation, SAT scores, and portfolios of work.

Colleges recognize the unique perspectives and talents that homeschooled students bring to their schools. Many admissions departments, including those at Ivy League schools, have set up special pages on their websites just for homeschooled students. They're not given special treatment or a higher acceptance level, but the colleges want to help homeschoolers have the best possible chance.

Take, for example, this excerpt from Princeton University's website: "We recognize that your experience as a homeschooled student will be somewhat different from students in traditional schools. We'll look at your academic record and non-academic interests and commitments within the context of your particular homeschool curriculum and experience."

While Princeton makes it clear that the percentage of homeschooled applicants is still small, the number of applicants is increasing each year. There is often a greater focus on test scores, such as the SAT and SAT II, as well as a request for greater documentation of their high school experience. Again from Princeton's website, "The more you can document for us and describe what you have done during your high school years, academically and otherwise, the better."[5]

Of course, not every homeschool student is aiming for Princeton, but the fact that so many colleges are open to and accepting of alternative educational backgrounds is a positive sign.

PREPARING FOR COLLEGE

If you're worried about competing for a college against students coming from traditional schools, take heart. Most colleges are looking for students who have applied themselves academically but also in a specific area of expertise. Being homeschooled gives your child a distinct advantage.

Shirag Shemmassian, a former college admissions interviewer and director of a consulting firm that helps students get admitted into highly selective colleges, shared that colleges aren't simply looking for the best students academically. In an attempt to set themselves apart by enrolling in advanced classes, getting the highest test scores, and joining all the extracurricular activities, students all end up doing the same thing, and subsequently no one stands out.

While his remarks were geared toward traditionally schooled children, there's something we can take from his experience and advice. He said, "What actually differentiates top applicants from the field is not necessarily what they do inside the classroom but what they do outside of the classroom."

If high school students spend all their time focused on academics, there is little to no time to pursue other activities. "We want teenagers to be teenagers," he added.

But it's not just well-rounded students they want. Colleges are looking for specialists. Kids become specialists in art, science, or sports by moving beyond the activity and taking it to the next level. This can look like mentoring others, volunteering in the community, and documenting their work in a portfolio. Time and investment in one's passion—and ultimately creating a new paradigm—can become the key to standing out and getting into the college of their choice.

Cal Newport, author and professor at Georgetown University, calls this the failed simulation effect. He said that "accomplishments that are hard to explain can be much more impressive than accomplishments that are simply hard to do."[6]

The best thing you can do as a parent to prepare your children for college, whether you homeschool or not, is to do the necessary research ahead of time. Visit college websites, visit schools in person, and inform yourself of the requirements.

CREATING A PORTFOLIO

As I write this, my eldest son is in his first year of high school. I knew this day was coming; I just didn't think it would come so soon. Since I started homeschooling him in second grade, there have been gaps in his education, to be sure. But there are gaps in any child's education; an education is never complete, no matter how comprehensive it claims to be.

But when you've raised a child to be a lifelong learner and given him the tools, the time, and the opportunities to solve problems on his own, there is nothing he cannot do. You can be confident that you're sending a success story out into the world.

My husband and I have done the research. We've prepared for this exciting season. And we've talked to Wyatt about what the next four years will entail and how we'll document it, regardless of what he decides to do after graduation. We're all excited about it.

We helped Wyatt create an online portfolio that showcases all his accomplishments and provides a living transcript of everything he's read, learned, studied, and achieved.

Blake Boles offered a basic recipe for creating such a portfolio of work:

1. Do hard stuff
2. Create evidence of the stuff you've done (such as blog posts, photographs, videos, short essays, websites, prototypes, etc.)
3. Publish evidence in an online portfolio
4. Network and market the hell out of yourself[7]

We're prescribing the subjects Wyatt must study this year as part of ninth grade. We give him freedom with the parts that are optional and work together on the ones that are not. In his online portfolio, he's able to integrate his reading lists on Goodreads, embed his videos from YouTube, create and link podcasts from SoundCloud, document photographs from Instagram, and post essays on a blog.

We're charting Wyatt's progress using a project management app so he can check off projects and move onto the next assignments. We're outsourcing his chemistry lessons with a subscription service, hiring a tutor to help with math, continuing his guitar lessons, and taking as many trips as possible to help his lessons on history and literature come alive.

We can stand in the very place where General Robert E. Lee surrendered the Civil War to Ulysses S. Grant, walk the Capitol Mall, where Martin Luther King Jr. gave his "I Have a Dream" speech, and hike the trails of the American Revolution.

All seven of us just got our passports, so we can soon visit the Globe Theatre in London and reenact Shakespeare or walk the beaches of Normandy as we study World War II. Our goal as a family is to obtain a living education, one beneath our feet, not just in a book.

Wyatt will certainly continue to develop his expertise in the areas that interest him at the moment—music, filmmaking, reading, and writing. I'm sure he'll form new passions and interests along the way. And all this will be documented in an online portfolio that he can use for college admissions, for whatever other pursuits he has, or simply for posterity.

Even if you don't have a high schooler preparing for college, you might enjoy building a portfolio of your kids' work throughout their entire homeschool experience.

Wild + Free mama Elsie Iudicello shared how she creates a portfolio each year. "Every time I set out to plan a new school year for my children, I imagine that I am getting ready to put together a quilt. I have colorful pieces of inspiration from many different sources laid upon the table and there are any number of patterns I can play with and consider. The final pattern eludes me since the creative execution depends largely on the hands of my fellow quilt makers, four wild and rambling boys of various tastes, personalities, and abilities."

Elsie lives in Florida, where homeschoolers are required to keep track of their work, but she uses the opportunity to document other aspects of their childhood journey as well. "The portfolio I turn in to the state is always a bit different from the version I keep for the family records. For our family, our yearly portfolios are a travel journal of sorts, markers on the path of who our children are becoming. There is so much learning happening within our homes that cannot be measured. Don't think of your portfolio as a static report filled with measurements. Instead, take a moment to think of your children and what makes them unique, everything from their sparkle to their struggles. Think of all the new discoveries they made about the world and their place in it. You get to document and preserve all this beauty!"

DIPLOMAS AND TRANSCRIPTS

Maybe you have a sinking feeling at the thought of no high school graduation ceremony, no cap and gown, and no diploma. After all, these are rites of passage for most teenagers. How else do you mark the completion of twelve years of education? Let's demystify the process a bit.

Graduation ceremonies are gatherings of friends and family to commemorate an academic accomplishment. You can do the same thing with your family and friends, get good seats, and skip to the best part of the ceremony. Caps and gowns can be purchased on Amazon, and diplomas are available at any educational supply store.

Homeschoolers receive diplomas from their parents rather than an accredited institution. Some homeschool co-ops and associations offer them to their participants, but it's not necessary. This doesn't hinder your child's ability to get into college any more than a state-issued diploma helps a student get into college. They are equal in all senses. But depending on the college, the homeschooled student may have to provide a more detailed transcript.

If you're not using a curriculum with a checklist to get in all of the required classes, putting together a transcript can be a bit more challenging, but it's not impossible. For every subject, you get to assign credits or hours, even for the more "experiential" ones.

For example, if you don't follow a curriculum for computer science, but your child spent countless hours creating stop-motion animations, you can give him a credit. If you don't use a language arts curriculum, but your child spent his days writing a novel, give him a credit.

Another way for homeschool students to receive credits is by taking classes at a local community college. Many families have found this to be a great way for the student to attend classes that the parents don't want to tackle at home, as well as receive credit that will transfer to colleges and universities. Wild + Free contributor Jennifer Pepito has relied on community college classes for all her teenage children during their high school years.

Many helpful resources for creating high school transcripts are available from veteran homeschoolers, including Julie Bogart of Brave Writer and Lee Binz, author of *Setting the Records Straight: How to Craft Homeschool Transcripts and Course Descriptions for College Admission and Scholarships*, and the members of Ambleside Online.

It's important to remember that we don't have to compromise an interest-led education for the sake of college admissions. We don't have to succumb to testing and alter everything we do just because we hit the high school years. Fitting in the core subjects takes very little time in the grand scheme of things, leaving plenty of opportunity to pursue personal interests. All of those things can be translated into courses for their transcript without infringing on their learning.

PREPARING FOR THE FUTURE

We don't know what path our children will take. No matter how strongly we are for or against college, our children will ultimately decide what they'll do. We can only help prepare them for whichever direction they choose. This doesn't mean piling up work for areas in which they don't have strengths but giving them time and space to become experts in their own interests.

"There has never been a generation when children have so desperately needed their parents' time, thoughtful creativity, and friendship."

—SUSAN SCHAEFFER MACAULAY

Susan Wise Bauer spoke at our Wild + Free conference in Williamsburg, Virginia. As a homeschool graduate and now a homeschooling parent and college professor, she talked about the gift of time her parents gave her and her siblings to explore their interests: "They let us do the bare minimum in some subjects so that we could develop our interests in other areas. And for every single one of us, this led us into the career that we now have."

The abundance of time we give to our children is a fertile seedbed for the individuals they will one day become. You can't possibly imagine how much this gift will impact them.

We all have our own set of quirks, blind spots, and weaknesses. The good news is that our children's futures do not rise and fall on our failures. We are raising children who have intelligent minds, creative passions, and limitless potential. They are resilient, amazing kids.

Let's dismiss the notion that we're not doing enough because that lie is based in insecurity and fear, not reality. You are exactly the mother and educator your child needs.

Bauer said, "Once your kids are in high school, you hear this little voice in the back of your head that says, 'You'll never get into college.' We all have this. I'm a college professor and I hear this voice all the time. That fear is present in all parents."

So take the pressure off yourself.

Stop thinking you can mess it up.

Because you can't.

If you're even a fraction as diligent at preparing as you are at worrying, you'll be just fine. Fear of the unknown keeps us from experiencing true freedom and the joy of this journey, and it has no place in our homes.

In so many ways, these are the best years. Don't lose heart or give in to the fear that homeschooling cannot work for the teen years. Your children may need you in less tangible ways, but that doesn't mean they need traditional school. This is the time when all of that hard work—slowly, magnificently—begins to pay off. Trust the journey and embrace this beautiful time of watching your teen's passions and talents collide into something amazing.

If college is your goal and it becomes your child's, you will find your way together. Take it one day at a time, one month at a time, and one year at a time, just as you did in the earlier years. Be intentional and faithful, but remember that learning is a lifelong journey. This is only the opening act.

THE MANNER

12 Discovering Your Homeschool Style

WHEN IT COMES TO HOMESCHOOLING, THERE IS no "one size fits all" approach. Homeschoolers come in all different shapes and styles, influences and interests, preferences and peculiarities. There are homemakers and business makers, book lovers and adventure takers, bread bakers and jewelry makers, curriculum creators and STEM researchers, fun makers and road-trippers. Depending on our giftedness, personality, and intricate design, homeschooling looks different for each of us.

The old model of homeschooling put everyone in the same category. But over the years, homeschoolers have discovered a plethora of educational models, from Waldorf and Montessori to the resurgence of classical pedagogy and the writings of Charlotte Mason. While there were many advantages in accessing a variety of methods, it also resulted in these camps circling their wagons and fostering a spirit of comparison and competition.

The tactile learners shook their silk scarves at the test takers, and the literature enthusiasts tried to drown out the memory drillers with their daily read-alouds. All of them upheld the legacies of their long-departed leaders as a testament to the "right way" to homeschool.

Division seemed to define the homeschooling community at large.

What makes Wild + Free different is that it embraces the values that unite us and celebrates the freedom we have in the nonessentials because everyone homeschools differently.

"Perhaps instead of spending so much time and effort trying to convince our children to move on the path we've designed, we could encourage them to get to their destination by allowing them a few minor detours."

—CYNTHIA ULRICH TOBIAS

We may not all homeschool in the same way, but we're in this together.

Our great joy as home educators is to discover the approach that ignites a passion for learning in our children. It's not always easy, but take heart—the answer lies in front of you. When the method and the child don't agree, believe the child.

If you are considering homeschooling, let me set you at ease. You don't have to fit a certain homeschooler profile to do it the wild + free way. You don't have to sign up for a co-op if it makes you feel bad or buy a big-box curriculum because it's the safe thing to do. You don't have to see yourself as a teacher type or wake up early to feel productive or schedule your day in blocks or buy vintage desks (although that's fun). And you don't have to adhere to a methodology just because you're surrounded by people who do.

You need only be willing to bring your personality, style, and gifts to the table and use them to create a unique learning experience for your children.

No matter what style we choose, may we never forget what this learning journey is really about—relationship, togetherness, real conversations, discovering passions, and living our own story. I love this simple reminder by Lisa Murphy: "The children are the curriculum."

Yes. So much yes.

STUMBLING INTO YOUR STYLE

You might have to try a few approaches before you find the right one for you. I call this "stumbling into your style" because it sounds better than what I did—running into brick walls.

When I first decided to bring my son home after his first-grade school year, I didn't know anything about homeschooling. I didn't know the insider talk, the distinctions between the different camps, or even that there were various homeschool styles at all. In fact, I didn't know the first thing about curriculums, let alone how to choose one.

My friend Stephanie Beaty was also planning to homeschool and had already done a lot of the research. Being the procrastinator that I am, I asked her if I could come by and look at what she had found. So, one evening after the babies were asleep, Stephanie gave me a debriefing of the major curriculums, and we discovered that we both wanted to take a similar approach to education: delight driven, literature based, and relationship rich.

We ordered the same big-box curriculum for the corresponding ages of our sons because it seemed like the best approach for our first year. For starters, it would guarantee the legitimacy of what we were doing. It would help us become capable teachers and give our children a certified education (albeit in a box), but it would also give us a foundation for guiding our children's education. We knew an education was more than the sum of its parts and that we could use as much or as little as we wanted. At the very least, we could get in the basics, read some good books together, and call it a success.

That first year, we both discovered a lot about our personal preferences and homeschool styles. I learned that reading great literature with my boys created meaningful connections and opened the door for incredible conversations. I learned that Wyatt had a natural knack for math and a voracious appetite for reading. I learned that Dylan was an eager learner, a natural linguist, and a clever contrarian. And I learned that I couldn't stick to a curriculum to save my life. Books were great, but everything else felt too scripted. I found myself coming up with creative lessons on the fly each day, despite the huge investment I had made.

A few weeks into our second year, I was sitting in my backyard on a beautiful fall day, talking to Stephanie on the phone. The sun warmed my face while the breeze made me pull my sweater a little tighter around my shoulders. The boys were building a teepee out of branches, and I relished the freedom this lifestyle offered us.

Stephanie and her family had recently moved to Florida, and I was missing our time together. Homeschooling felt a little lonelier without her close by, but this day felt like old times.

We talked about how things were going and how we had both found a rhythm that was working for our families. I

shared some of our adventures and
favorite activities, which included
nature hikes, handicrafts, and nature
journaling.

She said, "You're so Charlotte Mason,
Ains."

I had no idea what she meant by that, so she told me about a
book she was reading called *A Charlotte Mason Companion* by
Karen Andreola and recommended that I read it. I jotted down
the name, but two days later it arrived on my doorstep, despite
my never ordering it. (Thanks, Steph.)

That was the beginning of my journey learning about the
various styles of home education. I'm still learning, and I love
talking with friends about their preferred methods. While many
choose a style that resonates with them and pursue it in its
purist form, others take on a more eclectic style, pulling from
several different approaches.

You'll find that some homeschoolers don't care how
you define them, while many are fiercely passionate about
their style. You might hear some describe themselves as a
"classically bent Charlotte Mason home educator," a "Waldorf
homeschooler," or a "Reggio-inspired unschooler," and, like
me, many mothers all over the world are now referring to
themselves as "Wild + Free."

Understanding the different styles can give you a vision for
what you want your children's education to look like, give voice
to your desires, and help you tailor an individual education for
each of your children.

LET YOU BE YOU

Beyond the homeschool styles, there are many other terms
to describe the nontraditional schooling experience—

homeschooling, world schooling, nature schooling, road schooling, home educating, self-directed learning, and so on. For many people, these expressions have very distinct and important differentiations.

For example, some prefer *home education* to *homeschooling* because they want to differentiate themselves from school in the traditional sense. Others don't want to include the word *home* because they don't want to limit their learning to the home. They are always learning—in the world, in the forest, in their community—no matter where they are.

Still others don't want to imply that the parent is the teacher and the child the student, so they exclude any mention of education or schooling from their description.

Language is important because it forms our thinking, which in turn forms our beliefs and eventually our actions. But we don't hyperfocus on descriptors because our desire in whatever we do is to be wild + free, to break the chains of convention, and to live our own adventure. You are free to describe your journey in whatever way makes sense to you.

No matter what we call this thing we do, let's remember that learning is not a system, a methodology, or a checklist to get things done. It is an organic process that occurs when the conditions are right. Our role is part guide and part architect, creating an environment in which our children can not only grow but thrive. Moreover, we are colearners—learning with them, learning for them, and learning about them. Whatever method you choose, know that it will reflect your personality and, we hope, the personality of your child.

So here's to the mamas, the change makers and homemakers, the fun ones, the crazy ones, the silly and the serious ones. The fearless ones who blaze new trails. The broken ones who keep on going. The old souls and the free spirits. The planners and the fly-by-your-seaters. You are the ones making magic happen every day.

What makes your homeschool journey unique isn't what you do. It's who you are.

13

The Influences of Homeschooling

HOME-BASED EDUCATION ISN'T ABOUT "DOING school at home." It's about freeing our children to learn in their own way, at their own pace, within the most natural conditions. With access to ideas from around the world, homeschooling has progressed to incorporate multiple pedagogical styles, in which we're influenced by many approaches rather than limited by one. Just as we have the freedom to homeschool in the first place, we also have the freedom to adapt our approach to suit our teaching style, as well as the needs, learning styles, and personalities of our children.

While this is by no means an exhaustive study of the various methodologies, here are some of the more popular approaches that have influenced education over the past century and helped shape the values of what has become "the Wild + Free way."

CLASSICAL

The classical approach to education is rooted in the ancient worlds of Greece and Egypt, developed into a pedagogy during the Middle Ages by Martianus Capella, championed by both  Christian and secular scholars alike over the past hundred years, and upheld by many of the world's scholars today. If the definition of *education* is the "cultivation of wisdom and virtue by nourishing the soul on truth, goodness, and beauty," then a classical education takes on this endeavor by means of the seven liberal arts and four sciences.[1]

According to this philosophy, children learn in three stages: grammar, logic, and rhetoric. The early years (grades K–6) revolve around grammar, or language, at a time when children have a natural inclination for memorization through songs, chants, and rhymes. Children spend time absorbing the facts in various subjects such as science, math, geography, Latin, English grammar, history, and fine arts. This stage provides the foundation of all future education.

The logic stage is designed around a middle-grade child's desire to know the "why" behind everything. At this age, students begin to challenge authority and become more argumentative, so educators use this stage to teach logic, reasoning, and how to argue eloquently. In short, they are taught to think for themselves and apply logic to every subject—be it writing, reading, math, science, or history.

The rhetoric stage, during the high school years, also reflects the appropriate development of the child, focusing on teaching teenagers how to use persuasive speech and effective writing. This is when students apply all the knowledge and logic they have learned during the previous learning phases, or when they "learn to express themselves," as Susan Wise Bauer put it. This is the culmination of all the earlier years.

The classical approach focuses on providing a system for learning to take place, for teaching virtue, and for training the mind. Dorothy Sayers, a pioneer in the revival of classical education after its significant dwindling at the turn of the twentieth century, had a profound impact on furthering this philosophy, and many books, curriculums, and programs have been built on her influential words. She said, "Although we often succeed in teaching our pupils 'subjects,' we fail lamentably on the whole in teaching them how to think."

Classical education may be thought of by some as an outdated method, and by others as too stringent. But proponents of this approach see no fault in either its ancient origins or its rigor.

In fact, these only enhance its meaning and purpose in society today.

Susan Wise Bauer was integral in making classical education approachable at home with her books *The Well-Trained Mind* and *The Well-Educated Mind*. She asserted that rigorous study provides a child with a system to both develop virtue, instead of lazy habits, and "join what Mortimer Adler calls the 'Great Conversation'—the ongoing conversation of great minds down through the ages. Much modern education is so eclectic that the student has little opportunity to make connections between past events and the flood of current information."[2]

While the method has a hierarchy and a systematic structure, neither rigidity nor constraint is at the heart of a true classical education. In earnest, this way of learning offers freedom to embrace the "less is more" mind-set of modern education and to diverge from the teaching of separate subjects.

According to the CiRCE Institute, the work of classical educators is to guide their students through the contemplation of great texts and works of art, "believing that such contemplation will enable them to grow in wisdom and virtue," as well as to guide them in the "analysis of ideas via Socratic dialogue, believing that insight into the heart of things will enable students to grow in wisdom and virtue."[3]

This is no easy feat, but fostering a lifestyle steeped in ideas is a worthy endeavor.

Over the past twenty years, there has been a resurgence of classical schools, as well as homeschooling resources to inspire the classical way of learning at home. Among others, the Well-Trained Mind Academy, founded by Bauer, and the CiRCE Institute, started by Andrew Kern, are two leading organizations that provide resources, curriculums, and seminars for classical educators.

Many homeschoolers also use Classical Conversations, a program developed by Leigh Bortins, an aerospace engineer turned stay-at-home mom. She started the program in 1997 with eleven students, and today more than 45,000 families are enrolled in local chapters around the world, making her program one of the most popular iterations of classical education today.[4]

Classical Conversations, or CC, as it is commonly called, provides a practical framework for families to use the classical approach at home while coming together once a week to learn collectively from a tutor. The program follows the trivium and divides students into three levels: Foundations (grammar), Essentials (logic), and Challenge (rhetoric).

Wild + Free mama Bre Chang explained each level using the metaphor of moving. "I would describe Foundations as 'the packing phase.' The child's brain is like the moving truck. In the Foundations phase, you are filling up the truck as full as you can get it. The whole point of this phase is to fill up the truck. Essentials is 'the unpacking phase.' You take all of the info that was stored and start opening up those boxes, learning a bit more about what's inside, until you figure out which room they belong in. Challenge is where you start forming opinions and take that box into the living room and decide what you want to keep, donate, and how you really feel about that interesting piece of art. You start making the house a home."

For many home educators, CC offers a structured study plan they can easily implement at home. It covers subjects such as science, math, geography, Latin, English grammar, history, fine arts, and public speaking. But the program itself is simply a means to the greater purpose, which is to instill in children the ability to grow in both knowledge and the expression of that knowledge, to pursue virtue and beauty, and to learn how to think.

In her book *The Question*, Bortins noted, "Humans long for relationship, and thinking together in an interesting way about hard things is very rewarding."[5] Classical Conversations aims to create a way for our children to do just that.

Studying Latin is an important part of classical education. While most modern educators believe Latin is outdated and has little use in a child's education, classical enthusiasts argue the opposite. Not only do nearly all modern languages have Latin roots—over 50 percent of English vocabulary comes from Latin—it also reinforces learning the various parts of speech.

"I will say at once, quite firmly, that the best grounding for education is the Latin grammar," Sayers wrote in *The Lost Tools of Learning*. "I say this, not because Latin is traditional and medieval, but simply because even a rudimentary knowledge of Latin cuts down the labor and pains of learning almost any other subject by at least fifty percent. It is the key to the vocabulary and structure of all the Romance languages and to the structure of the Teutonic languages, as well as to the technical vocabulary of all the sciences and to the literature of the entire Mediterranean civilization, together with all its historical documents."[6]

Many would argue that the reasons for studying Latin go much deeper still. Andrew Kern, founder of the CiRCE Institute, said there is a difference between the benefits and the purpose of studying Latin. The benefits, while many, are lost without an understanding of the purpose—which is to learn and know Latin. Kern explained it this way:

It's not that everybody needs to learn Latin and Greek, only those who will engage in politics, law, theology, medicine, entertainment, philosophy, education, natural science, ethics, and the learned professions. Not every society needs to be permeated by people who know Latin and Greek, only those that love freedom and truth. I have no idea if Latin and Greek are innately superior to other languages. I only know that they are the languages in which people thought about the things listed above for over 2000 years. To lose that heritage is to become impoverished, homeless, and destitute.[7]

There is a reason why volumes of books have been written about classical education. Like most pedagogies, and maybe more so, it is difficult to condense into a brief summary. However, like other methodologies, it has many beautiful things to offer and deep meaning for those who pursue it.

Elsie Iudicello is a student of classical pedagogy and a director of Classical Conversations. She wrote, "Classical education changed the purpose of education for my family. We no longer looked at school work as dissected subjects, each separate and unrelated from the other. Learning became whole, harmonious and integrated. Math was a part of history and science and music and geography, each pouring into the other. Everything we encountered had a story and an origin and a meaning to us as individuals and as part of humanity. We walked away from the frantic cultural obsession of teaching as much material as possible, as early as possible, and instead focused on engaging deeply with fewer subjects, 'multum non multas,' in our own time. Best of all, we found the heart of our education in learning to cultivate wisdom and virtue. We are not learning for the purpose of churning out workers trained for one specific job.

We are nurturing souls and anchoring them to truth, goodness and beauty. This is learning for the soul and not the machine."[8]

It's easy to get caught up in the minutiae of educational philosophies, but it's more beneficial to see each one through the lens of the heart.

Andrew Kern reminds us, "Children are souls to be nurtured, not products to be measured."

And may they always be.

MONTESSORI

In 1936, an Italian educator named Maria Montessori stated in her book *The Secret of Childhood* that "the first aim of the prepared environment is, as far as it is possible, to render the growing child independent of the adult." Breaking conventions and becoming the first female doctor in Italy, Montessori wasn't one to look down on children for their youth. She believed they were capable of doing much more than society believed they could do.

Montessori espoused that the hand is the chief teacher of the child. Her experience in working with disabled children in free clinics allowed her to see the natural curiosity and intelligence within children—they wanted to touch and feel everything, especially the instruments she used to test intelligence. She began using these instruments as learning tools with the children and experienced great success.[9] As a result, she ended up opening her own school, but she never claimed credit for creating the Montessori approach to education.

"It is not true that I invented what is called the Montessori Method," she said. "I have studied the child; I have taken what the child has given me and expressed it, and that is what is called the Montessori Method."[10]

Her core principles of education included freedom, order, beauty, nature, reality, and the social and intellectual environment. She said that education was a "natural process carried out by the child and is not acquired by listening to words but by experiences in the environment" and that our senses are like "explorers of the world" opening the door to learning.

Today, Montessori classrooms are peaceful environments that offer a variety of spaces for children to learn and play— both independently and with one another. Children are free to move about the different spaces, cleaning up after themselves, while learning to interact with their peers by sharing, playing together, and dealing with conflict.

An important aspect of Montessori is that there is no focal point in the classroom, allowing for the environment as a whole to provide stimulation, and everything is scaled to a child's size—from furniture and shelving to art easels and wash stations. Often, there is only one item of each material, so children are working alone, waiting their turn to use certain items. While one child might be using knobbed cylinders, four are working together on a "world flags map" puzzle on the floor. Or three kids might be painting at an easel station while a few others are preparing the snack. All work, as Montessori preferred to call it, supports the child's need for free choice, hands-on activities, and independence.

The outdoor environment is equally important, and children spend a considerable amount of time playing in nature as a vital aspect of engaging the whole child.

Homeschooling mama Jessica Mueller described it this way: "The Montessori method is a holistic approach to educating the child based on observation and following the child's interests and abilities, rooted in hands-on materials and activities."

She said a few tenets of the philosophy are "to follow the child, freedom within limits, a prepared environment, respect and order, nature and reality, and abstaining from rewards."

Jessica was first introduced to Montessori in college when one of her education professors laughed at the philosophy, describing it as a "free-for-all environment with no structure where kids did whatever they wanted without intervention."

Jessica said, "Of course, that sounds like a ridiculous way to educate children, but out of necessity, I ended up teaching as an assistant in a primary Montessori classroom. As I began to experience Montessori firsthand and research it on my own, seeing the children interact, learn, and truly enjoy the experience, I knew it was what I wanted for my own children."

The Montessori method is primarily a school-based approach to learning because the environment plays a central role in the learning process, along with an abundance of sensory-rich materials. Additionally, the classroom is a necessary part of implementing the method wholly.

According to Eve Hermann, a Montessori-inspired homeschooler in France, "Maria Montessori imagined classes composed of different ages and with at least 30 children. It was not an option, but a necessary component for the proper functioning of the whole. She thought that the life of the class should reflect the society, like a hive, where every child works at his own construction, but also the good of all. This is why it is challenging to reproduce a Montessori environment at home."

Still, many parents, like Eve, choose to educate their children using the principles of Montessori despite being unable to recreate the classroom at home in its purest form. After all, purchasing expensive materials and strictly adhering to all aspects of the methodology isn't necessary to begin adopting the ideas of Maria Montessori.

Many mamas allow the philosophy of Montessori to guide their parenting, as well as their homeschool style, especially in the early years. There are lots of ways to create an environment at home that encourages children to take responsibility for their own learning and empowers them to become independent thinkers, creative problem solvers, risk takers, and respectful members of the community.

For example, parents might set aside spaces in their main living areas just for their children. By allowing them to bring their toys into the same space instead of banishing them to a playroom, we remind them that they are important and welcome in any environment.

Child-size shelving for toys and books, organized baskets, and trays make it easy for a child to see what is available and clean up appropriately. Open shelving for clothes that children can access is another element that is simple to implement within the home. The purpose isn't to create child-friendly environments for ease alone but to empower children to make choices, organize their items, and put them away appropriately.

Montessori believed that education was preparation for life, so she created an environment that was rich in sensory materials to allow children to experience the world around them. Through hands-on learning, children can explore a variety of subjects, such as math, language, science, geography, cultural studies, art, and music.

Gathering a collection of beautifully crafted toys and learning materials can take time, but it isn't impossible. The best way to start is by secondhand shopping, nature scavenging, and homemaking. Remember, you are creating an extension of your home, not building a stand-alone classroom, so quality over quantity is key.

In addition to the child-centered environments and well-crafted materials, many home educators love the approach that Montessori takes with math. It uses beautiful and tangible manipulatives to give children a visual representation of mathematical concepts.

Jessica shared that this was one reason she was drawn to this philosophy. "Maria Montessori believed 'the hand is the chief teacher of the brain,' and the materials are designed to move from concrete to abstract," she wrote.

"For example, to teach exchanging ones to tens, tens to hundreds, and hundreds to thousands, we use beads," Jessica continued. "A unit bead represents the ones, ten unit beads are exchanged for a 10-bar (ten beads strung together), ten 10-bars equal a 100-square (ten 10-bars), and ten 100-squares equal a 1,000-cube. So instead of simply seeing a one with a bunch of zeros, the child can see and work with the physical quantity of the number."

Another friend of mine, Michelle Garrels, incorporated a Montessori approach at home when she didn't see a natural inclination for math in one of her children.

"We had tried three other math curricula, and daily lessons were frequently met with groans," Michelle said. "I was familiar with much of the Montessori hands-on approach and the effect on brain development through some of the language arts materials we'd been using."

She loved the approach of learning the process first through tactile means, paving the way for memorization work later on, which is the opposite of most traditional math approaches.

Michelle said her child is thoroughly an artist, so she knew the natural beauty of the Montessori math materials and their tactile nature would be the right fit.

"I knew somehow this was my only chance to make math resonate," Michelle said, "by making it beautiful, playful, and touchable."

A Montessori-based curriculum focuses on mastery over memorization. It allows the child to learn at his own pace, regardless of age, so that he will move on to the next level only after he has mastered the material. This is why you'll often see various ages within the same Montessori classroom, which could be encouraging to the homeschooling mother of multiple ages. The one-room schoolhouse isn't a problem to be solved but a more practical way of learning.

Whether your goal is applying the Montessori method at home or simply understanding its philosophy so you can grow in your knowledge of educational models, it's impossible to deny the powerful impact that this passionate and profound thinker has had on early childhood development. If you take anything from this method, it's that children are worthy of our respect—both as human beings and as natural learners. In the words of Maria herself, "The goal of early childhood education should be to activate the child's own desire to learn."

Nothing more and nothing less.

CHARLOTTE MASON

At the turn of the twentieth century, an English educator named Charlotte Mason began sharing her vision for giving children a wide and liberal education. In her book *A Philosophy of Education*, she observed, "An education is an atmosphere, a discipline, a life."

This revolutionary statement is woven throughout all six of her volumes, laying the foundation for homes, families, and schools to build upon. It is also the motto that contributes highly in the ongoing work of Charlotte Mason education throughout the world.

Homeschooling mama Leah Boden, known by many in the Wild + Free community as the "Modern Miss Mason,"

explained it this way: "Miss Mason hands us three tools, or 'instruments' as she refers to them, to hinge our educating days upon. One does not outweigh the other but they evenly build a strong foundation on which to create an educated life. The 'Atmosphere' sets the tone; not so much the visual aesthetics of a house but moreover, the intentional or unintentional ethos that defines a family. 'Discipline' describes the taught rhythms and habits that bring longevity, strength and consistency to our days. And the 'Life' aspect of the motto pertains to the fuel (books) that feed a mind resulting in great ideas."

Mason's philosophies on education were shaped by her faith in God and her teaching experiences at a time when children were often dismissed in society, meant to be "seen but not heard." She maintained that children are "born *persons*," who should be treated as individuals and given the opportunity to have a full and rich education. From faith and habits to narration and nature study, her educational philosophy is replete with rich insights and practical applications and is used by thousands of homeschoolers around the world today, faith based and secular alike.

She was a teacher but believed that teaching got in the way of children's own self-discovery, so she encouraged giving children access to ideas and allowing them to do the thinking for themselves. She believed that providing children with an array of texts, hands-on experiences, and ample time to play freely would foster their imaginations and enable them to learn to think for themselves and understand the world in which they live.

Mason came up with the metaphor of "laying a feast" before children and allowing their minds to do the work of digestion. Boden said, "This is possibly one of the most powerful metaphors that Charlotte Mason uses with regards to the generous curriculum that we provide for our children. If all the best thought the world possesses is really stored in books, then our children deserve an abundance of literature and lives to inspire and feed their hungry minds; but not stored on our shelves collecting dust."

The image Boden conjures is one of delicacies strewn about the house in the form of great literature, nature study, art, music, handicrafts, and environments that foster learning.

"Our children need to hear these stories and ideas read aloud, have them scattered around our homes and piled up in baskets and on tables as we gather to learn," Boden said. "The feast is a collection of ideas, experiences and stories that nourish our children's heads and hearts with adventure and intrigue. The feast is a 'help yourself' offering of goodness and beauty brought to the child's eyes, hand, and mind by what we provide throughout their learning days."

Mason wanted to spark children's inner desire to learn, not bore them to death, so she advised using short lessons to awaken their enthusiasm—15 minutes for elementary students, 30 minutes for middle grades, and 45 minutes for higher grades—and then moving on to another subject before they grew weary. For her, the goal of education was not "How much has our child covered?" but "How much does he care?" and "About how many things does he care?"

To this end, she believed children should be left alone and that habit training was key to helping them take charge of their own education. If they formed healthy habits when they were young, they could become self-directed learners when they got older.

She said, "The mother who takes pains to endow her children with good habits secures for herself smooth and easy days." She resisted the idea of "teasing them with perpetual commands and direction" and preferred to let them go their own way and grow.

Today, rather than using textbooks, Charlotte Mason home educators read "living books," a phrase Mason coined to describe high-quality literature that would both ignite the imagination and give children a foundation in reading and writing. They include inspiring stories, quality writing, and admirable characters and individuals that children can emulate, breathing life into children and adults alike.

Wild + Free mama Amy Seegers summarized the Charlotte Mason method as "a learning style rich in art, history, nature, character building, and the Bible." She said she chose it for her family because it fit their style of learning and love of good books, art, and nature.

"For us," Seegers said, "it's getting out of the house and learning about the world around us, whether it's checking the ditches on our gravel road for milkweed, kayaking and stopping at every sandbar to find animal bones, or trying to catch the biggest fish, only to realize it was spawning, and then going home to watercolor or journal it all."

The Charlotte Mason method also encourages the practice of handicrafts, which is any activity that engages one's hands, requires a level of learned skill, encourages children to do their best work, and produces an end product that is useful. A few examples are woodworking, sewing, scrapbooking, crocheting, oil painting, leather tooling, quilting, pottery, calligraphy, knitting, flower arranging, and iron sculpting. Mason was passionate about helping children learn useful skills so they would always have a way to earn a living when they were older.

"My favorite thing about handicrafts is it doesn't feel like you are learning," Seegers said, "but you are. We've carved wood, sewed, learned how to latch hook, knitted, crocheted, and water-colored. I love showing my kids there is a deep satisfaction in making things with their hands."

Nature study is another tenet of a Charlotte Mason education. She recommended that families spend several hours a day—six, to be exact—outdoors. She even encouraged mothers living in the city to make this a priority by taking a train to the country or walking to a nearby park at least once a week.

In her book *For the Children's Sake*, Susan Schaeffer Macaulay wrote that "Charlotte Mason's ideal world for children had nature at the doorstep. She felt that organized

lessons should only take up the morning, so that children could freely play in and enjoy the gardens, meadows, woods, and lanes of England every afternoon."[11]

Charlotte Mason was a revolutionary educator who influenced not only schools but also mothers who educated their children at home. She wanted to set mothers and children free to learn according to their way. She believed in the role of mothers in raising lifelong self-educators. Nearly 150 years ago, she wrote, "There is nothing which a mother cannot bring her child up to."

And I couldn't agree more.

WALDORF

The Waldorf model of education was developed by artist, scientist, and spiritual philosopher Rudolf Steiner in the twentieth century, in the aftermath of World War I. Steiner was asked to create an educational model that would "promote peace among humankind." The first Waldorf school opened in 1919 for employees at the Waldorf-Astoria cigarette factory in Stuttgart, Germany.[12]

Steiner sought to educate the whole child—body, mind, and spirit. And the Waldorf curriculum is designed to mirror the basic stages of development from childhood to adulthood—moving from discovery of the world during the early years into artistic endeavors in the middle grades, and then into a scientific attitude during the high school years.[13]

Unlike many pedagogies, the Waldorf method focuses heavily on the imaginative aspects of a child. Developed at a time when education focused mainly on the physical world, this philosophy offered a holistic approach that was missing from children's learning experiences.

Today, there are over a thousand Waldorf schools around the world, and many homeschoolers use a Waldorf curriculum at home. Artistic presentation is a core value, so Waldorf-inspired classrooms and homeschools are infused with natural materials, child-led play, and various aspects of art, music, and movement. Many Waldorf practitioners set up seasonal displays, from chalkboards and nature tables to inspirational playthings and reading materials.

Ideally, all lessons are taught through storytelling and artistic expression and address the whole child. Every subject is integrated into the Waldorf curriculum, from math to science to spelling, and even the academic material is mostly presented through stories and images.

Wild + Free mama Rachel Kovac has been studying the Waldorf method since her fourteen-year-old was just a baby. She's now been homeschooling for six years and has found it to be a perfect fit for her family's lifestyle. She wrote, "A Waldorf education is a holistic education that seeks to nourish the whole child, body, mind and soul in an unhurried environment. Through beautiful stories that cultivate virtue, imaginative play, handwork, and integrating the arts throughout the curriculum, children develop a joy-filled and life-long love of learning."

At the heart of Waldorf pedagogy is the emphasis on imagination in learning and on infusing the intellectual, practical, and artistic development of children in a holistic manner. As a result, there's a big emphasis on fairy tales, myths, and stories that invoke the imagination.

Steiner wrote, "The need for imagination, a sense of truth, and a feeling of responsibility—these are the three forces which are the very nerve of education."

Another aspect at the core of the Waldorf philosophy is its aim to preserve and safeguard childhood. The understanding is that young children are not drawn into precocious intellectualism, so formal academic instruction is not recommended in the first stage of development.

Kovac put it this way: "Children have their entire lives to dedicate themselves to formal learning, but only this short window where they can be so immersed in the magical realm of imagination and deeply absorbed in play."

But that doesn't mean academics aren't important. As such, Waldorf educators aim to cultivate a child's intellectual, emotional, and physical beings at the same time. They call this the Head, Heart, Hands model, and as in the schools, Waldorf homeschoolers create a daily rhythm that is based on activities that nurture their child's head, heart, and hands.

For example, morning time usually focuses on academic main lessons, including grammar and math. When children need a mental break in the middle of the day, the focus turns to the heart or an activity that reaches them at the emotional level, such as music, art, or nature study. Finally, the afternoon is for hand-centered activities. Handicrafts or handiwork helps channel the energy of children while teaching them a skill, such as sewing, cooking, or building.

Wild + Free homeschooler DeAnna McCasland said, "For my family, Waldorf has been so much more than just a way to educate my children. It has been a positive lifestyle change as well. It is about peaceful parenting, getting back to simplicity and nature, and nurturing the child as a whole. The focus isn't just on their minds, but also on their hands and hearts. I want my children to know how to grow their own food and knit a hat just as much as I want them to understand long division."

Another unique aspect of Waldorf education is that students don't read textbooks or use workbooks. Rather, they create their own lesson books, one for every subject. They draw from the activities, stories, images, discussions, and experiences of the day and document what they are learning through their own pictures and words. There are no grades or tests, but students are encouraged to do their best work while given freedom to make it their own.

McCasland explained how this applies to language arts in her homeschooling. "Children learn the upper-case alphabet in kindergarten. So the night before the main lesson, we read a fairy tale at bedtime that relates to our new letter. The following morning, we discuss the fairy tale, and I introduce the letter and a chalkboard drawing that relates to the story and connects all of this back to the letter. The children draw their own version of the letter and connect it to the story in the main lesson book. For the rest of the week we practice writing the letter while out on nature walks in the dirt, made out of sticks or other nature findings. We bake bread in the shape of the letter or mold it out of beeswax. The child also plays games and draws the letters on my hand or back while I guess what it is and vice versa. There is also another game we play where I dust flour out on the grass in the shape of the letter and the child 'walks' the letter with their entire body. Poetry is introduced early on, and they grasp the sound of the letter by reciting poems and rhymes. This one lesson goes far beyond just putting it in their heads. We incorporate the hands and the heart as well."

Rudolf Steiner's philosophy of education was based on his spiritual philosophy, called anthroposophy, a formal educational, therapeutic, and creative system he developed that aimed "to use mainly natural means to optimize physical and mental health and well-being."[14] It focuses on the connection all humans have to the past, the natural world, and each other. It is not a religion per se but rather strives to bridge science, art, and religion into one approach.

While it is controversial to some that Steiner used his own spiritual views as the basis for Waldorf education, others choose to see the beauty of its pedagogy and separate the man from the method. Although anthroposophical views inspired the framework of its curriculum, the philosophy itself is not taught to children in most Waldorf schools.

Aside from the artistic and imaginative components, the phases of child development, the importance of establishing rhythms, the creation of main lesson books, and the methodology, the Waldorf method focuses significantly on the role of the teacher.

Steiner believed teachers played a key role in children's lives—both individually and as a whole. He believed in empowering teachers to use their natural gifts and insights and that they must cultivate their own imaginations if they were to help their students do the same. This could be done through research, meditation, and artistic expression.[15]

He also took an unconventional view when it came to teacher qualifications.

Kovac shared this about the role of teachers in Waldorf schools: "Rudolf Steiner did not specifically seek conventionally trained teachers to instruct at Waldorf schools. Instead he looked for inner qualities within the individual, and his teachers came from all walks of life."

"The first quality he looked for was a knowledge of child development in general," she said. "The second was an unending willingness to ceaselessly work on one's own inner development. The third was a desire to know and understand each particular child as an individual."

Steiner himself put it this way: "Where is the book in which the teacher can read about what teaching is? The children themselves are this book. We should not learn to teach out of any book other than the one lying open before us and consisting of the children themselves."

Indeed. Children are the curriculum.

REGGIO EMILIA

Reggio Emilia is a philosophy of early education that allows children to direct their own learning and express themselves in a multitude of ways besides speaking and writing—all in the context of relationships with other children and their surroundings. It was formed near the Italian city of the same name by a psychologist named Loris Malaguzzi in the aftermath of World War II.

This unique educational approach was introduced to the world in 1991 when a preschool in Reggio Emilia was listed as one of the top ten preschools internationally. Because the methodology argues that the location and community are fundamental for children's unique learning, any schools outside of Reggio Emilia that adopt its philosophies are considered "Reggio-inspired." They receive training in guiding their students but are encouraged to adapt to the needs of their individual communities. As a result, no two schools will ever look alike.

At the core of this approach is respecting children and their ability to be capable and active participants in their own learning. It is up to the teacher or parent to prepare the learning-rich environment and give thoughtful attention to their students' ideas and observations while allowing them to learn through the experiences of touching, moving, listening, and observing. Parents and teachers are colearners with the children.

Malaguzzi believed that teaching and learning shouldn't "stand on opposite banks and just watch the river flow by; instead, they should embark together on a journey down the water. Through an active, reciprocal exchange, teaching can strengthen learning how to learn."[16]

The goal is not to give children the answers but to encourage exploration, curiosity, and discussion. By documenting their thinking, showing interest in their ideas, asking questions, and providing materials for study, the goal is to help children learn to solve problems by discovery. Doing otherwise, they say, robs kids of the chance to develop perseverance and ingenuity.

Reggio teachers are encouraged to take on the role of colearner, being curious alongside their children and allowing mistakes to occur or initiating projects without a clear objective. In the midst of exploration, teachers interact with their students, listening carefully to their ideas, drawing them out through conversation, and respectfully repeating back the students' thoughts or theories. They often encourage children to represent their ideas in a physical form, as one of many expressions.

Sometimes a single question can lead to a widening body of exploration through dialogue and activity. In her book *Bringing Reggio Emilia Home*, Louise Boyd Cadwell explained it this way: "The first process causes the next, and then the next, like ever-widening concentric circles caused by a pebble dropped in a pond."[17]

Many homeschoolers have implemented a Reggio-inspired approach to their children's education and adapted the principles to fit their home culture. There is no preplanned curriculum, which can feel too ambiguous for some, but it offers children the freedom to pursue their own interests and can accommodate all ages and learning styles. With a focus on early childhood, this approach aims to value and nurture the whole child and all the child's capacities to learn.

Homeschooler Amanda Johns said that with a Reggio-inspired approach, "learning comes from the process unfolding organically. It's about the journey, not the destination."

The net result is weaving learning into life, with no need to separate the two.

Reggio Emilia teaches that speaking and writing are just a small part of how children make sense of the world and share their ideas. Given enough time, resources, and opportunity, children can make sense of the world and share their ideas through "one hundred languages."

"Pens, paper, and paint are not just for creating artwork," Johns said, "but can be an infinite database of language with which to help thoughts and ideas materialize."

The environment is just as important as the instruction. In the schools, two teachers are present, and the environment is considered the third teacher. The classroom is infused with natural light, organic materials, and beautiful, high-quality art supplies meant to inspire and invite children to explore with all of their senses and "languages."

But the environment also pertains to the geographic location and the community at large. Both have much to offer in where and how learning unfolds. This aspect is especially appealing to Johns, who said, "As homeschoolers, we have a great advantage to be able to be out in our community and in nature learning."

Homeschoolers who implement this philosophy at home start by creating a culture that respects the child's role as a learner. Parents provide ample time and materials, encourage exploration, ask thoughtful and open-ended questions, and allow the child to lead, at least some of the time. But they act more as a facilitator than a teacher.

As educators, parents must also be learners and allow the children to see them learning new things and nurturing their own souls. They get out in nature, exploring their community and discovering all there is to learn around them.

As a way to rebuild (literally and figuratively) after World War II, Malaguzzi developed this approach to value beauty, creativity, and the uniqueness of every child. He said, "Our task, regarding creativity, is to help children climb their own mountains, as high as possible. No one can do more."[18] At such a broken time in history, this educational model allowed children to lead the way in their own education while the adults took a back seat as sole imparters of knowledge.

This was more than just good pedagogy. It was an important reminder that children had something valuable to teach us as well. By focusing on experience-based, play-based, and interest-led learning, the Reggio Emilia approach gave children the freedom to chase wonder once again.

It's easy to see why this approach is gaining popularity around the world, especially as parents have begun seeing the pitfalls of the modern educational system. While the principles of Reggio Emilia were designed for early childhood, implementing these ideas at home in the early years can help shape the culture and learning environment as children grow. This approach can establish the foundation for all future education, regardless of pedagogy, at home or otherwise.

For families looking for concrete methodology with corresponding curriculums, this approach may not be as practical as others. But there is beauty in its open-ended pedagogy, and, regardless of style, becoming collaborators with our children in their education is a great starting point for any home-educating family.

UNSCHOOLING

Unschooling is less of an educational methodology and more of an educational theory that advocates for children to learn and grow by following their own interests without school or curriculum. The term was coined in the 1970s by educator and author John Holt as a twist to the popular 7 Up "Uncola" advertising campaign. Considered the father of unschooling, Holt was a teacher and advocate of school reform until he finally decided that true reform was not possible and turned his efforts to home education.

Holt defined unschooling as "learning and teaching that does not resemble school learning and teaching"[19] and called on parents to join him in liberating their children from formal education.

It was around this time that Dr. Raymond Moore, a Christian psychologist, also began advocating for homeschooling as a response to state-funded preschools and the push for earlier formal education. During the 1970s, Holt and Moore worked together to create the modern homeschooling movement, set up legal assistance for parents, and unite both secular and religious homeschoolers across America.

Many continued to follow Holt's unconventional ideas of freeing our children to learn without the constraints of formal education and allowing them to follow their interests. They distinguished themselves from the more traditional homeschoolers, resisting the idea of doing "school at home" by using the esteemed educator's term *unschooling* to define their efforts.

Holt's theories are based on years of observing students in Boston schools and homes. He espoused that "living is learning and when kids are living fully and energetically and happily they are learning a lot, even if we don't know what it is." In his book *How Children Learn*, he cites story after story of working with children and observing them in their own element. He said the key to children's learning was to trust them and the natural process that unfolded as they grew.

At a time when opting out of school was considered truancy in most states, Holt advocated for parents' rights. He believed that "people should be free to find or make the kinds of educational experience they want their children to have."

The unschooling approach is guided by the belief that learning happens all the time and that it cannot and should not be forced. Likewise, children cannot learn when they feel unsafe, shamed, or judged. As a result, unschooled children are free to go their own way, learn what they want, and discover new interests. Parents are there to support, guide, help them develop skills, and provide materials for them to explore.

This theory supports children making decisions for themselves—from what time they wake up and what they learn to how they spend their time and when they go to bed. It's about respecting children to know what they need. Parents understand that children can't do everything by themselves, so they are present to help them do things on their own, become self-directed learners, and attain the skills necessary for a successful life.

Wild + Free mama Louise Gibbens explained it this way: "Unschooling is really an entire way of life. It's about trusting that learning is natural and happening all of the time. True learning doesn't require coercion, nor should it be tedious or difficult. It's not about being taught or filled to the brim with knowledge, ready to take an exam, or reach a goal."

As a lifestyle, she continued, "learning should be fun, interesting, and meaningful. How we learn is as individual and unique as how we look. The real beauty of unschooling is that it takes all of this into account. It's a process that is truly child-centered and driven by interests."

When Gibbens brought her son home and began unschooling, it was an adjustment for both of them. "For quite some time after coming out of school, my unschooled eight-year-old was convinced that he wasn't learning anything. He was, of course, but all of a sudden, his learning wasn't forced or dictated, and he often had little or nothing to show for it on paper. Instead, he was doing the things he loved and was free to play." And now, she said, "The learning has become so much a part of the everyday that it's impossible to separate it from everything else."

Another principle of unschooling is that learning must be meaningful. Just as learning cannot be forced, "real" learning cannot occur when a person doesn't see the point or when they don't know how the information relates or is useful in the "real world."[20]

Author Lori Pickert believes that even very young children "have the capacity for inventive thought and decisive action. They have worthwhile ideas. They make perceptive connections.

They're individuals from the start: a unique bundle of interests, talents, and preferences. They have something to contribute. They want to be a part of things."

Our children don't want meaningless tasks or time-filling busywork. They crave meaningful work to connect their ideas and fully express their creativity.

To learn how to do something, Pickert asserts, "we need something real to focus on—not a task assigned by someone else, but something we want to create, something we want to understand. Not an empty exercise but a meaningful, self-chosen undertaking."

Unschooling practices vary from family to family, as well as the degree to which they are used. The reality is that about 50 percent of homeschoolers embrace some variety of unschooling, ranging anywhere from an "extreme hands-off approach to a moderate balance of incorporating self-directed learning while still setting some limits and goals for their children's education."[21]

A common misconception about unschooling is that because there is no structured learning time, unschooling families are lazy and undisciplined. Sometimes I'll hear a mother laughingly suggest that they are unschooling when they aren't able to fit in their regular subjects.

But for actual unschoolers, this approach is anything but negligent. And they would argue that unschooling isn't just an educational approach but a lifestyle. Parents and children who choose to unschool are both thoughtful and intentional about the activities and projects in which they engage, as well as the lack of rules and the focus on self-governing principles. Every decision is purposeful, even if it appears careless to outsiders.

Unschooling parent and former publisher of Holt's magazine, *Growing Without Schooling*, Patrick Farenga said he broadly defined unschooling "as allowing your children as much freedom to explore the world around them in their own ways as you can comfortably bear; I see unschooling in the light of partnership, not in the light of the dominance of a child's wishes over a parent's or vice versa."[22]

Still it can be difficult to discuss unschooling with critics. Without structured work, test scores, and a defined community, unschoolers often bear the brunt of criticism from outsiders.

Gibbens shared, "The hardest part about unschooling has been an unspoken pressure to prove to our close family, and even my husband at times, that the children *are* learning." But, she confirms, "They will learn what they need to, when they need to, and that, at times, this may be ahead of their schooled peers, and certain skills might develop later on."

Having a structured school day is just one way for children to learn. The standards that measure a student's performance can be the very ones that hold them back. Unschooling wasn't designed to hold children back. On the contrary, the intention is to help them soar.

BEAUTIFUL HOMESCHOOLING

The beautiful part about homeschooling is that we don't have to choose just one method, not for our own family and not even for each child. The best approach to homeschooling is one that suits our own personalities, our children's personalities, and how we best learn together. It should reflect not only our own interests but also the interests and gifts of our children.

Adopting parts of the various methods is valuable for some people, just as diving into one is meaningful for others. If we can discover that magical spark in a single pedagogy, great. But understanding all of them or adhering to a specific style is not necessary to homeschool well. Remember, we homeschool because of the freedom it offers us.

It's also wise to remember that every method of education was designed for a certain group of people at a specific time in history. Howard Gardner, a professor at the Harvard Graduate School of Education, wrote, "No matter how ideal an educational model or system, it is always rooted in local conditions. One could no more transport the Diana School of Reggio to New England than one could transport John Dewey's New England schoolhouse to the fields of Emilia Romagna. But just as we can now have 'museums without walls' that allow us to observe art work from all over our world, so, too, we can now have 'schoolhouses without walls' that allow us to observe educational practices as they have developed around the globe."[23]

You may start with one approach but discover that it's not right for your children. Or it might conflict with how you best teach your kids, your temperament, or your environment. Homeschooling can be a miserable experience when you're trying to do it someone else's way.

If something is not working in your household, don't be afraid to scrap it and try a different approach. When you figure out the best fit for your family, learning becomes a joy.

Wild + Free mama Amy Hughes talked about her shift from Charlotte Mason to unschooling and back again after she realized her younger children needed something different.

"For six years, I immersed myself in reading the six volumes of Mason's books," Hughes said. "I graduated my first homeschool student who had a full six years of a Charlotte Mason education and sent him off to college."

Hughes was a Charlotte Mason purist who had planned to do the same thing with her other kids until, one day, her eleven-year-old daughter threw the book *Madam How and Lady Why* against the wall and exclaimed, "I hate this book! Why can't I ever have a break?!"

My friend was stunned. It took her back to a time in her own childhood when she had threatened to run away from home with a note that read, "Because I'm not an adult and I can't have a break." She had been determined never to let her kids feel that way, but there was no denying what she was hearing. Hughes had planned out their days, their months, and their years. She had checklists and deadlines and even planned their summers and never took a break from math.

"I just couldn't believe I had unwittingly put us in this position when I had set out to homeschool for freedom from the very beginning," Hughes said.

She read everything she could on unschooling, told her kids there would be no more school, and "dove completely into the realm of absolute freedom for everyone." They played outside, read the books they wanted to read, and spent hours at the library, the park, and the beach.

And then, after about two months, boredom set in. They stayed home for longer periods of time. The kids started picking on each other and complaining. And the same daughter who had thrown that book at the wall two months earlier now begged her mother for something to do.

So Hughes pulled out the schedules again, made a few adjustments, and picked up right where they had left off. "I noticed something, though," Amy said. "My kids dove into their lessons with a voracious appetite. They were excited to be immersed back in their books. Their narrations were long and descriptive. They didn't even mind doing math. It was like that two months had refreshed and renewed them, bringing joy back into their lessons."

Today, Hughes doesn't consider herself an unschooler or a Charlotte Mason home educator because she goes back and forth between the two approaches. She joked that she doesn't mention this to many people because of how passionate the purists from both sides can be.

Sometimes it's good to try something new because we might discover a better fit for our families. But at other times, it just might confirm that we've been on the right path all along.

Homeschooling is about freedom. But not freedom just to do things the way we want. It's also about freedom for our children. Let's not hold on to our methodologies so tightly that we forget the reason we're doing this in the first place. Children are born persons, after all.

14 Finding Your Rhythm

RHYTHMS ARE VITAL FOR ANY FAMILY, BUT especially for homeschoolers. No matter what personality they have, children respond better to consistency.

Having healthy rhythms promotes peace in our homes, but it also speaks to our values. Our rhythm keeps us focused on what's important. Kim John Payne, author of *Simplicity Parenting*, wrote, "Meaning hides in repetition: We do this every day or every week because it matters."

Of course, life is unpredictable, and our rhythms can easily be disrupted from time to time, sometimes even for entire seasons. A new baby joins the family, the flu takes everyone down one by one, a loved one passes away, or you have a slew of appointments that you just can't miss. The interruptions can wreak havoc on our homeschooling routines.

This is why it's better to have a rhythm than a schedule.

A rhythm is not the same thing as a schedule. A schedule is inflexible. It doesn't breathe. A schedule dictates that you start at a particular time whether you're ready or not. Rhythm, on the other hand, creates a predictable flow to the day. It's driven not by the clock but by priorities.

Having a flexible framework, rather than a set of rigid requirements, allows your family to wade into the morning and flow from activity to activity throughout the day. If something interrupts the plan, you can easily adapt to the change rather than call the day a failure.

Life is full of change, and when we choose to homeschool, our children's education will have to ebb and flow along with the rest of life. That doesn't mean we shouldn't do our best to protect our family rhythms or politely let others know what times are sacred if needed. It simply means recognizing that things will come up that are completely out of our control. In those instances, you don't always have to throw the whole rhythm out the window. Often, you can choose what is most important or valuable to your family and focus on that for a season.

Say, for example, the kids are passing around the flu. Between tending to sick ones, caring for littles, and keeping up with meals and cleaning, you can't sit down for individual math lessons or meet everyone at the table for language arts and history. But maybe you can make lemon-honey tea and read to everyone for a few minutes on the sofa.

During busy seasons, mixed-up days, or downright hard times, focus on the activities that breed connection over getting the work done. One of the main reasons we homeschool is to foster relationships with our children, so when we prioritize the relationship over the to-do list, we are succeeding. Those seemingly small but meaningful moments will go much further in your children's hearts and minds than simply staying consistent in lessons.

Your rhythm may not look the same as anyone else's, and that's okay. Some families start the day early and enjoy big breakfasts together. Others sleep in and don't start homeschooling until late morning. Quite a few families travel full-time, making homeschooling an adventure. And still others

THE CALL OF THE WILD + FREE

keep adapting their rhythms to match the changing seasons of life.

Our family doesn't stop homeschooling altogether during the summer. My kids don't sleep in, much to my chagrin, and since we live by the ocean, we spend a considerable amount of time "summering" throughout the year. One year, I asked my kids whether they wanted to do nothing for three months and then lean in during the school year or drip the content throughout the year. They all chose the latter. Not that we wouldn't ever change, but for now we continue to do morning time, math, and writing exercises every day.

Of course, we take short breaks from formal learning throughout the summer as a way to refresh ourselves and breathe new life into our endeavors, but, in the words of my fun-loving friend Terri Woods, "No kid needs to go to the pool every day for three months."

Of course, if your family lives for summers off, that's okay too.

My friend and fellow Wild + Free mama Hannah Mayo said, "Each family, and even each year, is unique, and what works for one may not be right for another. I've discovered that I can find inspiration through the ways of other homeschooling families, but ultimately I've had to create a rhythm that fits my home, my kids, and the season of life we are currently in."

ESTABLISHING A RHYTHM

For young children, rhythms act as anchors throughout the day. Morning walks, snack time, family dinners, and bedtime read-alouds all become the cornerstones of their childhood. They provide security, peace, and comfort. As children get older, rhythms might not seem quite as important, but having consistency is just as important for teenagers as it is for toddlers.

Payne wrote, "It's appropriate for teenagers to begin to chafe at long-standing family rhythms. It is their job, developmentally, to complain. That doesn't mean that in response we should pack up our traditions and call it a day."

Your family rhythm isn't about control. It's not about dictating how everyone spends their time. Rather, it's a framework that fosters family connection and frees us to live and learn together under the same roof. As children become more independent and teenagers have activities or friends that pull them outside the home, we must learn to be flexible. Embrace this new stage of life and celebrate these amazing persons with whom we have been entrusted.

But just as there are exceptions, there can also be traditions that are upheld, such as family dinners. I recently spoke with a homeschooling father whose children are scheduled to leave for college every other year. He spent the past year gathering them around the dinner table each night to share a meal. At first, they recoiled at this expectation, a slight to their social lives, but as soon as the eldest son went off to college, they treasured the time they spent together.

When creating a framework for your daily rhythm, start simply and leave room for spontaneity to unfold. Here are a few things you could include in your framework:

- Breakfast
- Morning time
- Nature hike
- Snack time
- Main lessons
- Lunch
- Additional subjects
- Read-aloud
- Free time
- Dinner
- Family time
- Bedtime

Your rhythm might look different from this, but the good news is that you can constantly add to, take away from, and change your rhythm to suit what's best for your family. Don't be afraid to get rid of something that's not working. And don't hesitate to experiment with something new.

Unlike a schedule, a rhythm works for all personalities. For the checklist mamas, a rhythm provides a framework to follow. And for the spontaneous mamas, there is freedom to mix things up. Morning time can look different from day to day. You can take it outside to the park or play a game instead of singing songs. Main lessons don't have to be the same rote experience every day either. Alternate subjects, swap book work for manipulatives, or change locations.

There will always be nonnegotiables, like bedtime and mealtimes. And, depending on your children's personalities, you may have to become more or less flexible. That's part of being a parent. But having a rhythm rather than a schedule provides broad swaths of time that allow you to change things up and still provide your children with a natural flow and sense of expectancy.

It's not only daily rhythms that are valuable but also monthly, seasonal, and yearly ones. I participated in a Classical Conversations program for three years before I decided that my kids needed something different to keep learning exciting. Twice a year, we participate in a Wild + Free handicraft fair, which allows my children to make and sell their own creations. Once a year, we read a book together and then see the performance of that story at our local theater.

For years, we carried out "field trip Friday." As my kids got older, they lost interest in this once-favorite tradition, and with more activities outside of the home for music lessons, youth group, and get-togethers with friends, our Fridays are now quieter and more family focused.

For every homeschooling family, the calendar is a blank slate to fill according to your liking. All the social conventions get thrown out the window. There are no semesters, weekends, or holidays unless you choose to acknowledge them. No school bells, back-to-school shopping, or Friday night lights. To have a family rhythm, you'll have to create one or borrow it.

Don't be intimidated by the twenty-four hours staring back at you.

They represent a day of endless possibilities to inspire your children.

MORNING TIME

As your morning goes, so goes the rest of the day. As much as I hate to admit it, being the night owl that I am, mornings really do matter. That doesn't mean they need to start early, but they do need to start with intentionality. Believe me, I've tried it the other way. Once our children spring out of their beds, the tone of the day is established by how they spend the next few hours.

My friend and fellow Wild + Free mama Sharon McKeeman went so far as to say that her homeschool days begin with bedtime the night before: "I know this sounds counterintuitive," she said, "but the day you have tomorrow is shaped by how your children go to bed tonight."

I think she's on to something. When my kids are eased into bed with stories, songs, and gentle prayers, they wake up feeling loved, refreshed, and ready for a new day.

Mornings have a way of washing away the emotional residue of the previous day. No matter what happened yesterday, a rising sun can begin relationships and perspectives anew.

Morning time is a term coined by Cindy Rollins to describe this intentional time together with books, songs, and games. Also called *morning collective* by Jodi Mockabee and *morning basket* by Pam Barnhill, it centers our children and sets the tone for the day. Plus, there can be coffee, pancakes, and conversation about everyone's interests, which is a win-win for all.

Maybe you already have a morning rhythm that works for you, whether it's a big breakfast followed by chores and time outdoors or a more formal learning rhythm. In my early days of homeschooling, I discovered quickly that my boys were

much more apt to sit and listen to stories, practice their writing, or work on an art project if they got outside first thing in the morning to play. So, for many years, we started our days by getting out in nature, going on a hike, or building forts in the backyard. Our morning time didn't take place until after lunch, but it was still a profoundly meaningful time together. Every day for a couple of hours, life and learning intersected in a beautiful symphony of stories, poetry, music, handicrafts, and conversation.

As our boys got older, they didn't need to get outside first thing in the morning to get their "wild" fix as often as they did when they were younger. But the lack of a new rhythm in its place led to bickering and free-for-all activities with no accountability.

Because Ben woke up earlier than I did, and I had some morning responsibilities with Wild + Free, he decided to gather the kids around the kitchen table at the start of each day. At first, they complained about it. They didn't get to do what they usually did. It took a week or two for the habit to kick in, but they finally started gathering without any reminder at all. Ben took the opportunity to teach them life lessons, share perspectives on news stories, and read the Bible.

Several years later, I still gather everyone together in the afternoon to explore great books and work on meaningful projects, but morning time is going strong in our home, and it's become a mainstay in homes all over the world as well. Homeschooling just goes better when the day starts out in a positive way.

Wild + Free mama Rachel Carlisi said that morning time has been at the heart of her homeschool days. "During this time, we all come together and learn as a group," she said. "We read stories, poems, sing songs, play cards, movement games and board games, solve puzzles, eat snacks, and other activities. It sets the tone for our whole day. It feels less abrupt to begin our days with morning basket before any other learning activities, and some days it feels helpful to be outside where we have enjoyed many of our summer mornings."

Not everyone comes at morning time the same way. Sharon McKeeman uses the time to be productive with her best subjects. "A few years in, I found that what I needed for morning time was to teach the thing I love most at a time when I am the most energized and focused," she said. "So we stopped doing math first thing and started centering our days on our history, through which all of our literature, art, and writing are woven. I found that when I give my children the best I have to offer, there can be bumps in the rest of the day, but I feel fulfilled and they feel filled and grounded. We fit math and the other things into the rest of the day."

Gathering has become more challenging than ever for the modern family. Between taking the kids to soccer practice and piano lessons and spouses working longer hours and farther away than ever before, morning time is a balm to a child's heart. It might take a few weeks to teach them to come together each morning, but in time you won't be able to keep them away.

Whatever you call it or however you use it, morning time can help your day get started with the right tone and serve as the anchor for a beautiful homeschool rhythm.

SELF-DIRECTED RHYTHMS

As homeschooling mothers, our aim is not to bark orders and give commands or to assign our children mindless work for work's sake but instead to develop passionate lifelong learners. Creating a flexible framework gives our children the freedom to pursue their own interests and learn on their own while still fulfilling the requirements necessary for their education.

Eve Hermann said, "Homeschooling is more about creating good working habits than about academic learning. It's more about nurturing our children."

As a Montessori-inspired homeschooler, Eve designed her homeschool rhythm to give her daughters more time to explore on their own. "We work in the morning, but it's not strictly school work," she said. "It's a quiet time when the girls can choose what they want to do. It's an uninterrupted three-hour work period."

Eve's daughters always have projects they can continue, or there's material on the shelves from which they can choose. They can also decide to research something that arouses their curiosity, conduct an experiment, or decide on a read-aloud together. And if they don't have a particular interest at the moment, Eve is available to help offer ideas and guide them.

Morning time is also a vital part of Eve's day. She creates a soothing ambiance for learning with lighted candles and soft music playing in the background. After breakfast, they gather around the table to talk about their interests and schedule their day together.

"I love that they can have the power to decide for themselves, and my goal is that my children become more and more independent and self-directed in their learnings," Eve said. "I hope one day they won't need me anymore, or if so, just for the fun of working together."

Eve is careful not to get in the way of her children's learning. She believes that if they choose what to study, rather than have it forced on them by her, they will actually enjoy learning and seek to do more of it. "When the child is beyond the need to know, she discovers the pleasure that hides in learning," Eve said. "The path is more exciting than the end, than the knowledge itself. The pleasure lies between when we don't know and when we know."

Eve knows that familiar rhythms help children know what to expect throughout the day and feel relaxed and safe in their environment. But giving them the freedom to choose their work within this flexible framework "gives them access to the pleasure of great work."

Eve explained, "The great work described by Maria Montessori happens when the child is so deeply and fully involved in his work that he can't see what is going on around him."

As with any homeschooling family, Eve's family's rhythm sometimes falls apart. But she is quick to pull her girls aside and find out how they're feeling. When given a say in how to reframe the day, they come at learning with greater zeal and excitement. In fact, she said she has to remake their rhythm two or three times during the course of a school year. Whether it's a slight tweak or a major overhaul, she can see a noticeable change in the girls' motivation.

Isn't that what we all want for our children—to love learning? If we can instill this one gift in them during childhood, there is nothing they cannot do, no obstacle they cannot overcome, and no challenge they can't face. Our greatest aim of homeschooling will have been accomplished.

"If my children could experience this at least once," Eve said, "it would stay inside them for the rest of their lives. Being able to learn is more important than the knowledge itself."

Let the children be your guide.

KEEPING IT CREATIVE

We get to decide what our children learn. We get to decide when they learn. We get to do what's best for our children. And we get to create the schedule. So why not get creative with it?

My friend Raimie Harrison is a homeschool mama who was also homeschooled growing up. She has a pretty good grasp of how to do it based on her own experience, so she created a weekly rhythm that would make learning fun, mix things up, and yet uphold family traditions.

Most of her days include math, journaling, reading, and language arts. But here is how she frames each day of the week with other activities to supplement their learning:

SWEET SUNDAY

Worship, hospitality, board games, and family walk

MAGIC MONDAY

Baking, teatime, poetry, art, and music

TIME TRAVEL TUESDAY

History and geography

WORK AND WONDER WEDNESDAY

Cleaning, writing letters, and time for wonder

THUNDER THURSDAY

Adventure, nature collecting, and audiobooks

FAVORITES FRIDAY

Library, nature journaling, and science and studies at Nana's house

SKILLFUL SATURDAY

Homestead work, Wild Explorers Club, and Sunday prep

You might incorporate activities that aren't part of conventional schoolwork but are just as meaningful nonetheless. In our household, for example, my children spend at least an hour each day doing neurological therapy to improve their brain activity. This season won't last forever, but we're working through some challenges in their reading comprehension.

My friend Hannah is passionate about growing her own food and eating healthfully, so her children are learning how to cook as an integral part of their homeschooling life. And my friend Stephanie discovered that her second oldest son has a remarkable talent for gymnastics, so her weekly rhythm includes plenty of time at the local gym, where he can develop his abilities.

For my friend Elsie Iudicello, her daily rhythm includes cleaning the house. But to help her children actually enjoy the experience, she blasts music through the stereo system and calls it the Blessing Hour. She recently shared this humorous story with the Wild + Free community: "I was about 8 months pregnant with boy number four when I lost my mind. I didn't stop to ponder 'What Would Charlotte Mason Do?' At that moment, Charlotte Mason was simply a childless British school teacher from the 1800s who didn't have cankles and sciatic pain flaring up every time she had to wipe pee off the floor. So she pretty much sat this one out.

"I lined the boys up on the couch, their little feet barely clearing the edge, and I lowered myself onto the coffee table and gave them a good dose of pregnancy stink eye before unloading on them. Not my best moment. I think I ended the tirade by crying. They instantly huddled up around me and stroked my swollen hands and patted my cheeks with concern and kissed me, which made me cry more.

"'Boys, we get to bless our family today. We are going to clean our little apartment together. We are going to clean the bathroom and sweep the floors and put away dishes. We are going to work together to get everything beautiful so that when Daddy comes home we can spend lots of time playing with him.

Now, let's go around, and you can each say a job that you already know how to do and one job you want to learn how to do.'

"This was how the Blessing Hour was born. It evolved slowly but steadily. I realized that as long as I took the time to teach a skill well, they were capable of handling a great deal."

Just as teachers have websites where they can purchase lesson plans from other teachers and homeschoolers have boxed curriculums and programs they can incorporate to fill their weeks, you have the same remarkable freedom to choose a rhythm for your children. The fact that someone else created a rhythm doesn't give it any more validity than if you did. So flip over the napkin and start scrawling your ideas. Dream of what your ideal homeschool life could be.

HOMESCHOOLING THROUGH HARD TIMES

The biggest causes of stress are known to be the death of a loved one, marital trouble, the loss of a job, an increase in financial obligations, getting married, and moving to a new home.

And in the summer of 2010, I looked square in the face of five out of six of them.

Not to mention, I had just delivered my third baby and our rental house was infested with cockroaches. Yes, 2010 will forever go down in history as the worst year of my life.

I was on the cusp of homeschooling, trying to figure out what I thought of being away from my children all day and why no other parent around me seemed to mind.

A few months later, my mother was diagnosed with terminal brain cancer. At first, she opted out of surgery, but then it grew so painful that she changed her mind. The spiderweb-like sprawl of the tumor was so embedded that the intervention offered her only six more months to live, and even then, it left her never the same. She passed away exactly when they said she would.

My marriage was nearly over. Ben's job took him away from us every week, and with the stress of a new business, the heartbreak of my mother's illness, and the struggle to keep the lights on, it stretched us to the breaking point. A police officer once pulled me over because he saw a distraught mother weeping behind the steering wheel, trying to drive her children home. He offered to escort me home. Grocery store clerks and random strangers would ask me if something was wrong. It didn't take much to see it in my eyes.

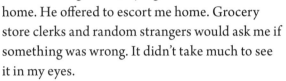

Despite all this, and the fact that many friends asked if I was still planning to homeschool, the thought of not homeschooling never crossed my mind. I had spent the past two years in the rat race, driving kids to and from school, juggling little ones and class parties, rushing home to meet the bus, getting homework done, and taking the boys to soccer practice on time.

As I've interacted with the Wild + Free community for the past few years, I've seen mothers lost to cancer, husbands lost to divorce, homes lost to tragedies, and hearts crushed by the brutal circumstances of life. And yet, in spite of all these challenges, I've seen brave mothers stand up to difficult times and vow to not let their children be lost as well.

Homeschooling mothers are some of the most courageous people I know.

Earlier, I mentioned Jennifer Schuh, who decided to homeschool her children after getting divorced. At first, she kept her children in school, trying to be at home for them as much as she could. Since her expenses were low, she worked part-time, three evenings a week, at a fine dining restaurant. While she worked, a member of her family looked after her kids.

Everything worked on paper, but Jenn could tell her daughter was still grieving the breakup of their family. This was not how Jenn wanted it to be. It was during this time that she noticed all sorts of single-parent homeschools. They were able to decide their own rhythm, dive into topics their children were interested in, and invest in their talents. "I secretly envied them," Jenn said.

"Finally, one woman asked me, 'If this is your desire, why not just do it?' And so I did. I made the plunge, pulled my child from public school, and officially began our own homeschool."

Something similar happened to Andrea Pratt when she lost her father to cancer. She didn't think she could muster the strength to continue homeschooling in the wake of grief. Questions flooded her mind: "How will I maintain our schooling rhythm? How can I protect my children from this pain? How will I manage with no help? How will I be able to do enough in this season?"

Andrea acknowledged that while she couldn't be the kind of homeschooler she wanted to be during this season, she knew she could do enough.

"When I did nothing but lie on the floor near my three children while they played, I did enough. When our day consisted of making cookies and reading picture books, I did enough. When I cried in front of them because it was impossible not to, I did enough. When I had a neighbor help me get my children dressed because I could not do it myself, I did enough."

She said that what her children saw and learned during that difficult season cannot be measured by any standardized test. "They saw what love really looks like," Andrea said. "They learned and experienced compassion because we extended it to each other every day. They saw friends, family, and people we hardly knew surround us and hold us up while we were in pain. They learned how to grieve in a real, healthy, and necessary way. There is no curriculum more beneficial than those experiences, and to me, that is more than enough."

RELATIONSHIPS OVER RHYTHM

Beware the nagging doubt that looms over every homeschooling mother's head. Even when you're not navigating grief like Andrea or struggling through heartbreak like Jennifer, your biggest challenge will be escaping the unavoidable feeling that you're not doing enough.

The antidote is not to fill your days with strenuous activities and "outwork" the local public school. It's not to construct a schedule and force your children to comply regardless of tears or complaint. Your only job is to foster a peaceful environment and encourage a love of learning.

Your children will take care of the rest.

This is why flexible rhythms are so important. When something conflicts with the joy of learning, put down the books. When an activity isn't working out, try something else. When your days become stale and routine, change things up. Rhythms allow you to follow your children into their areas of passion. The lessons actually stick, and you're all better for it.

At the same time, rhythms give your family a sense of direction each day. Rhythms help our children feel secure, focused, and accountable.

You won't have to worry about whether you're doing enough because the rhythm is your guide. The flow of your day, your week, and your year incorporates all the learning you hope to do. The guilt goes away because you know you'll get to it. You don't wake up with shortness of breath or end the day in a panic because of what you didn't accomplish.

Your rhythm is your friend. If it's pushing you too hard, you can tell it to back off. If it's not pulling its weight, you can have a heart-to-heart and set the expectations higher. But you are in charge of your rhythm. Go ahead and ask a friend. Read what the "experts" say. Borrow one from someone else. Just be sure the rhythm you choose is the right one for your family.

At the end of the day, homeschooling is about relationships. If you're debating the priority of virtue over academics, character over curriculum, let me try to settle this for you. As Wild + Free homeschoolers, we're betting all our chips on relationships. They are the only thing that matters.

15 Creating a Family Culture

EVERY FAMILY HAS A CULTURE, EVEN IF IT'S NOT intentional. It's the way things are done in your family, the experiences your children have, and what will mark them for the rest of their lives. Some families are rigid and strict; others are freewheeling and fun. Some are full of joy and tradition; others are full of sadness and brokenness. However it looks in your family, your children are being raised in an environment that will impact them and their children's children for generations to come.

You can be intentional about setting a healthy family culture and shape the environment in which they live and learn. It starts with reflecting on your own background. What are the things you hope to reclaim? The things you want to redeem?

My parents upheld the importance of education and the belief that I could accomplish anything if I put in the time and hard work. I was given a childhood with access to nature and the freedom to explore the neighborhood and waterways behind my house, to go to summer camp and away with friends on ski trips. Sometimes I marvel at the amount of freedom I had.

My father instilled in me a desire to accomplish meaningful goals. He had me running 5K races by the time I was five years old and reading books beyond my age. My mother gave me a nurturing spirit that loves to rescue animals, care for my sick ones, and hold all the newborns.

I have memories of wonderful Christmases when both of my parents dressed up in elf costumes, and I'll confess that I have a hard time not doing the same for my own kids.

As a couple, Ben and I have had to merge our family cultures, and it hasn't always gone smoothly. When we have friends over for dinner, Ben goes around the house turning on all the lights, and I go around dimming them all because of how our respective parents entertained guests. When it comes to holidays, I'm drawn to traditions, while Ben shuns them. It took time and intentionality to create our own family culture based on what we mutually love and value.

When I was fourteen years old, my childhood was rocked by the divorce of my parents, which became a part of my family culture whether I liked it or not. I spent my teen years shuttling between my parents' homes in different states, struggling to find normalcy, navigating relationships, and doing my best in school. While there are many wonderful aspects I want to reclaim from my childhood, much of what I want to redeem in my own family is restoring a sense of security and togetherness for my children.

As parents, we have the remarkable opportunity to shape a family culture at home. We're already passionate about how we want to educate our kids, but we can extend this same intentionality to all aspects of their childhood. I talk to women all the time who wish they would have valued childhood more when their kids were younger. They lament the lost years and time spent away from their kids. They want to know if it's too late, even for their teenagers.

Let me assure you that it's not.

If your family culture isn't what you want it to be, you can start with small daily decisions that will change the course of your family life. It won't be easy, and it may not happen overnight. In fact, you may take one step forward in a key area and take two steps back in another. But don't give up. You can remake your family with small, intentional decisions each day.

Here are a few questions you and your spouse can ask yourselves as you think about the kind of culture you want to create for your children.

DO OUR CHILDREN KNOW THEY'RE LOVED?

Connecting with my firstborn came so easily to me. When it was just the two of us, we spent our days strolling through neighborhood trails and visiting farms to pet the animals. We did everything together, and we were buddies. We didn't even have to say anything. We ate our grapes and swung our feet from atop the jungle gym and wished the days would go on like this forever.

There was no doubt about my love for him and his love for me.

When I became pregnant with my second-born, I was elated, but sometimes as I read to my darling boy with his hand on my burgeoning belly, I felt a lump in my throat and wondered how I could possibly love another child as much as this. It sounds silly now, but it was a serious concern for me at the time. As any mother who's been there will tell you, loving your child, whether the second or the seventh, feels just as natural and new as the first. Sometimes even more because you know so well the fleetingness of time.

Still, five kids later, it's all I can do not to mother them like a herd. I have to work hard to carve out quality time with each child, but most of the time it's group outings. While I know that each child regards me as his or her mother alone, not within community, the practicalities dictate that our time be spent together. And the days go better when everyone stays in formation and doesn't act out.

The challenge with parenting and, to an even greater degree, with homeschooling is making sure that each of our children knows he's loved. Adding to the complexity, each child gives and receives love differently. Thanks to the insightful work of Dr. Gary Chapman, we know there are five love languages through which every person feels valued and cherished—words of affirmation, quality time, gift giving, physical touch, and acts of service. When people want to express love, they tend to do so in their native "language," and when they want to feel love, they need to receive it in the same way or it's hardly noticed at all. Their love tank goes empty.

Children are not often enlightened about love languages, so their cries for affection usually come in the form of disciplinary problems—talking back, lashing out, or getting into trouble on purpose. It may not achieve the desired results, but it gives them the attention they crave.

My third-born son was endowed with a love language to which we were thoroughly unaccustomed—acts of service. While Ben and I both recognize that housework needs to be done, we view it as an inhibitor of our quality time together rather than a contributor to it. Our ideal weekend mornings are spent drinking coffee in bed together for as long as we can.

So when it was time to leave the house or put the kids to bed—the times when blood pressures are high or energy levels are low—Cody chose those moments to express his frustrations. He refused to tie his shoes or put on his pajamas or brush his teeth.

At best, we were baffled. Why would our most action-oriented, competent kid suddenly refuse to do anything for himself? At worst, we thought it was outright rebellion. Why wouldn't he cooperate? But after this happened for months on end, Ben and I wondered if there was something amiss. We began experimenting with our responses to see if it made a difference.

As it turned out, Cody wanted to see if we would love him by serving him in those moments. So we tied his shoes and spread the toothpaste on his brush and made his bed in the morning, and suddenly we had a different boy. He became much more loving and cooperative and even began doing things around the house that we never asked him to do.

One of the foundational works of homeschooling is to make sure our children know they are loved. When they feel secure in their value, when they know they're cherished, their hearts are joyful, more compliant. The day goes better. A child who is well loved is a delight to educate.

Sometimes this comes in the form of the five love languages—an encouraging word fitly spoken, a caring touch on the neck or the arm, or even a special gift when they least expect it. But it can also be as simple as saying the words "I love you." This new generation of parents seems more likely to speak those daring words than parents in the past, but it can still be a rarity in many households. Unloving parents beget unloving parents who beget unloving parents.

Creating a family culture means breaking with bad habits and replacing them with good ones. If you came from a home where the words "I love you" were never spoken—maybe they still aren't, maybe you end phone calls to your parents with silence on the other end—break the cycle. Muster the courage to let those empowering words leave your mouth and forever change the course of your family. Your great-great-granddaughter will say "I love you" because you did.

DO WE CELEBRATE OUR
CHILDREN'S UNIQUE IDENTITIES?

After my father's military career, he became a business consultant to CEOs, Fortune 500 companies, and the Special Forces, specializing in the application of the Myers-Briggs Type Indicator (MBTI) in all aspects of an organization. Not only did I grow up knowing the nuances of my personality type, but I was also celebrated for the strengths of my wiring.

So it was only natural that when I brought Ben home to meet my dad one weekend, he sat him down at the kitchen table and gave him the MBTI. It must have turned out well because he raised no objections at the wedding. But I never knew how powerful personality types could be until we had to navigate the differences in our personalities in the first few years of marriage.

For example, I'm a perceiver, and Ben is a judger, so he lives by a to-do list, a calendar, and a scheduling app on top of it. I prefer to go with the flow, respond to life as it comes, and wait as long as I can to make decisions in the likelihood that new information might come along. Ben makes lists and uses them; I make lists and lose them.

Early on, our evenings out sounded something like this.

"Where would you like to go to dinner?" Ben would ask.

"Oh, I don't know. How about Outback Steakhouse?"

"Great. I love Outback," Ben would respond. "Let's go."

"Or we could go to that new Mexican place," I'd say, "and try their guacamole."

Ben would swallow something invisible and nod his head.

"Okay. Perfect. The new Mexican place it is."

"Great, I'll get my coat," I'd say and then turn around. "You know, I'm craving Pad Thai."

And then Ben's head would explode.

We finally figured out some tactics that would serve us well throughout our marriage. For example, I tell him what I definitely *don't* want for dinner and let him make the call. We still have some bumps along the way, but we're doing better.

Introduce five children. All homeschooled. All distinct in their personality types. And all combustible with the tensions that rise and fall in the course of a day with seven people.

Homeschooling families are basically reality shows without the cameras.

Some of my kids prefer consistency in their days, and others need a frequent change of pace. Some need time alone to recharge their batteries; others need hearty discourse to feel their best. Some need instructions explained step-by-step; others need the big picture to understand.

We can't possibly thrive at homeschooling without understanding how our children are wired. In traditional schools, they are all taught in the same way. But we get to understand how our children are wired and then adapt their education to their personalities. We get to value who they are and meet them where they're at.

So observe them. Study them. Watch how they express themselves, and take note.

Go Jane Goodall on your children.

DO WE CREATE TRADITIONS AS A FAMILY?

As a mother, I wasn't always a fan of Halloween. I've trained my kids to abstain from sugar and usually steer them away from talking to strangers, let alone taking candy from them. But somehow Halloween has become one of our most cherished traditions as a family. We string lights in our courtyard, make vats of chili and hot apple cider, and invite everyone we know. As much as it surprises me, it's one of those traditions that we can't *not* do anymore.

That's the way family traditions come about, isn't it? We do something one time, often by accident, and it turns into a meaningful family ritual that we repeat year after year.

When I was a junior at the University of North Carolina at Greensboro, I was devastated by the tragic events at Columbine High School. As a volunteer leader with the organization Young Life, I couldn't *not* do something, so I piled into a car with three friends and drove to Littleton, Colorado, where we delivered hundreds of notes from high school kids to comfort the surviving students. We ended up staying in Colorado and volunteering at a Young Life camp in the Rockies. I helped build cabins and run the ropes course, enjoying one of the most beautiful places on Earth.

I decided that if I ever had a family, I would bring them back there to experience what I did. Twenty years later, I got my wish. We signed up for a family camp, and it was everything we hoped it would be. We loved it so much that we decided to make it an annual tradition.

For the past four years, we've hosted Wild + Free family camps at Trail West Lodge in Buena Vista, Colorado, and hundreds of families have experienced the same thing we did. My kids relish this time in a wild, familiar place, and we could never not do it as long as they're with us.

We've done the same thing each September with the Mayberry Days Festival in Andy Griffith's hometown, nightly read-alouds of The Lord of the Rings Trilogy by J. R. R. Tolkien, and picnic dinners at the beach throughout the summer with friends. Traditions make our children's lives a special experience and create a culture that will live on in their own families.

Homeschooling can sometimes make you feel as if the walls are closing in on you. It's easy to become housebound and stick to the same old routines. But homeschooling is also loaded with opportunities to craft special moments that make your children's lives unforgettable. Maybe it's pancake morning on Tuesdays, hot tea and scones for the weekly poetry reading, or handicraft fairs in the fall.

You can establish a treasured family culture by celebrating the smallest occasions in big ways. All you have to do is identify what your children love, and repeat it. A tradition doesn't have to be significant in order to be meaningful. It's important because your family says it is.

DO WE PLAY TOGETHER AS A FAMILY?

One of the challenges in a family of seven is that every hobby we undertake costs seven times as much. Staying home made good sense for a lot of years until we realized we weren't having any fun. So, last summer, we finally broke down and bought beach cruisers for the entire family. If John Muir were raising children in Virginia Beach, he might say, "The boardwalk is calling, and I must go." Or maybe not, but that's where you'll find us on many summer evenings.

One night, clouds were rolling in while the members of our "chain gang" pedaled their little hearts out for twenty blocks toward the smoothie shop. It seemed suspicious that nobody else was enjoying the open bike lanes, cool salt air, and white crests of the crashing waves.

Then the rains came. And I don't mean just any rains. Torrential rains. We're talking the scene from *The Notebook* with Ryan Gosling and Rachel McAdams but without the kissing.

At first, there were tears. Then anger. Then blame, as it seemed that perhaps none of us would survive. And then surrender. And finally, elation and laughter as we enjoyed this spectacular moment of fun together as a family. We will never forget that experience.

At the heart of every child is the need for play. Play is important for creativity, learning, and interacting with peers. But it's also the way children communicate. If we want to show our children we love them, we need to play with them. Play is the magical portal to connection.

Playing with our children isn't about enjoying the activity as much as it is about connecting with them. Much as with love languages or personality types, understanding how our children play is critical. Author and psychologist Lawrence J. Cohen, the author of *Playful Parenting*, wrote, "Play is important, not just because children do so much of it, but because there are layers and layers of meaning to even the most casual play."

He pointed out the various layers of a father and son playing catch—from developing hand-eye coordination and the joy of learning a new skill to the bonding time the two are sharing.

"The rhythm of the ball flying back and forth is a bridge," Cohen wrote, "reestablishing a deep connection between adult and child; and comments like 'good try' and 'nice catch' build confidence and trust."[1]

It's complicated, though. Playing like children isn't easy. It's hard work, and most of us have forgotten how to do it. On top of that, it's difficult to switch gears after a long day of work to exert the kind of energy children crave. But if play is how our children communicate, it behooves us to stop and listen.

At the very least, playing together is a great way to bring our families closer together. It might sound counterintuitive, but plan for play. A lot of families love game nights. Others bond over movies. Our family is currently enjoying a season of playing flag football. When you discover what your family loves to do together, make it a priority to do that. Being intentional to include regular times of play can significantly enhance the culture of your family.

DO WE MEET OUR CHILDREN AT THEIR LEVEL?

There is so much wisdom at thirty thousand feet. We can see the whole of the landscape, where the pitfalls are, the dangers. As parents, we spend much of our day trying to get the little ones to

see things at our level—don't touch the
stove, look both ways before crossing the
street, don't misbehave in public.

We are the General Douglas
MacArthurs of our households, field
marshaling the troops into the best
strategic formations because we can see
the master plan at our altitude.

It's a constant beckoning to rise up to our level.

But children feel cherished only at their own level.

When we sit on the carpet with them, time stands still. When
we play their games, we enter into a hidden universe where they
feel seen for who they really are. Is it any wonder that most of the
great children's stories are set in a world where parents merely
peek through cracked bedroom doors at night to make sure all
is quiet but never get to enter the wardrobe? And yet children
want nothing more than to enter the secret garden hand in hand
with their parents.

But sitting on the floor tests our patience. Stopping to play
a childhood game raises our blood pressure. We've got things
to do, deadlines to meet, dinner to cook, duties to uphold. And
then there's the great new modern appendage, the smartphone,
rewiring our brains and expanding our obligations to include
liking and being liked by people we've never met.

The best part about homeschooling is that entering into
our children's world is part of the curriculum. It's not stated in
any textbook, but it's the natural outflow of this organic lifestyle.

One reason I detest replicating the classroom at home is that
it requires children to assume the posture of adults. We bend
their bodies into the "learning position" as if they're already
working in cubicles. I don't know how your children sit at the
dining room table, but mine look nothing like how the chairs
are shaped. And telling them otherwise does me no good.

Children invite us into their world in small, delicate ways
each day. They stand before us, board game in hand, looking up

into our eyes as if maybe this time might be different. Children are resilient. They ask, get rejected, and then ask again.

Imagine being surrounded by giants all day, looking up at the underside of their chins, and then experiencing the sheer delight when one of them crouches down to join our activity.

Childhood is so fleeting. Before we know it, they will indeed stand as tall as us and perhaps see things the way we do. But by then, it will be too late. Their childhood will be gone.

May we learn to enter their world before they stop inviting us.

DO WE CREATE A SAFE PLACE FOR OUR CHILDREN?

We have an unfair advantage as parents. We have the keys to the house, the car, the bank account, and our children's freedom. And if we're not careful, we can misuse this power.

I can't help but laugh when I think of the scene in the movie *Matilda* when Danny DeVito's character said, "Listen, you little wiseacre, I'm smart, you're dumb. I'm big, you're little. I'm right, you're wrong, and there's nothing you can do about it."

I laugh because, by the end of the movie, Matilda comes out the victor. But in many households, children don't always fare so well. There are many kids who can't speak their minds, talk about their feelings, or feel confident in who they were created to be.

If anything can be said of our homeschools, may it be that they are safe places for our children. Places where they can be encouraged in their gifts and comforted in their struggles. Places where they can share their fears and express their sorrows. Places where they can be heard and known and taken seriously.

I was visiting a masseuse the other day and told her where my muscles felt sore. Without warning, she put her hand on my back and dropped to her knees so her face was at my eye

level and she could truly hear what I was trying to say. It was so unexpected, such a rare occurrence, that I nearly couldn't finish speaking. No one usually listens to me with such rapt attention. It inspired me to go home and be a better mother, to listen with not just my ears but my whole being.

We create a safe family culture, first of all, by letting our children express their range of emotions without consequence. To crack down on frustration or sadness or even anger creates a policy that "true emotions will not be tolerated here," no matter what they are.

In his book *Playful Parenting*, Lawrence Cohen mentioned boys' special needs for empathy and emotional connection. "To help boys connect, you can play anything at all, especially games that require some interaction. Even better, play what they want to play. You can't communicate the idea that what they want to play is stupid and violent and antisocial, and then expect them to talk to you about their inner feelings."[2]

There are often underlying feelings that need to be worked out through daily interactions. Take, for example, the game of catch between father and son. The son throws the ball as if he wants to hurt his dad. Sound familiar? It's easy for the father to peg him as angry and frustrated. But Cohen suggests that the son is really asking his dad, "Can you catch what I throw at you? Are my feelings too much for you? Am I safe from my own impulses, my own anger?"

Second, we create a safe family culture by saying we're sorry when we're wrong. Parents aren't perfect. Most children figure this out, but sometimes the parents never do. We exercise our highly developed skills in rationale and logic to fortify our position as the all-knowing, all-seeing authorities of the household and threaten our children for even questioning it.

Saying "I'm sorry" makes us human. It puts us at the same level as our children and helps them know that they can be sorry too. We need more people in the world who are willing to be sorry. More marriages and families need them too. "Sorry" is the grease that helps the gears of relationships to keep running smoothly. Let me warn you now, as a homeschool mother, get used to apologizing. The sheer amount of concentrated time you spend with your children will compound the number of infractions for which apologies will be needed.

Finally, we create a safe family culture by setting an example with our actions, not just our words. It's easy to say we value something. It's another thing to do it. And our children always, always pay attention to what we value. I have been horrified by the number of hypocrisies that have been reflected back to me by the actions of my children. On those occasions, I can't speak one word of correction because I know I am the one to blame. To fix them, I have to go first.

DO WE PURSUE MEANINGFUL ENDEAVORS?

Children are hardwired for adventure. They are born to love fairy tales and fantasies, rescues and redemptions. It's why kids love video games in which they can act out their natural-born desires and movies in which they can relate to characters who fight to survive against all odds.

Life was meant to be a wild adventure, and yet we've domesticated it with nine-to-five routines, standardized learning, and organized activities that homogenize our lives with everyone else's. But our passion for adventure never goes away. We simply trade it in for standards of living.

Know this: children will find adventure whether we're the ones who give it to them or not. If they can't find it in their families, they'll look for it elsewhere. They'll find it with friends, their girlfriends, their boyfriends, and even other families. Our children will find their tribe.

Last year, Wild + Free launched a campaign to raise money to purchase land for what we're calling the Wild + Free Farm

Village. Our dream is to create a place where women, children, and families could come to experience the beauty of nature, host retreats and gatherings, connect with other like-minded families, and let our children run wild + free.

In just five months, the Wild + Free community raised $400,000 toward the project, and we've begun searching for the perfect location. Our family has spent the past year traveling to different parts of Virginia along the Blue Ridge Mountains, visiting different plots of land.

We've hiked along mountain streams where black bears are spotted in the spring. We've climbed up mountains to explore the ideal spot for a zipline. And we've sat in town hall meetings with community members as they've asked questions and raised objections to our plans.

And our children have been right there with us through all of it.

We're pursuing this dream because we want a place that Wild + Free can call home. We imagine homeschooling mamas coming for weekend gatherings and farm-to-table dinners. Kids coming for nature school and forest school. Teens coming for writers' retreats and gap years. And families coming for much-needed time together. In time, perhaps we'll have "farm villages" in beautiful locations throughout the country. But in the meantime, our family is turning this season of searching into an epic family adventure.

Kids may not act as if they want to go on adventures. They'll beg for movies and screen time in the car. They'll complain about the heat, the bug bites, and the boredom of the in-between times. But nobody grows up and regrets the time they spent together as a family. No one longs for the good ol' days of playing video games and killing time in the cul-de-sac.

At the core of every parent is the desire for our children to be happy. But maybe that shouldn't be our goal. As we all know, there's a difference between happiness and joy. And while children often believe that doing things for themselves will make them happy, the opposite is actually true. Studies show that people who engage in meaningful endeavors have more joy.

Helen Keller wrote, "Many persons have a wrong idea of what constitutes happiness. It is not attained through self-gratification but through fidelity to a worthy purpose."

You were born to be an adventurous family. Go forth.

WE ARE FAMILY

You know the feeling. You wake up one day and realize you don't like how things are going—the way your family members speak to each other, the bad habits that have emerged, the stuck rhythms of life. You know your family culture isn't what you want it to be, what you were made for.

You think that if you could only quit your taxing job, move to Wyoming, and buy a homestead, everything would be different; things would go better. Myriad things would have to fall into place for you to make the needed changes in your family, and it all seems impossible.

But these external arrangements can't fill the hole in your heart. And they don't need to. Whether you homeschool or not, you have everything you need to reshape the culture of your family. It starts with a vision of what you want your family to be and moves into small everyday decisions that bring this vision to life.

Maybe it's the inclusion of morning time at the start of each day. Maybe it's trips with friends to the nearby state park. The introduction of handicrafts or nature journaling into your weekly rhythm. Or a nightly read-aloud with your children before bed. You might face a revolt from your kids at first, but persist, dear mama. Integrate these treasures into your regular routine without making a big deal of it, and watch your children fall in love with a new family culture in time.

Creating a family culture takes sacrifice, intentionality, and constant reevaluation as your children grow, priorities change, or things fall away from the difficulty of day-to-day living. It's easy to fall back into default mode. When this happens, as it inevitably will, take time to talk to your family about your relationships, your values, and your goals—and get back on track.

A family culture offers a framework for your children to thrive, a sense of identity, values to uphold, and traditions to honor. It's the difference between becoming who you were meant to be and becoming what society wants to shape you into. And oh, does society have a plan for your life. It offers a ready-made, cookie-cutter approach that will shape you into the mold of every other stressed-out, overextended family out there. It will require less work, less thought, and less guilt than forging your own path. You simply plug in to the system and let it do its thing.

But your family was made for more.

You were made to be wild + free.

THE METHOD

16 The Wild + Free Way

IT'S TAKEN ME A WHILE TO ADMIT THERE'S
actually a Wild + Free way. I never wanted people to
think they were being given a formula, prescribed a
solution, or forced into a box. After all, those are the very
things we're trying to avoid. So I held my ground and
said we are a community that supports all of the other
homeschooling approaches. It was true. And it still is.

But no matter how hard I resisted, others chose
to claim it as their approach. Just as people refer to
themselves as Charlotte Mason home educators,
unschoolers, or Waldorf-inspired homeschoolers, a
new generation of mothers all over the world has begun
identifying as Wild + Free mamas, Wild + Free learners,
and Wild + Free homeschoolers.

In time, I've come to realize that Wild + Free is a
philosophy as much as it is a community. The way we
approach it varies from family to family, but our daily
lives celebrate the values of this tribe. And just as our
inclinations, passions, and yearnings are all universal,

the Wild + Free philosophy transcends geography, race, and culture.

We can be Wild + Free *and* follow the classical, Charlotte Mason, or Waldorf approach. We can be Wild + Free as well as Montessori based, Reggio inspired, or radical unschooled. What makes us Wild + Free is not dismissing these styles but believing in the fundamental truths that have guided the growth and education of our children since the beginning of time.

When I first began homeschooling, I knew I didn't want to replicate the classroom or study my old teachers' textbooks from college. Instead, I sought out the founders of philosophies and discovered there was a whole world of pedagogical inspiration to devour.

I studied the great educators—Mason, Montessori, Steiner, Dewey, Piaget, and others. I filled my gunnysack of knowledge with their ideas and sage insights. And I still go to them for wisdom from time to time. But as I observed my children in those early days, I could see the curriculum coming to life before my eyes. By learning alongside them every day, experience became my greatest teacher. And I discovered the natural tools that are at every mother's disposal.

Through this journey, five values began to emerge.

I watched as the School of Nature cultivated my children's physical and cognitive abilities. I saw the Power of Story weave its way into their souls. I witnessed the Pedagogy of Play fulfill its purpose in their growing minds and characters. I tipped my hat to the Curriculum of Curiosity as it taught them more than I could ever dream of showing them. And I stood in awe as the Magic of Wonder captivated their hearts and imaginations.

Slowly, ever careful not to capsize the boat, I backed away from the syllabus and allowed these natural phenomena to become the precepts of our homeschooling. We've embraced these five values—Nature, Story, Play, Curiosity, and Wonder—

along with the proven science behind them, and what has emerged is the philosophy itself.

Wild + Free is not a formula but a journey of conviction. It's one of intentional practices unique to every family. No matter your academic approach to homeschooling, natural tendencies are at work in your children. Don't fight them. Tap into them. Nurture them. And whenever your chosen method isn't matching up with your child, go back to the basics, and let these principles be your guide. We may not all do it the same way, but we are in this together.

17 The School of Nature

IMAGINE SITTING DOWN WITH THE MOTHER OF young children and presenting two options for their education. The first option has her kids sitting inside at desks for six hours a day. They stare straight ahead, with little to no interaction with the other children, while an adult teaches them as a group, asks an occasional question, and creates artificial experiences (textbooks, digital screens, and worksheets) for them to learn about the real world. When they do go outside, it's for a quick thirty-minute break on the playground.

The other option is to structure their school days to include music, reading, shared meals, and art projects. They go outside to play. The kids come in red-faced, happy, tired, and hungry. The mother makes lunch. They eat together. They talk about the adventures of the morning. They tell her about the fort they built or the mud pies they made. Oh, and the robin watching them from the fence. She wonders aloud whether it was standing guard because they were close to its nest. Maybe there were eggs. Did they know robins' eggs are blue?

They want to see. She pulls out the nature journals and the bird guides, and they spend a few minutes studying them. She suggests they draw something from the book. Or whatever they'd like. The bird, the nest, the eggs—the day.

On paper, it's not much of a choice, is it? Nature wins every time.

Nature unlocks the imagination and inspires creativity in ways that a schoolroom never could. Artists and architects are inspired by the designs they see in nature. Poets describe its beauty in exquisite detail. Mathematicians find geometric patterns in natural phenomena, and scientists look to nature for answers to the mysteries of the universe. We see this truth in the work of Thoreau, Emerson, Frost, Whitman, Matisse, Gandhi, Pascal, Wright, Keats, Einstein.

Nature is the best classroom we could ever hope for, and yet our education system has determined that it should play no part in it. Every decision—from cutting recess to discouraging tag games and even running on the playground—shows our children that nature has no place in their education, let alone their free time. In an era when our lives are becoming more digitized by the day, our children need time to explore the natural world. They need contact with living things, fresh air in their lungs, and an understanding of what sustains them.

Scott Sampson, the author of *How to Raise a Wild Child*, wrote, "If children are to grow into healthy, well-adjusted adults, nature needs to be integral to their everyday lives, from place-based learning at school to unstructured, unsupervised, even risk-prone play around home. Nature isn't just a bunch of far-off plants, animals, and landscapes to learn about and visit once or twice a year. It's an environment to be immersed in daily."[1]

Somehow, we have been swindled into believing that nature is a preoccupation of the past, something to be enjoyed by woodsmen and explorers rather than those who are blessed with the benefits of modern conveniences and progress. But nature is an essential tool for both our overall well-being and education today, especially for those who live in urban places, where it is sparse.

Jennifer Dees often writes about exploring nature in the city for Wild + Free. She lives in Los Angeles, where her search for nature takes her family under highway overpasses and along graffiti-covered canals.

"It is so easy to think that if we only lived somewhere else, we would spend more time in nature study—somewhere with more open space, more water, more trees, more trails," Jennifer wrote. "But we have to make ourselves actually do nature study no matter where we live. Each part of the country has a different kind of beauty and a different wealth of animals and plants."

"*All children need nature, not only those whose parents appreciate nature, not only those of a certain economic class or culture or set of abilities. All children and future generations have a right to a nature-rich future and the option to share in the responsibilities that come with that right.*"

—RICHARD LOUV

And that is the great challenge, isn't it? To incorporate nature into our homeschools when there isn't a national park close by and the weather is inclement. Still, it's entirely possible, even in small doses. We don't all have to live on a working farm, in an off-grid cabin, or in the Alaskan bush to give our children a nature-rich upbringing and education. The goal isn't 100 percent immersion in this lifestyle but just enough of it. And that's something any parent can do.

Susan Schaeffer Macaulay wrote, "We all have limitations and problems. But I must never think it is all or nothing.

Perhaps I'd like to live in the country, but I don't. Well, maybe I can get the family to a park two times a week, and out to the country once every two weeks. Maybe I have to send my child to a not-so-good school. Well, maybe we can read one or two good books together aloud. If you can't give them everything, give them something."[2]

That's it, then. If we can't give them everything, let's give them something.

THE BENEFITS OF NATURE

I grew up in West Point, New York, a tight-knit military community nestled along the grassy western banks of the Hudson River. For a few memorable years, I called a modest townhome, with a small side yard and a wooded hill across the back alley, home. When ordinary life was too much, I went outdoors and found a friend in solitude. In the wild, life made sense to me.

It was on the hill behind my house, among the spruce and fir trees, that I figured out who I was. Sitting atop a giant rock perched on the sloping scape—no matter that civilization was just a stone's throw away—I discovered a safe space where I could think, dream, and simply be.

As I look back on my forty years of life, I realize I have always felt most at home when I am a little lost—in the wilderness, in crowds, in my thoughts. The words of John Muir have always resonated with me: "Everybody needs beauty as well as bread, places to play in and pray in, where nature may heal and give strength to body and soul."

I've seen it with my own kids too. They light up when they are bounding down a trail or making their own path through the trees. Even the ones who don't get quite as excited about exploring seem to come alive after spending time outdoors. Time in nature is not a luxury. It is a necessity. And we must give our children time to explore and get to know the Earth.

We must let them spread their wings and explore without interference. Let them chase butterflies, sunsets, and dreams. Let them build and climb, get dirty and wet. Let them feel what it's like to play in the rain or dance under a full moon. Let them be wild. Let them be free.

And by all means, let them be children.

There are endless benefits to children being in nature. Being in natural settings stimulates the brain and restores cognitive function. Experts have seen significant benefits for children with autism, attention deficit hyperactivity disorder (ADHD), depression, and other conditions when they spend time outdoors. Not to mention, nature encourages imaginative play, curiosity, and other qualities necessary to spark a love for investigation and learning.[3]

Children who spend time in natural settings interact better with kids of all ages and learn to solve problems more easily. They build muscle and coordination and fend off obesity. Among other things, it cultivates a sense of responsibility to care for the Earth—derived not from lectures but from natural activities, such as splashing in waves, jumping in lakes, walking through forests, and chasing friends through the fields. Being in nature is the most organic way to preserve a sense of wonder in children and adults alike, and it fosters curiosity, imagination, and the other qualities necessary to spark a love for investigation and learning.

Scott Sampson wrote, "Compared to kids confined indoors, children who regularly play in nature show heightened motor control—including balance, coordination, and agility. They tend to engage more in imaginative and creative play, which in turn fosters language, abstract reasoning, and problem-solving skills, together with a sense of wonder."

He went on to say that "nature play is superior at engendering a sense of self and a sense of place, allowing children to recognize both their independence and interdependence. Play in outdoor settings also exceeds indoor alternatives in fostering cognitive, emotional, and moral development. And individuals who spend abundant time playing outdoors as children are more likely to grow up with a strong attachment to place and an environmental ethic."[4]

The benefits of getting kids outside reach beyond the desire to see them play, gain agility, develop social skills, and nurture their emotional health. The fact is, the lack of time spent climbing trees, playing tag, exploring creeks, and making tree forts in the woods is also taking a toll on our children's physical health.

> "We do not inherit the Earth from our ancestors; we borrow it from our children."
>
> —NATIVE AMERICAN PROVERB

Richard Louv summarized the dilemma for most modern families when he observed in his book *Last Child in the Woods*, "Parents are told to turn off the TV and restrict video game time, but we hear little about what the kids should do physically during their non-electronic time. The usual suggestion is organized sports. But consider this: The obesity epidemic coincides with the greatest increase in organized children's sports in history."[5]

The answer isn't to raise more athletic kids. Let's face it: sports aren't for everyone. The goal is to get our kids to become more active—in play, in imagination, in nature.

One recent study that tracked the movements of children throughout a day in Denmark and New Zealand showed that sports weren't all that significant for children's health; rather, "self-organised physical activity" accounted for most of their exercise. Sports researcher Glen Nielsen said, "It was very surprising how great a part of children's physical activity comes from free play, while organised sport only made a small contribution to the overall level of activity."[6] If we want to keep our kids physically healthy, we must give our children more opportunities for free play, not organized sports.

Any seasoned homeschooler will tell you that when children lose their focus or struggle to stay engaged, send them outdoors. There is no trouble that an hour outside won't cure.

Charlotte Mason believed that "every hour spent in the open is a clear gain, tending to the increase of brain power and bodily vigour, and to the lengthening of the life itself."

She contended that children (and their mothers) should spend at least six hours each day outdoors. This may seem preposterous in this day and age, but perhaps it's even more important today than ever before. From the rising number of behavioral and learning disabilities to the lure of the glowing screen, children need a provocative alternative. And shooing kids out of the house for thirty minutes a day may not be enough. Children need to reawaken their sense of wonder, uncover their desire for real-life danger, and nurture this aspect of family culture.

Being in nature awakens the senses, stirs the emotions, and raises the body's vibrational frequency, which is important for having an overall sense of well-being, not to mention fighting disease and mental illness. John Burroughs understood its necessary place in his own life when he mused, "I go to nature to be soothed and healed, and to have my senses put in order."

We go to nature to become our best selves.

CREATING A FAMILY CULTURE IN NATURE

I am the offspring of two bookworms. We didn't go camping even once as a family when I was growing up. Still, I grew up in the 1980s, when kids had the freedom to roam their neighborhoods without supervision. Even in the midst of suburbia, I found my own pieces of the wild. From the fringes of the backyard to the undeveloped wilderness on the outskirts of our neighborhood, nature could be found anywhere. And then there were trips to the seaside.

I spent some of my most formative years visiting the ocean every summer. The mere cry of a seagull or whiff of salty air causes the memories to come flooding back. I remember when the winds and tides created a sand wall before we arrived. I would play below the "cliffs" for hours, hidden from the view of adults, lost in my own make-believe world of island mermaids.

But looking back, I realize these trips weren't as frequent as the impressions are deep. Those personal encounters with the natural world left a mark on my heart and mind.

From the time my eldest son was very young, long before we ever lived near the ocean, I watched something awaken in him whenever we visited the shore. It seemed as if the heaviness he experienced with his health challenges and speech delays was washed away in the ocean waves, as if he could finally be his true self. Being in nature will do that to you.

I've seen my children learn and grow from frequent visits to the ocean. From the sensory stimulation of sand and water to the organic education that happens in discovering nature and wildlife, these discoveries open the door to curiosity, creativity, and learning for years to come. The ocean is a big part of our life, but every family has its own unique place. For you, maybe it's a local creek, a lake house, or a cabin in the mountains. Being in nature together as a family creates memories and bonds that last a lifetime.

You have only to find your place.

There is a Japanese practice called *shinrin yoku*, or "forest bathing," in which people go to natural areas for relaxation and to promote mental and physical well-being. The Swedes have a practice called *friluftsliv*, which loosely translates to "open air life."[7] No matter which natural area you prefer, being in nature will restore you as a person. Biologist Rachel Carson wrote, "There is something infinitely healing in the repeated refrains of nature—the assurance that dawn comes after night, and spring after the winter."

You don't have to be athletic or outdoorsy to be a family that gets outside. And you don't have to hike the Swiss Alps or climb Mount Everest to experience the wonder of nature. My own family hasn't done any better to uphold the time-honored tradition of camping. We hate mosquitoes, prefer indoor plumbing, and have a penchant for particular pillows at night.

"Nature is an unfailing source of children's curiosity and delight."

—RAYMOND MOORE

But we're suckers for enjoying peaceful evenings at the ocean, taking walks through forests, and lying flat on our backs on picnic tables to take in the stars over Buena Vista, Colorado.

These experiences aren't just fun pastimes for us. They enrich our time as a family.

As Richard Louv wrote, "Nature does not steal time; it amplifies it."[8]

LEARNING TO LOVE THE OUTDOORS

I've had mothers tell me, "My children don't like being in nature." And I always assure them I can relate. My first child was born while we were living in a northern Virginia suburb with a parking lot for a yard. We took him for walks on the sidewalks that meandered through the neighborhood, usually strapped in a baby carrier or pushed in a stroller. Unintentionally, we rarely gave him the chance to explore the natural world on his own.

In some ways, I was the antithesis of a Wild + Free mama.

At the time, I could have cited our living situation as an excuse for not spending more time in nature. But truth be told, it just wasn't a priority for me. Sometimes I wish I could go back to those early years of motherhood for a do-over. I cringe when I think about the opportunities we had at our fingertips, the farms and fields around us, if only I had made the most of them.

Seven years later, I longed to give Wyatt the childhood he deserved. We brought him home, established our homeschool (which we named the Young Explorers Academy), and spent every waking hour exploring the backyard and going on nature expeditions at a local state park, an aquarium, and museums. We took up nature journaling and got lost in good books. I created a "wall of weird" for our nature finds, and Wyatt thrived. His natural wonder began to return and subsequently his childlike innocence. Still, had you asked him, he would have told you that he didn't like nature, hated being dirty and hot, and despised bugs.

I decided not to remind him of that when he was chasing fireflies at dusk or watching with wonder as a butterfly emerged from its chrysalis on our back patio.

Being mindful of children's needs and supporting our children's interests is vastly different from catering to their every whim, emotion, and desire. We can help foster a love for nature in their hearts and minds, even if they feel otherwise. We don't need our children's affirmation for every little thing on this parenting journey. Some kids need our passion to push them through. Kids need nature. Whether or not they see its value doesn't change the fact that it is vital to raising healthy individuals.

Wild + Free mama Rachael Alsbury talked about the challenges she faced in getting her reluctant children to enjoy playing outside. She had visions of lightning bugs in Mason jars, long hours of survival play, and old-fashioned games such as hopscotch and jump rope.

"Instead, my girls shrieked at every bug they saw," Rachael said, "refused to step foot off the patio, and wailed at the back door on perfect seventy-degree days."

She realized that one of her jobs would be to show her girls how to enjoy spending time outside. With so many stimulating activities and devices competing for their attention, outdoor play was something she had to deliberately nurture, in both herself and her children.

"After one year of consistency, we emerged victorious," Rachael said. "Most days, you will find my girls outside, naming birds, holding ladybugs, and immersed in imaginative free play."

When asked how she did it, Rachael said she committed to being outdoors for one to two hours a day. For a time, she prioritized this goal over formal, academic learning.

"A big portion of our first homeschool year was spent dealing with phobias surrounding dirt and bugs," Rachael said. "We read piles of library books about ants, ladybugs, flowers, birds, and gardening. Reading beautiful picture books together helped unlock the wonder of nature."

She also started finding things they could enjoy in their own yard.

"We spruced up our mud kitchen with new pots and pans and put air in deflated bike tires," Rachael said. "I stocked up on bubbles, sidewalk chalk, and bug-catching supplies."

She also tried to reduce the amount of overstimulation that gets in the way of enjoying nature. "It's hard for the slow, meditative activity of being outdoors to compete with nonstop exposure to handheld devices, flashing imagery, and instant gratification," Rachael said. "Purging excess toys and reducing our screen time for a season helped reawaken our

POSITIVE WAYS TO TALK TO KIDS
ABOUT THE WEATHER

By Josée Bergeron[9]

If it's **COLD** try saying . . .
Come and look out the
front door! Can you see your
breath? That means we need
to wear our warm clothing
today.

If it's **SNOWING** try saying. . .
Wow! Look at all those
beautiful snowflakes. Let's
go outside and see if we can
catch some on our tongues.

If it's **WINDY** try saying . . .
Can you see the trees
swaying in the wind? Today
would be a great day to fly
a kite.

If it's **RAINING** try saying . . .
Rain is wonderful for plants
and animals. It's a perfect
day to jump in some puddles.

If it's **CLOUDY** try saying . . .
The clouds are hiding the
sun. Today would be a great
day to look for shapes in the
clouds.

senses and wean us from our dependence on technology for entertainment."

Whether they balk at the mosquitoes, itchy grass, or unappealing weather, it behooves us to find creative ways to engage our children outdoors.

French Canadian mama of three Josée Bergeron runs a blog about getting kids out into nature. She wrote, "The way we talk to our kids about the weather has a big impact on their interest in playing outside. When we talk about the weather negatively, using it as an excuse to stay inside or blaming it for thwarting our plans, our kids learn to do the same thing. Our kids are really good at copying us!"[10]

Kids can play outside in all sorts of weather. The greatest hindrance isn't a lack of interest, a disdain for dirt, or an apathy for adventure. Often the biggest obstacle for our kids' loving nature is us.

If you want to raise explorers of the wild, you have to be one yourself. Get outside. Get dirty. Start oohing and aahing. Begin wondering and wandering again. Be afraid. Be adventurous. If you lead the way, I promise, before you know it, your children will be leading you.

THE ENEMY OF TIME IN NATURE

Kids need to be outside, but the competition is real. From television and video games to indoor play and peer pressure, we have to work against a culture that is working even harder to steal the wonder from our children's lives.

In 2009, Oxford University Press revised the *Oxford Junior Dictionary* for children and removed nature terms such as *heron, magpie, otter, acorn, clover, ivy, willow,* and *blackberry.* In their place, they included *Blackberry, blog, MP3 player, voicemail,* and *broadband.*[11] While most people might never notice and some would argue that language must change to reflect the current environment, the revision speaks volumes about the reality of children today.[12]

The good news is that we get to choose whether words like *acorn, buttercup,* or *conker* make it into our own children's vocabulary. Let's face it, Oxford doesn't have anything on a homeschool mom.

That said, keeping my kids off screens is not the goal. Technology is most likely their future. Their own mother runs an online organization, manages social media on her phone, and is writing this book on a laptop. I spend a considerable amount of time using technology every week. I have to create healthy boundaries for my own health, and so will they one day.

For now, we are their guides, albeit flawed. We are doing our best to form healthy habits alongside them, so they will learn how to do this for themselves as they grow in maturity.

Last summer at family camp, my then fourteen-year-old son made a new friend who lived across the country. At the end of the weekend, they exchanged contact information.

"Do you have a cell phone?" the boy asked Wyatt.

"No," my son replied sheepishly.

"Okay, how about Instagram?"

Wyatt laughed. "Not that either."

The kid was giving it his best shot. "Okay, what do you have?"

"Email," Wyatt said with a grin.

"Email it is!"

I want my children to know how to create and write and communicate in the real world. Taking away these tools doesn't benefit their future; it holds them back.

But as their parents, we still get to choose how much or often they are on their devices. My kids don't have phones, but they chat with their friends in Google Hangouts during certain times of the day. They don't play violent video games, but they crash into waves and play football in the sand with friends until the sun sets on summer evenings. They don't get to watch unlimited television, but we have a weekly family movie night and other special times to catch a favorite show.

They look forward to the moments when they get to hop online with friends, watch movies, and play their favorite video games. But when you fill your life with exciting activities, creative endeavors, and frequent adventures, it leaves little time to think about television.

Even now, my eldest son is writing his next book. My middle son has moved into live-action filmmaking and scoring his projects with electronic music on his laptop. My youngest son is learning how to fly a drone and capture video with it. And my six-year-old daughter has mastered the art of drawing unicorns on a digital sketchpad. The only reason they've been able to develop these skills is that we've given them time on computers.

Now, I'm well aware of the dangers of the internet. We have family policies that facilitate their use—such as certain hours for using screens, no devices at the dinner table, and their other work must be completed. But I am constantly in awe of what they create each day. Sequestering my children from all opportunities to learn and engage with the world isn't the answer.

> "Look deep into nature, and then you will understand everything better."
>
> —ALBERT EINSTEIN

As Peter Gray wrote, "The route to getting our kids outdoors is not to throw away the computer or television set, no more than it is to throw away the books we have in our homes. These are all great sources of learning and enjoyment. Rather, the route is to make sure kids have real opportunities to play freely outdoors, with other kids, without interference from adults.

"Kids in today's world need to become highly skilled with computers, just as hunter-gatherer kids needed to become highly skilled with bows and arrows or digging sticks. To develop such skills, they need freedom and opportunity to play with computers, the primary tools of today. But for healthy development, they also need freedom and opportunity to play outdoors, away from the house, with other kids. The key words here are *freedom* and *opportunity*—not coercion."[13]

David Sobel, an advocate for place-based education and author of *Nature Preschools and Forest Kindergartens*, wrote,

"Yes, we need to acculturate children to life in the modern, technological world, but we also need to have them bond with the earth so they can learn to balance ecology with technology."

Screens are not the enemy. They are essential to helping our kids prepare for the future. But their pull is powerful, and children need help managing them, in the early years especially. The solution is not to ban devices from our households but to provide more compelling alternatives.

This is why my family spends at least three nights a week at the ocean during the summer. It's why we go to Colorado each August as a family. And it's why I incorporate nature hikes at our local state park throughout the school year. We are constantly trying to sabotage our domesticated, indoor, technology-driven life for the sake of becoming a Wild + Free family.

If we want our children to get outside, we have to take them. It's not always convenient. And it's not always easy. But it's always worth it.

NATURE AS OUR CLASSROOM

 The beautiful part about homeschooling is that you can create your very own forest school or nature-based environment for learning. After all, nature is the ideal classroom.

There is no other place that can both calm and stimulate the senses. No other place where judgment, comparison, and fear of failure are nonexistent. And no other place that can ignite the imagination and silence us with wonder all at once. Nature never bores, never disappoints, and never tires of delighting us with its marvels. One look at a sunset, one splash in a creek, one firefly in cupped hands before bed gives us the chance to collide with wonder.

Nature is the greatest teacher you'll ever find, but only the curious will learn.

So how do you prioritize getting out into nature with your kids? No matter where you live, there are natural places all around you—forests, parks, gardens, streams. In urban environments, there are city parks and conservation areas, or you can take a day trip out of the city. Find them. Mark them on the map. Take your children there. Give them a childhood that breaks the rules and defies the statistics. Give them a childhood, for their future's sake.

"The child should be taken daily, if possible, to scenes—moor or meadow, park, common, or shore—where he may find new things to examine, and so add to his store of real knowledge."

—CHARLOTTE MASON

The simplest way to get your children in nature is to go with them. Start in your backyard. If you don't have one, find the nearest park, creek, or forest, and visit the same spot whenever it's possible. Take time to get to know the world around you. As your senses come to life, you'll begin to notice things. Birds chirping. Frogs croaking. Sun streaks shooting through the trees like golden swords. The smell of a skunk, sting of a bee, or flutter of a hummingbird's wings.

Time in nature turns into the study of nature, and before you know it, this becomes a natural part of your education. But know that this practice starts small. It begins with going outside. Charlotte Mason wrote, "An observant child should be put in the way of things worth observing."

NATURE JOURNALING

Nature journaling is a great way to foster curiosity about nature and deepen our knowledge of it. It's why Charlotte Mason encouraged mothers and children alike to do it. She wrote, "Consider, too, what an unequalled mental training the child-naturalist is getting for any study or calling under the sun—the powers of attention, of discrimination, of patient pursuit, growing with his growth, what will they not fit him for?"[14] It's why John Muir Laws wrote that nature journaling "is the single most powerful tool to supercharge your observation, memory, and connection with nature."[15] And it's why we've included nature journaling tutorials in every one of Wild + Free's monthly content bundles for the past five years.

Nature journaling doesn't need to be complicated. You don't need artistic skills, fancy pens, or expensive journals to get started. All you need is a curious spirit, a pencil, and a notebook. Call them nature journals, field guides, or whatever you like. But go into the fields, walk into the woods, and sit by the streams. Listen, watch, and sketch what you see. Include the date, time, and location. Include lists, quotes, or pressed flowers in your pages if you'd like. And fill them with the observations of your outings. In time, the habit of nature journaling will nurture a love for nature in both you and your children.

LIVING CURRICULUM

Nature is meant to be a part of the living curriculum, not relegated to weekend camping trips or vacations when Papa is off work. Nature is the work. Nature is the curriculum.

Wild + Free mama Greta Eskridge said, "I have never considered our nature days to be wasted days. That mind-set has been crucial all along."

If we desire to see our children connect with the natural world in earnest, it can't always be our idea. It has to be theirs. This means we have to provide the kind of environment that offers time and opportunity to explore. It means setting an example without expectations.

For a few weeks every spring, the garden becomes our classroom. Last year, my daughter Millie could hardly wait to join me in the dirt. Together, we plotted out where everything would go in our garden and then read the directions for planting different types of seeds. She discovered the delicate balance of loosening roots from the plants, how deep to dig, which seeds to scatter in rows, and which ones to count and drop in intervals.

She learned the names of wildflowers such as milkweed, goldenrod, bluebonnets, and sunflowers. She discovered the familiar scents of mint, rosemary, and basil in the tray of starter plants. And she learned to count to five as we dropped cucumber and carrot seeds into small holes and covered them with soil. But most important, she uncovered wonder in the world of her own backyard, made meaningful connections with the Earth, and achieved a sense of purpose from working alongside her mama.

What if I had viewed her involvement as a nuisance? What if I had scolded her when she accidentally broke a stem or dropped a handful of pea seeds in the grass? What if I had tried to do as much as I could alone when she was preoccupied with worms? What if? Benjamin Franklin said, "Tell me and I forget, teach me and I remember, involve me and I learn."

Every experience in nature doesn't need to be about education. But the education will come through experience. So we can relax and let our children find delight in nature, not see it as one more subject or chore. As conservationist Anna Botsford Comstock urged in her *Handbook of Nature Study*, "If nature-study as taught does not make the child love nature and the out-of-doors, then it should cease. Let us not inflict permanent injury on the child by turning him away from nature instead of toward it."[16]

INCORPORATING NATURE
INTO HOMESCHOOLING

We can incorporate nature into our homeschools by thinking small, rather than big. Keep it simple and close to home. Show them that nature isn't something to see out the car window while driving to Grandma's house or on a once-in-a-lifetime trip to the Grand Canyon.

Throw open the windows to listen to the birds singing in the morning. Go for a walk after a spring rain—or during, for that matter. Jump in puddles, save the worms, and catch raindrops. Point out a cluster of trees in the neighborhood park and suggest making a wilderness fort with the fallen branches. Pick the dandelions springing up through the cracks of the sidewalk.

Bring the books outside. Ditch the desks for climbing trees. Spend the day hiking with friends. Go to the creek to learn about the water cycle. Learn the names of things no longer found in the *Oxford Junior Dictionary*. Cultivate a "wild life" for you and your children.

Plant a garden to see what will grow in your backyard. Walk in the woods looking for animal tracks. Start a rock, wildflower, or insect collection. Raise monarch caterpillars and feed them milkweed until they transform into butterflies before your very eyes. Set up a bird-watching station at your front window equipped with binoculars, notebooks, and bird guides.

Visit the local nature center, not once, not just twice, but until the employees trust you enough to pull back the proverbial curtain and show you the good stuff. Cancel the cable and use the funds to purchase memberships at the local zoo, aquarium, and botanical gardens instead. Start a Wild + Free group and meet each month at the nearest trailhead.

Find a secret swimming hole. Build a tree house in the backyard. Get bikes for the whole family, and take them on the paths less traveled. Bring nature inside the home—display it, study it, label it, make art with it, and mail it to friends. Clean up trash at the local park.

Run in fields with your shoes off. Wade across creeks with your boots on. Go for a nature walk each morning, like my friend Leah Boden, to start the homeschool day. Create a mud kitchen in the backyard, like my friend Rachael Alsbury, and let your kids make pies.

"Mud is the most poetical thing in the world."

—R. H. BLYTH

Read living books about nature like Greta Eskridge, or take up nature journaling like Kristin Rogers. Make land art like Pacha Hornaday and nature crafts like Katrien van Deuren.

Every once in a while, go big. Skip the Disney vacation and rent a cabin in the woods. Take up wake-surfing like my friend Paula Caggiano, or visit the national parks like Naomi Ovando.

But no matter what you do, make time for nature. Schedule it into your week. Don't let it become an afterthought, the thing you do only after the "important work" has been done. It is *the* important work. Being in nature, as Louv wrote, helps children "realize that school isn't supposed to be a polite form of incarceration, but a portal to the wider world."

Allow them plenty of time in their special places, as Louv calls them,[17] be it a treehouse in the woods, a secret spot at your favorite beach, a cluster of bushes in the backyard, their very own garden plot where the fairies come out to play, or a giant rock up on the hill behind your house. These are the encounters with nature that will leave lifelong impressions.

Dear mama, don't let society tell you what's important for your children's education. Decide for yourself. And may the peace of the wild things call you back to the very place you belong.

18 The Power of Story

I'M THE SORT OF PERSON WHO WOULD WEAR A T-shirt that said, "The book was better." Books are always better. Not just the tactile experience of reading words on pages, but the experience they offer to our emotions, intellect, and soul. My favorite gifts are books. My favorite date nights are in bookstores. I have thousands of titles stuffed into my Amazon cart with no hope of acquiring them all, but it feels cathartic to put them there.

If you walked into my home, you would quickly see what our family values. You wouldn't find much decor on the walls because we focus our attention on trips and experiences outside the home. You wouldn't find sufficient tools for cooking because we prefer time around the dinner table to time around the stove. My guests always complain about the lack of good steak knives or saucepans when they visit my house. I once lived with a broken oven for over a year. I found I could cook everything from a roasted chicken to a homemade pizza in my toaster oven.

But one thing you would find is books. Lots and lots of books. You would also see my children nestled around the furniture in our living room writing books, outlining manuscripts, diagramming plots, and storyboarding the movie versions of their ideas.

Even my third-born son, Cody, who doesn't yet read or write, has a collection of books that he implores us to read over and over again. Lately, he's been crafting his own short stories and dictating them for me to write down. In fact, he told me the other day that he wants to include a DVD in the back of each book so that "children who don't yet read can listen to the stories."

On top of it all, you would see the crown jewel of our house—a magnificent book nook we constructed in the corner of our living room. It's lined with titles from floor to ceiling, with adjustable lights, and a comfy couch situated in the middle of it all. Whenever we have guests, they sit in the nook for hours, combing through the stacks and reading what they fancy.

Books are at the center of our family culture. If our children don't turn out to be writers, they will at least be voracious readers. Either way, they'll have stories of adventures, mysteries, and fantasies intermingled with the memories of their childhood.

It only makes sense that books would be at the center of our homeschool life too. Before I knew exactly what to do as a homeschooler, I would gather my kids in the living room or around the kitchen table, prepare a healthy snack, serve hot tea, and read.

I've read so many books aloud that my children will never be able to separate the voice of Laura Ingalls Wilder or Ishmael in *Moby Dick* from the sound of their own mother. Their father once read *The Hobbit* each night before bed without breaking from the Irish and British accents that distinguished the characters. It had to be some kind of Guinness World Record.

The power of story reaches far beyond the moment in which a child hears it for the first time. It ignites a creative process of imagining and storytelling within her mind and heart.

Sarah Clarkson wrote, "Consider that for every children's classic written, there are countless versions of it to be found within the minds of the children who read it, and no two of them are the same. The imagination of each child is unique, creating a new image to fit the words he or she reads. Because of this, to read a story is to set in motion a swift growth of new images within the mind of a child. Every book read adds to that stock of inner imagery so that a child who is a great reader has a mind crammed with landscapes and people, trees and fairies, castles and mountains unique to his or her own thought."[1]

What comes from all this reading isn't just a love of reading but also a love of learning. In her book *The Read-Aloud Family*, Sarah Mackenzie commented, "If you want a child to know the truth, tell him the truth. If you want a child to love the truth, tell him a story."[2]

Stories lodge themselves into the corners and crevices of our hearts and minds, never to be forgotten, delivering timeless lessons like a wise old friend who accompanies us throughout our lives. There is quite possibly no better tool for imparting knowledge than great stories.

And yet I understand the challenges of reading to our children at home. We're exhausted. They can't sit still. There's no time. The home theater system proves to be a worthy adversary. And for many homeschoolers, it doesn't feel as important as learning math or science.

Reading can feel like a "soft subject," something on par with gym class or home economics. It doesn't always offer hard facts or a way of measuring our progress. The reading contests at the library are regarded as extra credit at best. But the proof is in the results.

Teach me a fact, and I'll probably forget it tomorrow.

Tell me a story, and I'll remember it forever.

CREATE A CURRICULUM
OF LIVING BOOKS

As homeschoolers, we have the privilege of using actual books, rather than textbooks, in our children's education. A textbook is a condensed secondhand version of events that's structured to be taught in a classroom within a limited amount of time. A modern convenience, at best, created to convey information, instead of igniting a desire to learn.

For most subjects, textbooks are like processed food for thought.

In his book *The End of Education*, Neil Postman wrote that textbooks are "enemies of education, instruments for promoting dogmatism and trivial learning."[3]

Living books, on the other hand, tell the truth in real time, expressed through the lives of their characters and the details of their storylines. They contain layers of meaning, touch the emotions, and ignite the imagination while teaching you about a particular topic. They bring subjects such as science and history to life in a context where the application is immediately apparent.

Charlotte Mason first coined the term *living books* and advocated them as a part of her educational philosophy. She regarded anything else as "twaddle." She wrote, "Self-education by means of real books, narration, first-hand experience, and observation is such a very satisfying and rewarding process that it naturally continues throughout life."

Charlotte Mason home educator Leah Boden described living books as "books that tell a story, engage a child, and reach out a hand of friendship in order for the reader to be able to form a lasting connection, which ultimately impacts their thoughts and ideas."

The groundbreaking revolution of homeschooling is that you can teach your children with living books. You don't need textbooks. They might seem like an easier option, a catalog that covers all the bases. Kids can use them to memorize facts or pass a test. But a literature-rich education brings learning to life through the all-encompassing curriculum of experience.

My friend Rea Berg has a passion for teaching history through living books. She wrote, "History has effectively been taught through literature since ancient times. Just the last century or so has this vibrant subject been robbed of its human connection by the ubiquitous textbook."

If we want to give our children an organic, living education, we must provide them with nutrient-dense food for thought. To give them a rich heritage of literature and create passionate lifelong learners, living books are the only way to go.

Educator and author Jim Trelease asked the question, "So how do we educate the heart?" He continued, "There are really only two ways: life experience and stories about life experience, which is called literature. Great preachers and teachers—Aesop, Socrates, Confucius, Moses, and Jesus—have traditionally used stories to get their lesson plans across, educating both the mind and the heart."[4]

When you use living books as your framework for studies, there is no need for textbooks, worksheets, or even formal curriculums. Of course, there's nothing wrong with using a packaged program to get started. Beginner mamas often prefer someone else to do the legwork of preparation. But remember, everything is merely a guide. Doing it all is neither necessary nor required. With a little bit of time and research, you can easily create your own living syllabus.

Living books are often, but are not limited to, the classics. Some examples of living books include *Black Beauty, Little House on the Prairie, The Adventures of Tom Sawyer, Anne of Green Gables, The Chronicles of Narnia,* and *Mrs. Piggle-Wiggle,* among others.

How do we know what constitutes a living book?

Gladys M. Hunt, author of *Honey for a Child's Heart,* said they should be "stories that make for wonder. Stories that make for laughter. Stories that stir one within with an understanding of the true nature of courage, of love, of beauty. Stories that make one tingle with high adventure, with daring, with grim determination, with the capacity of seeing danger through to the end. Stories that bring our minds to kneel in reverence; stories that show the tenderness of true mercy, the strength of loyalty, the unmawkish respect for what is good."[5]

"And all the time we have books, books teeming with ideas fresh from the minds of thinkers upon every subject to which we can wish to introduce children."

—CHARLOTTE MASON

The good news is that there are living books for nearly every subject—from history and science to geography and math. A quick internet search will lead you to a number of living book lists for nearly every subject, genre, and age group.

I understand that relying solely on living books can feel like a risk. We already feel the pressure of holding our children's education in the palm of our hands. But what would you rather have—a child who begrudgingly recites data and can't wait for school to be over or a child who falls in love with learning and doesn't know exactly when school ends and life begins?

As Jim Trelease said in *The Read-Aloud Handbook*, "What we teach children to love and desire will always outweigh what we make them learn."

This is why we host book clubs as part of our homeschool experience. We want not only to read the great books but also to relive the stories with friends. We want to churn butter like Ma Ingalls, whitewash a fence like Tom Sawyer, and take turns reciting poetry like Anne Shirley.

It's why we make popcorn and huddle in the living room each afternoon to read the Green Ember series, *The Lord of the Rings*, *The Swiss Family Robinson*, and the Little Britches series.

It's not a break from learning. It's not an interruption in the school day. It *is* school.

It's why we use literature for science, history, geography, art, and even math at times. That's not to say we don't practice applying the Pythagorean theorem, rehearse our multiplication tables, or make our own Archimedean levers in the backyard. But living books help us apply these disciplines in the meaningful and memorable context of stories.

Literature, after all, helps us learn.

LANGUAGE ARTS THROUGH LITERATURE

There is nothing that teaches language arts better than reading great literature. We become better writers by reading skilled writing. We improve our spelling by seeing words in print. And we expand our vocabularies by being exposed to new words. The same goes for punctuation, sentence structure, and grammar. The kinds of books our kids read determine how they write.

Julie Bogart, the founder of Brave Writer, recommends teaching formal grammar and language arts only twice in a child's education—once in elementary school and again in middle school before they enter the application phase of high school. You will eventually identify a style that works for you, but never underestimate the power of literature as a primary teaching tool.

One practice I began early in homeschooling was to have my children keep "morning journals." These exercises in writing at the start of each day allow them to express whatever they want to say without being graded or evaluated. The purpose is to get them writing.

In the beginning, I often gave them writing prompts. They were sometimes creative, at other times practical, but they were always voluntary, meant to get their juices flowing. There were no requirements for what to write about, and they didn't even have to show me what they wrote.

Sometimes they fought the assignment, saying they couldn't think of a topic. But with the blank page staring at them and Mom's gentle encouragement, they always figured out what to write.

And write they did. Over the past eight years, they've filled page after page with accounts of their lives and of road trips, gripes about their parents, an original poem, details about the worlds they've built in Minecraft, reasons why they hate Shakespeare, and anything else you can imagine.

We've also adopted the practice of "copy work." By copying poems and passages from great books, my children see not only how the words are constructed but also how they feel coming off the ends of their pencils. This is a practice that aspiring writers of all skill levels employ to improve their writing technique. Not to mention that it improves their penmanship.

Along with copying worthy passages of prose and poetry, we practice the "art of narration." Asking children to summarize the meaning of a story, a passage, or a book allows them to digest the "mind food" they receive through living books. You never know what children are actually learning until they try to repeat it back to you.

There are numerous resources for beginning this practice in your own homeschool. The best part is that even children as young as four or five can retell a story, fable, or science lesson.

Jodi Mockabee incorporates narration into her homeschool rhythm but takes it a step further by having her children create their own lesson books. "I was drawn to the Waldorf philosophy in which students build their own curriculum through main lesson books," she said. "These are designed to record narrations and illustrations from stories their teacher has shared."

Jodi begins by reading a passage of a book aloud while her children listen and decide what to illustrate. Once they have chosen a subject, they find an illustration of higher artistic capability to copy. Jodi works with them to improve the scale, proportion, and other details of their art.

Once they've finished their illustrations, they join their mother at the computer to narrate what they just heard. They explain the details of the story while Jodi types, working to improve the quality of their writing as they go. When the typed narration is finished, she prints it out and has the children copy their narration onto the illustrated paper using their best penmanship. She calls this practice of capturing their narration in a documented form "notebooking."

"Notebooking is a treasured activity that has taught the children that diligent, hard work pays off in rewarding and fruitful ways," Jodi said. "We have folders lining our bookcases filled with beautiful illustrations and narrations that serve as records of what they have learned."

Narration can take many forms, not just oral or written. It can occur in pictures, dramatic play, and organic conversations. And while it is good to practice the art of narration to give our kids the necessary tools they will later use for writing, we must be careful not to turn every reading experience into an outlet for formal narration. We don't want to kill a child's love of books. Let much of it be personal to the child. Leave something to magic.

Susan Wise Bauer wrote, "Read to the child, explain where necessary, and discuss those things that seem important, but don't try to make every text an opportunity for a lecture, or you'll lose the child's attention."

Much like the rest of their education, what our children learn will seep out into everyday life as they process it in their own time. When you immerse yourself in a lifestyle of living learning, life becomes a never-ending narration.

READING ALOUD

Reading aloud is the cure for so much that ails childhood. For children who are lonely or feel like outcasts among their siblings or friends, it brings them together for a bonding experience around books. For overwhelmed children, it provides a time of peace and centeredness as the stories wash away their concerns. For children who are going through a difficult season and can't complete their studies in earnest, it allows the natural teaching of literature to fill their minds with all its rich knowledge and goodness. For all children, "literature can help children think about what life is like before they live it as adults," as Susan Schaeffer Macaulay wrote.[6]

And for children who can't stand books at all, reading aloud offers the same benefits of literature without their having to do the hard work on their own. They can sit back, listen to the story, and enjoy all the rewards that a passionate reader would receive.

And this doesn't even touch on the benefits for those who can't yet read on their own. Developmental disabilities such as auditory processing disorder, dysgraphia, dyslexia, and ADHD, among others, pose significant challenges for children. But we can give them a childhood steeped in literature through reading aloud. They don't have to miss out on a story-rich experience before their abilities catch up with their age.

Reading to young children fosters a deep love for books that will prepare them for reading in the future. Jim Trelease pointed out that "the single most important activity for building the knowledge required for eventual success in reading is reading aloud to children."[7]

According to Child Trends, reading to children develops literacy skills and an awareness of language long before they're able to read: "Since language development is fundamental to all areas of learning, skills developed early in life can help set the stage for later school success."

Without these skills, children tend to fall behind in school and are more likely to drop out.

In an international study involving fifteen-year-olds from fourteen developed countries, students whose parents had read books to them on a regular basis during the first year of elementary school scored an average of fourteen points higher on comprehensive reading assessments. Also, children who come from read-aloud homes have a larger vocabulary, higher levels of phonological, letter name, and sound awareness, and better success at decoding words.[8]

But the success stories are more than scientific. Take the word of children who grew up in families who read together. My friend and fellow Wild + Free mama Danielle Jones fondly remembers growing up homeschooled and experiencing family read-alouds.

"Share good books with children. It is a magic door of contact between a child and some of the most interesting and creative people our culture has enjoyed."

—SUSAN SCHAEFFER MACAULAY

She wrote, "One of the most treasured and important memories from my own days as a homeschooled student was my mom reading to my siblings and me after lunch. She would pour herself a cup of hot tea, and we'd settle on the couch. I couldn't wait to find out what would happen next to my favorite character, while being transported to another time or place by the power of Mom's voice, as it became that character."

The best part about Danielle's story is that her mother didn't stop reading aloud when her children were old enough to read on their own. "My relationship with my mom was enriched and nurtured by the simple investment of reading out loud," Danielle said. "Our daily read-aloud times were something I always looked forward to. It kept our relationship intact from elementary through the teen years, keeping the lines of communication open. Consistency was key. It served as an anchor in the day, something I could always look forward to when we were home."

Read-alouds are a balm to the soul of a teenager. We don't always know what's going on in their minds and hearts, and we can't always get them to articulate their feelings, but when we come together to read good books aloud, our families become whole once again.

Danielle said, "Reading out loud created a context for discussing deep and thought-provoking themes that various books brought up. From conversations about what it means to be a faithful friend in *Charlotte's Web* to the nature of good and evil in *The Strange Case of Dr. Jekyll and Mr. Hyde*, reading together gave a platform to talk about things that matter."

Reading aloud is about more than just telling great stories to your kids. It's about growing their literacy, giving them a love of books, and making meaningful connections with them.

INSPIRING RELUCTANT READERS

If you have a reluctant reader, take heart. The goal isn't to get our kids to love reading as much as it is to have them fall in love with stories. The text itself doesn't hold the power, but rather the story within. Books are beautiful—troves of goodness, celebrations of language, and preservers of stories. But the treasure is in the means, not the end. We mustn't forget that stories began as an oral tradition, and stories will remain when all the books are gone.

While we hope that our children will gain the affection for reading, we must allow the process to unfold in its own time. In the meantime, there are a few things we can do to inspire a love of stories in our reluctant readers.

Experiment with Different Genres

While my children are young, I never know what books will capture their interests. My eldest son, Wyatt, prefers fiction and fantasy. It's not easy to get him to read nonfiction. There was a season when he read every book in the Hardy Boys series. The books probably wouldn't make Charlotte Mason's description of *living*, but they brought him delight, so I spent two years searching for used copies so he would keep reading.

My second-born, Dylan, prefers sociodramatic stories, comic books, and graphic novels. It's challenging to get him to read a novel (I think he read a total of two last year), but at least he's reading. My third-born, Cody, prefers biographical stories, historical fiction, and nonfiction, particularly books about natural disasters. And my daughter Annie prefers stories that speak to her heart—children trying to survive tragic circumstances without their parents and lost animals trying to find their way back home.

Introduce Audiobooks

Audiobooks are great for nonreaders. But they also work wonders with reluctant readers, as the power of story can weave its way into their souls without them knowing. We frequently play audiobooks during lunch, on rainy afternoons, or while driving in the car. When my boys were younger, we listened to the entire series of Lemony Snicket's A Series of Unfortunate Events in the car. Not a one would get out of the car until there was a chapter break. Readers or not, they were hooked on story.

Find a Series and Whet Their Appetite

Pick a series that you think your child would be interested in, and read the first book aloud. If it works its magic, it won't be long before he's devouring the rest of the series on his own. For my eldest, the series was Little House when he was eight years old. For my second son, it was The Hunger Games when he was twelve.

Watch the Movie First

Did you have to read that twice? I can relate. If you asked my children, they'd all tell you that I am a stickler when it comes to reading the book before watching the movie. Whether it's *The Lord of the Rings* or *Harry Potter*, I always make my kids wait until we finish the book before watching the movie together as

A FEW OF OUR FAVORITE CHAPTER BOOKS

Charlotte's Web by E. B. White

Heidi by Johanna Spyri

The Railway Children
by Edith Nesbit

Pippi Longstocking
by Astrid Lindgren

A Wrinkle in Time
by Madeleine L'Engle

Charlie and the Chocolate Factory by Roald Dahl

A Little Princess
by Frances Hodgson Burnett

The Yearling by Marjorie Kinnan Rawlings

Little Women by Louisa May Alcott

Little Men by Louisa May Alcott

A FEW OF OUR FAVORITE BOOK SERIES

Thornton Burgess Animal Stories
by Thornton Burgess

Little House
by Laura Ingalls Wilder

The Boxcar Children
by Gertrude Chandler Warner

The Chronicles of Narnia
by C. S. Lewis

The Lord of the Rings trilogy
by J. R. R. Tolkien

The Little Britches series
by Ralph Moody

The Harry Potter series
by J. K. Rowling

The Green Ember series
by S. D. Smith

The Mysterious Benedict Society
by Trenton Lee Stewart

A FEW OF OUR FAVORITE PICTURE BOOKS

Roxaboxen
by Alice McLerran

Blueberries for Sal
by Robert McKloskey

Children of the Forest
by Elsa Beskow

Annie and the Wild Animals
by Jan Brett

Miss Rumphius
by Barbara Cooney

Frog and Toad
by Arnold Lobel

Children of the North Lights
by Ingri and Edgar Parin d'Aulaire

a family. But it's okay to make exceptions, and I'll tell you why. Our brains can process images faster than words—in fact, sixty thousand times faster, to be exact.[9] So reluctant readers might need to be drawn into stories before they are drawn into books.

Last year, I broke my rule and we watched the movie *Wonder* together as a family. Dylan was so moved that he immediately pulled the book off our shelf and devoured it in three days. When he was done, he asked his bookish brother what he should read next.

Discovering books that capture his attention has been challenging, but he's finding his way in his own time. And I believe the same can be true for all reluctant readers.

FOSTERING A LOVE OF READING

To foster a love of reading, it is tempting to use a system of rewards and mandates to motivate our children, but when we do, we rob them of their intrinsic desire, which leads to a decline in motivation altogether. A study published in the *Journal of Research in Education* reported that "when reading is portrayed as something one has to be forced to do, students may draw the conclusion that it is not the kind of activity they want to engage in when given free time."[10]

Erica Reischer, author of *What Great Parents Do*, wrote, "Compelling children to read may improve their reading skills, which is undeniably important, but mandated reading does not bring the same benefits as when children themselves choose to read. Worse, it may even diminish their interest in reading at all."[11]

Research shows that a love of reading determines whether our children will become lifelong readers.[12] And kids who read for the pleasure of it excel academically.[13] Reischer pointed out that "recreational readers tend to have higher academic achievement and greater economic success, and even display more civic-mindedness."

So how do we foster a love of reading in our homes? How do we transition our homeschools from textbook-driven classrooms into literature-rich learning environments?

First, we model a love of reading in our own lives. I'll confess that I always have a book with me—in my purse, in the car, or on my nightstand. I read to my children throughout the day and before bedtime. They hear me talk about my love of books, and I'm always picking up reprinted classics to read again and again. I agree with Gladys M. Hunt, who said, "No book is really worth reading at the age of 10 which is not equally worth reading at the age of 50."

Children are more likely to read when they see their parents doing it.

Second, we fill our lives with experiences involving books. We visit the library or bookstore nearly every week. We limit screen time and celebrate a day "wasted" by reading all day. We go to live reading events, theater productions of great works, and book fairs.

We also host book clubs with our friends. Nothing gets children excited about doing something more than knowing their peers are doing it too. If you have teens, let them facilitate the book club themselves. Who cares what they cover, as long as they talk about the book.

And third, we continue to search for books that will spark our children's interests and ignite their imaginations. I never force my kids to read, but that doesn't mean I'm not deliberate about getting books into their hands. Sometimes I introduce them to new titles and fail miserably. But I never give up. I keep searching for books that will capture their interest. I share the same belief as Maya Angelou, who said, "If you don't like to read, you haven't found the right book."

CREATING A CULTURE OF READING

Giving our children a textbook-driven education looks different from giving them a literature-rich education. You can tell the difference when you enter someone's home—grading charts on the wall, textbooks stacked in the schoolroom, and a mama who's worried if it's all getting through.

A literature-rich education, on the other hand, looks like a welcoming environment, an inviting place for children to learn—interesting books strewn around the living room, cozy reading spaces throughout the house, and plenty of reading time prioritized during the day.

How we structure our homeschools determines our children's love of reading. The goal isn't to pile books on top of everything else but to replace the things that are running us in circles with the slow and steady mind-set of a lifestyle steeped in stories. As Sarah Mackenzie wrote, "Either we create a space where reading is something that is done for the joy of it, where the imagination is cultivated and allowed to wander and stretch and grow, or we deaden our children's natural love for the written word."[14]

Every day offers a chance to create a family culture of reading in our homes. Practice the art of strewing. Place books throughout the home for your children to discover. Bring them back from the library every week, and leave them in an obvious place. Make sure you're offering a variety of reading material, from fiction and picture books to nonfiction and comic books. Read aloud together. Host a book club with friends. And don't give up or become disheartened if something doesn't strike their interest. For every book they reject, there will be another one that captures their attention.

At first, it's not so much about the kind of reading as the love of it. The goal is to get our children reading. Don't worry if your kids aren't always reading living books. While they are superior in many ways to other types of books, they're not always the starting point for some kids. Jim Trelease said, "Allow children to choose the books they wish to read to themselves, even if they don't meet your high standards."

If we help our children fall in love with literature, it will leave them never the same.

19 The Pedagogy of Play

HERE LIES THE CHILDHOOD PASTIME OF PLAY.
Oh, we don't mind play so long as it comes after the work and doesn't hinder our child's academic progress. We're okay with play as long as it doesn't affect their test scores. Yes, play is just fine as long as our children's education comes first.

What have we done to childhood?

Just as the frog in the pot doesn't feel the temperature slowly rising, families have been slow to sense the increasing pressures heaped upon their kids in education. We press into their childhoods in the same way we increase our time on the treadmill or apply more rigorous standards in the workplace. Before we know it, our children are left without a childhood.

David Sobel wrote, "We want our children to splash in mud puddles, but we also want them to score well on those first-grade entrance evaluations. And deep down, we want our children to go to good colleges, and therefore, it's never too early to get them on the right path."[1]

It doesn't seem to matter that research shows that social and emotional readiness in a child produces better academic achievement in the future. In fact, a study conducted by the University of North Florida found that children who attended academically driven preschools had lower grades by the end of fourth grade than those who attended play-based preschools.[2]

As a result, researchers revealed that early academic instruction "may actually slow down learning if it's presented before children are developmentally ready for it." In other words, bring back the mud puddles! They're more valuable to a child's development than we think.

We've got it stuck in our heads that if it doesn't look like work and act like work, then it must not be productive at all. But what if play were essential to preparing a child for academic success? What if children's natural desire to be carefree were critical for developing their potential?

In their book *Lens on Outdoor Learning*, Wendy Banning and Ginny Sullivan shared that "children's self-directed outdoor play provides opportunities for developing initiative, persistence, invention, and problem solving—the foundations of academic success."[3]

I get it. It feels counterproductive to let kids be kids. Especially when everyone else is putting their children in prestigious schools and full-day kindergartens and upholding a rigorous schedule with advanced math, foreign languages, and private tennis lessons.

But don't be fooled by the folly of the do-more mentality.

Kids fly farther, faster, when given a childhood full of play.

Vince Gowmon wrote, "If you trust play, you will not have to control your child's development as much. Play will raise the child in ways you can never imagine."[4]

Peter Gray agreed when he wrote, "Play is nature's way of teaching children how to solve their own problems, control their impulses, modulate their emotions, see from others' perspectives, negotiate differences, and get along with others as equals. There is no substitute for play as a means of learning these skills. They can't be taught in school. For life in the real world, these lessons of personal responsibility, self-control, and sociability are far more important than any lessons that can be taught in school."[5]

> *"Children cannot bounce off the walls if we take away the walls."*
>
> —ERIN KENNY

What a scandalous realization—that play is actually good for children. That plenty of free time, even boredom, prepares them for the future. That time to dream and explore on their own, without agenda, without schedule, molds their character and makes them better adults.

Long live childhood.

BETTER LATE THAN EARLY

Pushing our children to excel more, achieve more, and learn more, as early as they can, is tempting because most kids can handle it. Their dials go "up to eleven." But that doesn't mean it's good for them. They were given this tremendous capacity for learning in order to explore, discover, and play, not sit in artificial environments as if they were chickens, mass-fed the same diet, kept on the same schedule, and expected to pop out "results" at the same time.

Let my people go.

The trouble with our modern version of childhood is that it strongly resembles the lifestyle of adults and comes at the expense of play. It takes a conscientious community to restore childhood to its original condition, which means sabotaging our selfish ambition, slowing down our children's early education, and restoring play to its central role in their lives.

Nancy Carlsson-Paige is an early childhood development expert who taught teachers at Lesley University in Cambridge, Massachusetts, for over thirty years and is the author of the book *Taking Back Childhood*. She reminds us that the most important competencies in young children can't be tested, as we already suspect, and confirms the important role of play in a child's development.

"It takes a long time to grow young."

—PABLO PICASSO

She wrote, "We have decades of research in child development and neuroscience that tell us that young children learn actively— they have to move, use their senses, get their hands on things, interact with other kids and teachers, create, invent."

She goes on to say, "Play is the primary engine of human growth; it's universal—as much as walking and talking. Play is the way children build ideas and how they make sense of their experience and feel safe. Just look at all the math concepts at work in the intricate buildings of kindergartners. Or watch a 4-year-old put on a cape and pretend to be a superhero after witnessing some scary event.

"But play is disappearing from classrooms. Even though we know play is learning for young kids, we are seeing it shoved aside to make room for academic instruction and 'rigor.'"[6]

In their book *Crisis in the Kindergarten*, Edward Miller and Joan Almon state, "Skepticism about the value of play is compounded by the widespread assumption . . . that the earlier children begin to master the basic elements of reading, such as phonics and letter recognition, the more likely they are to succeed in school. And so kindergarten education has become heavily focused on teaching literacy and other academic skills, and preschool is rapidly following suit."[7]

And yet this general belief is widely disputed through research.

A study of kindergartens in Germany compared fifty play-based classes with fifty early-learning centers and found that the children who played excelled over the others in reading and mathematics and were better adjusted socially and emotionally in school. They also excelled in creativity and intelligence, oral expression, and industry.[8]

A study in New Zealand found that children who learned to read later caught up to children who began reading at age four or five, and they were found to have better reading comprehension and a greater motivation to read for pleasure.[9]

The same study reported that countries such as Sweden and Finland have "better academic achievement and child well-being, despite children not starting school until age 7."[10]

Time for play equates to higher-performing, more capable, better-adjusted kids.

David Whitebread, a developmental cognitive psychologist at the University of Cambridge, said, "Play shapes children's brains. It strengthens their competencies as they spontaneously experiment with learning and emotions without worrying. It is fundamental to human creativity."[11]

Children, as it turns out, need a childhood.

Charlotte Mason spoke of childhood as a "quiet growing time." Does that sound like what we've given them? And yet she wasn't the only educator who believed that formal education should wait. Maria Montessori, Rudolf Steiner, and many of today's leading psychologists all advocate for waiting until the age of seven for any formal education.

The number one question we get on the Wild + Free Instagram account comes from mothers of young children who want to know what they should do with their two-, three-, and four-year-olds for school. And my answer, every time, albeit with more diplomacy, is to do nothing. Read with them, spend time with them, and let them play.

Let them explore.

Let them discover.

Let them have a childhood.

WORK THAT FEELS LIKE PLAY

Contrary to popular perception, children don't despise work. Not at all. They'll do the hard labor of solving problems, thinking critically, and recalling information, but under one condition: it has to be meaningful. Is that too much to ask? That it serves a purpose? That it's relevant? Those are very likely the same requirements you have of your own job or work at home.

I know what it's like to assign books for my children to read only to have them complain and moan about it. I know what it's like to give them an assignment they don't want to do. Of course, there's a time and place for all kinds of work, but I suspect that much of it is meant to abate the guilt that's inherent to homeschooling, the inner voice that says we're not doing enough. So we pile up the rote copy work and mindless memorization just to feel better about ourselves.

Susan Schaeffer Macaulay wrote, "Many schools excel in wasting time. Time is like a fortune; it is wrong to allow it to be buried. Children are tired out with busy work. They are talked at until their attention habitually wanders, and maybe nine-tenths of their time is wasted."[12]

I witnessed this firsthand when my eldest son was attending public school. Despite having wonderful teachers and enjoying many subjects, he was bored to death by the time spent waiting on disruptive classmates, waiting in line, and waiting for the next meaningful thing to do. I'm sure it equally frustrated his teachers, but they were at the mercy of a one-to-thirty ratio in the classroom. At home, we have the ability to make moments meaningful, even if they occur in short bursts throughout the day, and to give our children opportunities to do purposeful work.

Not only does teaching suffer when the work isn't meaningful, but learning doesn't happen either. It becomes a futile exercise in parental authority, a battle of wills, and no one's the better for it. What if we took a step back and evaluated our educational activities by what mattered?

After Helen Keller overcame the challenges of being born blind and deaf to graduate from college, she reflected on the wisdom and intentionality of her beloved teacher, Anne Sullivan.

It was because she seized the right moment to impart knowledge that made it so pleasant and acceptable to me. She realized that a child's mind is like a shallow brook which ripples and dances merrily over the stony course of its education and reflects here a flower, there a bush, yonder a fleecy cloud; and she attempted to guide my mind on its way, knowing that like a brook it should be fed by mountain streams and hidden springs, until it broadened out into a deep river, capable of reflecting in its placid surface, billowy hills, the luminous shadows of trees and the blue heavens, as well as the sweet face of a little flower.[13]

Anne Sullivan knew when to lean in and when to pull back. She knew when to follow a trail and when to return home. She didn't try to control the learning experience. She followed it. And what unfolded was a living, natural education that bridged Helen's passions with learning.

As homeschooling mothers, this is our opportunity, our mandate, to make work meaningful. Learning is a natural desire within every child. We need only take the time to listen and notice where their interests collide with their capacity to learn.

They'll show us where to go.

MAKING WORK MEANINGFUL

Meaningful work happens when children become engaged with what they're learning. It moves beyond "being taught" into self-directed learning. Meaningless work stops when the lesson is over or the school day is done. But meaningful work is the starting point for curiosity and discovery.

Children who engage in meaningful work don't want to stop exploring. It's the child who is given a piano and spends countless hours teaching himself to play. The child who is given a microscope and can't stop asking for new specimens to study. The child who is given a particular book and after finishing it begs to read the rest of the series.

When children are young, play is their meaningful work. By doing the things we often deem unproductive, kids develop problem-solving skills, eye-hand coordination, and vivid imaginations. I get it. We can't help but want our children ahead of their peers. We see how quickly they learn, and we load them up with assignments to make the most of their capacity.

Lori Pickert wrote, "Children, even when very young, have the capacity for inventive thought and decisive action. They have worthwhile ideas. They make perceptive connections. They're individuals from the start: a unique bundle of interests, talents, and preferences. They have something to contribute. They want to be a part of things."

But as developing individuals, they don't always know how to do this. They need to learn how to become learners. Rather than assuming they'll eventually figure it out, we can help them.

Pickert wrote, "It's up to us to give them the opportunity to express their creativity, explore widely, and connect with their own meaningful work." This isn't just a skill to get through their education. Our goal is to "help them live a life based on learning and doing."[14]

> "I do not teach my pupils. I only provide the conditions in which they can learn."
>
> —ALBERT EINSTEIN

If given the chance, kids will find meaningful projects in which to engage. But we can also encourage meaningful work with the way we teach them. By giving them a chance to shape their own education, helping them develop healthy habits, and showing them how to find answers, we can help them create something beautiful and engage with a topic in a way that sticks.

As our children grow older and show an interest in doing other kinds of work, we can introduce age-appropriate opportunities to tackle new challenges. Before we know it, our kids will take off on their own learning journeys, and we'll be there just to guide and encourage them.

What an accomplishment that would be—to resist the shallow lure of doing meaningless busywork and instead show our children how to do meaningful work that lasts a lifetime.

SKILLFUL PLAY

With the right amount of passion and commitment to practice, our children are capable of becoming experts in their fields of study. They do the hard work of inventors and mathematicians through a complicated process called play. Let's call it "skillful play."

There are many types of cognitive and social play, as you've probably observed in your children over the years—sensory play, pretend or sociodramatic play, building play, and games with rules, to name a few. Jean Piaget contended that children are like little scientists, constantly observing, experimenting, and interacting with the world around them. As parents, we can nurture their intelligence by providing opportunities for them to play.

As you become a student of your child, you will see their unique gifts and passions bloom. They already have a pretty good idea of how to go about this, but there are many ways to encourage skillful play—from math manipulatives, sensory activities, and gross motor exercises to board games, card games, art, music, and outdoor play. There is nothing holding you back from creating a play-based curriculum except a little research and creativity.

HANDICRAFTS

Another wonderful way to help our children work toward mastery is to introduce the practice of handiwork. Charlotte Mason referred to them as handicrafts. The Waldorf pedagogy uses terms such as *handcraft*, *handwork*, and *craft*—each describing a different level of skill.

Regardless of what you call it, this kind of work is any activity that engages one's hands, requires a level of learned skill, encourages children to do their best work, and produces an end product that is useful. The concept of usefulness will vary from family to family, but let's not get hung up on any definition that strips joy from a project.

MAKE SPACE FOR PLAY

YOUNGER STUDENTS

Dramatic play—child-size kitchen with dishes and silverware, dolls, dollhouses, doll clothes, tea set, play food, play silks, cardboard houses, costumes

Engineering—wooden blocks, wooden train sets, wooden craft kits (cars, planes, etc.), child-size tool bench and tools

Art—easels, paints, brushes, smocks, canvases, pastels, paper, scissors, glue, window crayons, sidewalk chalk, clay, modeling beeswax

Math games and manipulatives—story cubes, board games, card games

Science—microscope, telescope, nature nook, magnifying glasses, cabinet of curiosities, petri dishes and test tubes, a book of child-friendly experiments, magnets, terrariums, aquariums, science and discovery centers

Physical—natural playgrounds, tree stumps, balance beams, gardening tools, hula hoops, play silks, rope swings, treehouses, climbing ladders, tumbling mats

Reading and writing—books, typewriters, paper and pencils, record player, iPod and earbuds for listening to audiobooks, write and draw books

OLDER STUDENTS

Maker spaces—scraps of wood, cardboard boxes, metal scraps, soda bottles, soldering tools, jewelry-making materials, PVC pipe, art books, cigar boxes

Music centers—instruments, microphones, recording equipment

Writing nook—bookshelf, quality paper, good pens, quotes, newspapers, magazines

Tech corner—computers, iPads, gadgets, drones, circuits, solar panels

EXAMPLES OF HANDICRAFTS

Calligraphy

Woodworking

Jewelry making

Leather tooling

Pottery throwing

Flower arranging

Iron sculpting

Oil painting

Quilting

Crocheting

Hand stitching

Watercolor painting

Branch weaving

Papermaking

Finger knitting

Peg doll making

Paper bead making

Woodburning

Wood carving

Scrapbooking

Candle making

Sewing

I never force my children to do handiwork, but every few months, I introduce a new project and we work on it together in the afternoons. If they seem bored or need something to occupy their hands as I read aloud, I often suggest they work on a handicraft project. But overall, I let them decide how far they will take their new skill. As a result, my kids have learned how to dip beeswax candles, whittle wood, and finger knit—to name just a few. The practice of handiwork isn't about any one particular skill but is meant to instill a curious confidence in learning new things.

My nine-year-old, Cody, has been asking for several years to use the old sewing machine he discovered in our linen closet. I kept putting him off, thinking it wasn't an age-appropriate activity. But one day it hit me that there was a good chance he would stop asking all too soon, and I would have missed giving him a wonderful opportunity to try something new. I realized the biggest barrier to my saying yes was more likely my own inadequacies when it came to sewing.

So I promptly pulled the machine down and let him start tinkering with it. We asked a neighbor who is a seamstress to come over and show him the basics, and she gladly obliged.

I don't know how long his interest will last or how far he will take this new desire, but these are the kinds of experiences that give a child a chance to grow in confidence, foster curiosity, and explore new avenues of creativity. As parents, we can't teach our children everything, but we can provide resources, release them into their flow, and revel in what they create.

I can't say this enough—real work begins with play.

Observe when your kids are hard at play. That, my friend, is the spirit we all need to do great work. Be careful not to squelch it in them, but rather look for ways to support it. You may wish for them to show the same passion for all their subjects, but rest assured they are developing the work ethic they'll need to accomplish other things throughout their lives.

PRIORITIZING PLAY

I used to worry that what we did for homeschool didn't look like work. I don't anymore. I used to become insecure when other parents described how long it took their children to do their homework at night. Now I feel sorry for them. When children's play intersects with their desire to learn more and deepen their understanding, it *is* work.

The other day, my eldest son was noodling on his laptop when I told him to put it away. He was researching animation techniques, and it wasn't the designated time for him to be on it.

"But you're on *your* laptop," he said.

"I'm doing work," I explained.

He bit his tongue as if he might burst.

"But so am I!" he erupted.

I paused for a moment, looked into his eyes, and realized he was being earnest. Just as I thought the importance of writing this chapter preempted all other activities at the time, Wyatt felt the same way about his research. And he was right. What he was doing may not have looked like work, but that didn't mean he wasn't working. I watched him adjust his characters, trying to make their movements appear more natural. I observed him studying the experts, trying to apply their techniques to his own projects. It looked like play, but I concede that he was doing actual work.

Purchase a curriculum if you must. Schedule your days for peace of mind. But remember that fostering relationships, engaging with your children in their natural habitat, and encouraging curiosity and wonder in them are more important than you could ever know.

And make time for play.

Whenever possible, spend time outdoors, the Earth's natural playground. A fallen tree, a cluster of boulders, and a rippling creek will offer hours of discovery-rich play for your children.

Go to the library and announce a free shopping spree for any books they'd like. Of course, they're all on loan, but revel in the wonder of plundering the stacks of whatever fancies them.

Read good books together. But forget trying to capture their rapt attention. Give them sensory activities to occupy their hands and time while you read. Let them get lost in play.

Get together with friends for science experiments and then let the afternoon slip away with unplanned activities. Let the children play tag, run up and down hills, and chase each other, and don't think for a minute that you are wasting their day. They are doing the important work of play.

Set the table at night with watercolor paints, homemade play dough, moon sand, and leaves, and let them awaken to the delights of these items in the morning. Surprise them with fun.

Separate beans, shells, and rocks into different containers and care not a bit whether they stay organized. Let your children feel the satisfaction of making messes out of order.

Surprise your children after dinner with Mason jars and challenge them to catch all the fireflies at dusk. Make fairy houses, build birdhouses, and set up mud kitchens.

Make music. In fact, make your own instruments. See who can make the craziest, most unexpected instrument out of the materials you have lying around the house.

Set up a bird-watching station at the front window. Include the necessary bird books and binoculars, of course, but don't forget the kazoos and party poppers to celebrate the birds' arrival.

Make story stones with prompts and symbols for telling great stories. Build boats and float them down the gutter on rainy days. Learn finger knitting or needle felting.

Raise monarch caterpillars and celebrate their transformation with a party.

Celebrate the important holidays during your homeschool day. Why not celebrate the unimportant ones too? Nothing makes a day go better than honoring National Donut Day.

Let the little ones make messes, and make cleanup time fun. Bake together, experiment together, and don't worry if it doesn't turn out perfectly. Create art out of anything and everything.

Take field trips and road trips and spontaneous trips just for fun. Climb trees, go on hikes, and decorate walking sticks. Go to local nature centers, zoos, and aquariums when the other kids are in school.

Have family dinners. Take evening walks. Say wishes and prayers. Make your compliments long and your goodbyes longer.

Tell bedtime stories. Tell bedtime jokes. Laugh together. Be together. Make thankful jars and count your blessings. Play music in the house. Sing and dance together.

Begin the day with gladness. Make seriousness forbidden.

Let it be known that, as for you and your house, you will play together.

20 The Curriculum of Curiosity

THERE IS A GREAT DIVIDE THAT SEPARATES THE interests of children from their academic studies. This is why heavy metal bands can write chart-topping songs about how school's out for summer and why Ferris Bueller can take a day off and throngs of people will go watch a movie about it.

Any teacher worth her salt is on a quest to bridge that gap. Teacher of the Year awards are given to those who get close. But only homeschooling mamas are in a position to actually give their kids that freedom. After all, the conventional school system is held accountable for a standardized curriculum. It's one course of study for every child, whether they're interested or not.

In homeschooling, our children's curiosity can actually become the curriculum. We can work with our kids to develop an educational approach that engages their interests and makes them want to learn more. But unfortunately, even homeschoolers fall into the trap of mandating coursework that conflicts with our children's interests. We cling to homeschool styles for help, but they almost always have to do with *our* preferences, not those of our kids.

Children have their own way of learning and coming at life. Children are natural-born learners. They aren't ignorant about what they need to learn, even if they can't put it into words. But they have their own unique personalities, learning styles, and interests. It behooves us to take time to discover what those are and then develop a child-led curriculum that keeps them engaged and interested in learning for the long haul.

This is the beautiful scandal of homeschooling—we get to learn what fascinates us.

"You can teach a student a lesson for a day; but if you can teach him to learn by creating curiosity, he will continue the learning process as long as he lives."

—CLAY P. BEDFORD

There are gaps in any education, whether it's at Yale University or Yonkers Community College. In fact, the Texas State Board of Education recently decided to remove Helen Keller and John Hancock from the required academic studies, leading to the erasure of those figures from the minds of Texas schoolchildren.[1]

As homeschoolers, we get the privilege of choosing our gaps too, or at least we can rest in the grace that we haven't messed up. When we focus on instilling a love of learning over a list of requirements, we can almost guarantee that our children's education won't end when they leave our homes.

Curiosity is what makes children want to learn. They won't learn unless they're interested. Sure, they'll memorize the material. They'll figure out how to pass the test. But they won't really learn.

Curiosity helps shape a more child-friendly curriculum. In fact, their curiosity becomes the curriculum.

CULTIVATING CURIOSITY

Why do we ask children to care about only seven specific subjects and then gauge their academic aptitude on those fields of study? Children have their own interests, and while it takes some longer than others to sort them out, it's our job to help them discover what those are.

Finding their passion should be children's lifework.

And while they're still at home, it should be our work too.

We have the wonderful, yet arduous, task of helping to draw out our children's best qualities,

helping them to identify their strengths and gifts in a nurturing environment, free from the labels and peer pressures they might encounter in a traditional school setting. We can help our children narrow down and define their interests without negative stereotypes being imposed on them.

But what lights up our children will not necessarily be what interests us. If we want our kids, especially our teens, to care about what we love, we have to care about what *they* love.

There is a process to figure this out. Just remember these four words: *foster, identify, encourage,* and *invest.*

First, we can foster their curiosity by exposing them to new subjects, activities, and fields.

Our homes can become laboratories where children are free to explore their passions without consequence. The environment we create becomes an important part of this process.

We don't know the exact conditions that made up Albert Einstein's learning environment as a child, but on the basis

COLLECT YOUR OWN LOOSE PARTS

NATURE ITEMS

Acorns

Rocks

Shells

Sticks

Driftwood

Branch slices

Pine cones

HOUSEHOLD ITEMS

Wine corks

PVC piping parts

Cardboard pieces

Toilet paper rolls

Paper towel rolls

Egg cartons

Wooden spools

MUSIC CORNER

Egg shakers

Triangles

Pots (makeshift drums)

Thundersticks

Keyboard

Guitar

Tree stump (stage)

CREATIVE DOODADS

Wooden beads

Glass beads

Nuts and bolts

Old keys and locks

Peg people

Buttons

Ribbons

String or rope

Wooden kitchen utensils

NIFTY CONTAINERS

Buckets

Crates

Cardboard boxes

Flowerpots

Ice cube trays

Muffin tins

Wooden bowls

Trays

of his reflections, we can guess that it included time to think, an abundance of books, and a copious amount of freedom to explore and discover on an individual basis. He was constantly looking for ways to stay out of school and to be free to think and dream, read books, and spend time in nature. In short, he created his own wild + free homeschool.

In 1971, Simon Nicholson published an article titled "How NOT to Cheat Children: The Theory of Loose Parts." He maintained that children need environments that have an abundance of "loose parts" at their disposal. These range from natural or recycled materials, such as rocks, acorns, cardboard, and wood, to abstract notions such as music, gravity, and playing with words.[2]

He wrote, "In any environment, both the degree of inventiveness and creativity and the possibility of discovery, are directly proportional to the number and kind of variables in it."[3]

These variables can include access to sewing machines, woodworking tools, sudoku books, typewriters, or musical instruments, among other things. By giving our kids "loose parts" to explore, they can figure out what they love, what they don't love, and what they excel in.

One of the best things I've ever created for our homeschool is a collection of loose parts, using items I've found at thrift stores, collected on nature walks, and uncovered around the house. I store them on a shelf in our den and pull them out for my kids to explore with their hands and tickle their imaginations. You could store them on a rolling cart, display them on shelves, or hide them in a cabinet to pull out when you need an activity.

Depending on their age and temperament, kids jump from interest to interest throughout their childhood. But in time, certain interests will become clearer while others fall away, as their true passions emerge and grow stronger.

The second part of the process of finding out what our children love is to help them identify what ignites their passions.

From the loose parts we offer them, our children will show passion or promise for certain fields. When we gave our son Dylan an iPad, we never dreamed that he would start creating short videos that he scored with music. When we bought him a small electronic keyboard to make it easier, we never thought it would foster a love of playing the piano.

But sure enough, he dove into music, learning to play by ear and copying songs from YouTube. We realized he had a gift and enrolled him in music lessons to refine his talent. There's hardly an hour each day when he's not sitting at the baby grand in our living room.

Third, we can encourage children in their continual development by allowing them to play, which is how children get better at what they do.

And fourth, we can invest in their futures.

We may not be able to take credit for our children's talents or interests, but we can certainly be patrons of their passions. As parents, we get to decide how we spend our resources—time, energy, and money. How much of those resources go toward our children's futures?

Homeschooling mama Tara Skogen once told me the story of how her son became an apiarist. He came across a book on bees that he couldn't put down.

"His curiosity turned into an ever-deepening interest," Tara said. "You could sense the excitement of what he was learning. Oftentimes, he would track me down to share all of his new bee knowledge. It didn't take long for the planning and research to begin. We determined where we would place the bees, the type of hive we would build, its actual construction, how many bees he would have, whether he would get a nuc (a partially established hive), and so on."

After weeks of planning, they purchased all the necessary supplies. Not many families would go to such lengths to foster their children's interests, especially accommodating a beehive in their backyard, but it's the very nudge our children need.

"Homeschooling grants us the opportunity to slow down and try new things," Tara said. "It gives us the time to explore our interests and learn more about them. It gives us time to sit and read for almost as long as we want, which is exactly how this love of bees started for my son."

We may not know exactly what will come from investing in our children's curiosities, passions, and talents, but we can be sure of one thing—it will never be wasted.

CHILDREN CAN BECOME EXPERTS

Childhood is widely regarded as a time of frivolity, immaturity, innocence, and ignorance. It never dawns on us that children can become experts, but it's true. Children can undertake meaningful projects, develop valuable skills, and comprehend important concepts as well as any adult. Childhood needs better public relations. And homeschooling mamas are the ones to provide it.

> "Play is the shortest route between children and their creative calling."
>
> —VINCE GOWMON

We can't teach them into expertise, of course. It has to come on their own terms. When we give them opportunities to pursue knowledge in the areas that interest them, find answers to questions that stump them, and create things that are important to them, they take ownership.

This is why fostering curiosity is so important to their education. When they are given autonomy throughout their day, with plenty of time to experiment, explore their ideas, and pursue their own interests without mandates, they get better at what they do. They become experts.

Lori Pickert wrote, "Creative work requires big chunks of unscheduled time. It requires freedom to explore, to try different things, to just think and imagine—and it requires a relaxed mindset. It is impossible to take your time and explore an idea in many different ways if you feel pressured by a lack of time or someone else's expectations."[4]

It all starts when children are young, with the independence we give them. But not the sort of independence that comes from making them cry alone in the dark or telling them to toughen up when they're scared. Independence comes from knowing they're secure, just as my three-year-old Millie runs away from me at the beach, looking back over her shoulder as if to say, "I'm running away, but you'd better be watching me." They need to know they have our protection at every moment.

This isn't the mushy logic of a doting mother but the conclusion of a scientific study.

In his book *How Children Succeed*, Paul Tough wrote, "Babies whose parents responded readily and fully to their cries in the first months of life were, at one year, more independent and intrepid than babies whose parents had ignored their cries. In preschool, the pattern continued—the children whose parents had responded most sensitively to their emotional needs as infants were the most self-reliant. Warm, sensitive parental care, [the study] contended, created a 'secure base' from which a child could explore the world."[5]

As children grow, what we teach or don't teach them in the developmental years makes a difference as well. Tough wrote, "What matters most in a child's development, they say, is not how much information we can stuff into her brain in the first few years. What matters, instead, is whether we are able to help her develop a very different set of qualities, a list that includes persistence, self-control, curiosity, conscientiousness, grit, and self-confidence."[6]

During the teen years, fostering their independence is even more important.

I love being the mother of a teenager. It brings me so much joy thinking about my little towheaded boy who has always been my sweet companion, old soul, and gentle teacher. Watching him discover what he loves and is good at is both humbling and exhilarating.

One thing I've learned is that teens will do the necessary hard work when it comes to their passions. We can set them up for success by giving them the freedom to pursue their interests and the time to figure out what those are. An abundance of fruit comes from us strewing experiences, art, books, and ideas through our words, home, and lifestyle.

Walter Isaacson, author of the biography *Einstein*, wrote, "Throughout his life, Albert Einstein would retain the intuition and the awe of a child. He never lost his sense of wonder at the magic of nature's phenomena—magnetic fields, gravity, inertia, acceleration, light beams—which grown-ups find so commonplace. He retained the ability to hold two thoughts in his mind simultaneously, to be puzzled when they conflicted, and to marvel when he could smell an underlying unity. 'People like you and me never grow old,' he wrote a friend later in life. 'We never cease to stand like curious children before the great mystery into which we were born.'"[7]

May we keep childhood forever alive in our kids.

MAKING CURIOSITY THE CURRICULUM

Our children possess the desire for beauty, appreciation for the good, and the ability to do hard things. But we can suck the potential right out of our kids by the way we educate them.

Ken Robinson, author of *Out of Our Minds: Learning to Be Creative*, said that children enter school with virtually

98 percent genius levels at divergent thinking, but this capacity is nearly halved after five years of formal schooling and declines significantly more after another five years.[8]

As mothers, we can get their genius back. We can give our children opportunities to pursue worthwhile endeavors, access to nature, art, and handicrafts, and exposure to the broader constituents of the arts—books, music, painting, poetry, theater, dance, and more.

If only we would stop thinking of free time as wasted time, self-directed learning as unproductive interests, and hours of play as frivolous activity. The subjects of a child's curiosity are not "electives" or "extracurricular activities" but the guiding foundation of their education.

The beautiful thing about homeschooling is that we can create our own kinds of gifted programs and magnet schools, which only a special few can attend in the public education system. Of course, we have to include the core subjects that are important for satisfying state requirements. But we can explore the curiosity-invoking side of every subject.

In science, we can study the periodic table of elements, but we can also conduct kitchen counter experiments to show how gases are formed. In math, we can study the multiplication tables, but we can also arrange pine cones or acorns into a living abacus.

We can take our time getting our little ones started in homeschooling and allow them to get advanced placement in the subject of play. We can finally say no to the rote worksheets and turn their lessons into something meaningful. We can give our kids a choice in what they study by choosing our own gaps in education and leaving out the things that aren't relevant.

We can cultivate a supportive, creative environment where we encourage our children to follow their interests, going deeper and deeper until they become experts. We can provide books and objects throughout our homes that beckon our children to try something new.

We can identify their strengths and passions and fuel their development by investing in resources and providing ample time to explore them. We can give them tools to sharpen their skills, investigate their interests, and experiment with new things.

We can invoke our children's curiosity, even with the boring stuff.

We can make homeschool captivating.

21 The Magic of Wonder

OUR CHILDREN ARE BORN WITH ALL THE SENSE OF wonder, curiosity, and adventure they will ever need. We cannot bestow these gifts on them. We can only provide the conditions in which they can thrive. We are the preservationists of childhood.

In 2011, I began homeschooling my son Wyatt in the belief that I could give him something he could never receive in the mainstream school system—a childhood. Today, my belief in the wonder of childhood is stronger than ever before.

"What is wonder?" you might ask. According to the Merriam-Webster online dictionary, wonder is "astonishment at something awesomely mysterious or new to one's experience."

Wonder isn't some lofty ideal that we hope to impart to our children if we can. It's the natural tendency to look at the world and want to explore it. Wonder is triggered by beauty, new discoveries, and our imaginations. Children live in a constant state of wonder. They're always learning, exploring, and discovering new things.

Last summer, I was walking up the path to our home when the sight of something heart-wrenching stopped me dead in my tracks. A baby bird lay lifeless on the path. At first, I was inclined to hide it from my girls, keep their hearts free from sorrow, and spare us an afternoon of unnecessary pain. But I decided to let them experience the raw reality of nature instead.

My two-year-old daughter insisted on holding the hatchling in her chubby little hands until we convinced her that a burial was best. She stood beside the funeral plot behind our shed wailing for the tiny creature. My heart was heavy for her, but I couldn't bear to strip her of the greater gift of wonder. I didn't try to teach her about the circle of life or survival of the fittest. I simply let her exist in the state of not understanding or knowing.

And I chose to cry with her.

> "If I had influence with the good fairy who is supposed to preside over the christening of all children, I should ask that her gift to each child in the world be a sense of wonder so indestructible that it would last throughout life."
>
> —RACHEL CARSON

Wonder is the birthright of every child. It is not limited to IMAX movies, lunar eclipses, and Christmas light displays. Wonder is the everyday inclination to look at the world through fresh eyes and desire to experience, learn, and explore. If given the chance, children will spend much of their time in a state of wonder.

In his book of essays called *The Defendant*, G. K. Chesterton observed, "The fascination of children lies in this: that with each of them, all things are remade, and the universe is put again upon its trial. As we walk the streets and see below us those delightful bulbous heads—three times too big for the body—we ought always to remember that within every one of these heads there is a new universe, as new as it was on the seventh day of creation."

Then how is it that we seem to be losing our sense of wonder?

THE LOSS OF WONDER

Everyone and everything seems to be working hard to destroy wonder. Schools focus on assessing and ranking our children. They teach that playtime equals break time and that learning and playing are separate entities, with the latter getting very little attention at all.

Before long, the wonder is schooled right out of them.

In 2016, science teacher Matt Pritchard gave a TED Talk called "The Quantum State of Wonder." He likened wonder to quantum physics in that it dwells in the realm of probability and possibility. He shared how wonder is the "wow" that leads to the "how." He asserted that children should be allowed to hover in that in-between state.

As an educational tool, Pritchard said, "there's power in wonder, in serious play, because wonder beckons us and whispers, 'I wonder—what if?'"

He explained that by giving our children the answers and dismissing the chance of wonder, we inadvertently take away any internal motivation to learn and swap it for the external "carrot on a stick" motivation. We rob them of the magic, the not-knowing, the experience of learning.

"Education is not about giving the answer," he argued. "Education is about finding the connections between different things and forging new connections. Education is about giving the confidence and skills to go and explore the world themselves."

If all learning begins with wonder, then this should affect how we educate our children. Our tools should work more like magic wands than Mason jars as we look for ways to keep them flying, not contain them. We are not in this to manufacture products but to raise whole persons. One day, our children will have grown up. And they will undoubtedly feel the need to ground themselves in more concrete realities, to forget the parts of their childhood that birthed their futures into existence. But, for now, it's up to us as mothers to restore what has been lost.

It's up to you and me to reclaim the wonder of childhood.

Now, I know what you're thinking. In the midst of temper tantrums, incessant arguing, bad moods, and, yes, even when the kids aren't behaving all that well either, it's hard to take responsibility for reclaiming wonder. As homeschooling mamas, all of us have challenging moments. There are days when nothing seems to be getting through. In these difficult but ordinary times, may we return to life-changing pursuit of wonder.

When was the last time you imagined what it was like to experience life as a tiny wildflower growing in the middle of a field, a butterfly in the garden, or a tree swaying in the wind?

Children do this all the time, which is why their potential to learn is endless. It's why they are able to change the world with their imaginative ideas. And it's why Albert Einstein repeatedly credited his discoveries to his childlike thinking, even as an adult.

He wrote, "The most beautiful thing we can experience is the mysterious. It is the source of all true art and science. He to whom the emotion is a stranger, who can no longer pause to wonder and stand wrapped in awe, is as good as dead—his eyes are closed."

When was the last time you imagined what it was like to experience life as a child?

I wonder what our homeschools would look like if only we would.

WHERE WONDER CAN BE FOUND

Wonder is not to be found in the mad dash of curriculums and coursework. It won't be discovered on chalkboards or checklists. When our children memorize vast amounts of facts and dates, it may swell our hearts for a season, warding off fears that we haven't completely messed up their lives by this daring decision to homeschool. But it will never restore wonder.

"The most unfathomable schools and sages have never attained to the gravity which dwells in the eyes of a baby of three months old. It is the gravity of astonishment at the universe, and astonishment at the universe is not mysticism, but a transcendent common sense."

— G. K. CHESTERTON

The conventional metrics of education may help us fulfill the state's requirements and stave off the critical remarks of grandparents and grocers. It may give us hope that our children will somehow be better off by being schooled at home. But it will never save childhood.

Wonder can be found only in the wide-open pastures of time and freedom to be a child—the last remaining expanses on Earth where imaginations can gallop without fear of being captured and where concepts such as progress and performance are replaced with memories and moments.

Why do we fear letting our kids be kids? Rhodes scholars aren't made in the third grade (or the ninth, for that matter). Novelists and Nobel laureates aren't created with a curriculum. Our children's futures come from something infinitely more personal—the awareness of self, the love of learning, and the freedom to follow one's interests into greater areas of passion.

Let's release our children back into the wild where they belong. Giving them time to be kids does not detract from their potential, not at all. It gives them roots with which to drink from the deep springs of knowledge. Not the kind of knowledge that shows up on achievement tests but the sort that shapes their futures and enables them to make an indelible mark on the world.

The consequence of growing up with a fully realized childhood is a healthy disregard for impossibility and the deliberate avoidance of the status quo.

Let us not fear how long it takes our children to grow up, to act like adults. Their maturation will come soon enough and, once attained, can never be reversed. Childhood becomes like the attics and tree forts from long ago that shaped our youth but now exist only in distant memory.

As my youngest son struggles to learn how to read and write because of his dyslexia and fears being surpassed by his younger sisters, I mourn for his frustration. I grieve for the angst it must cause him to see a street sign and not be able to read it or to be around peers who talk about reading books and not be able to join them.

But I have no concern whatsoever about whether he will succeed in life. I feel no pressure to rush his childhood or advance him beyond his age. His time will come. His capabilities will catch up with his years. And his creativity will continue to flourish. In the meantime, it is my duty to give him a lush, fertile childhood from which the rest of his life will spring.

As Karen Andreola said, "A plant blooms from within. When the environment is right, the plant flourishes because it is living."

THE BENEFITS OF BOREDOM

Kids will often say they're bored when faced with the time and space to experience unbridled wonder. But boredom has its benefits. Let us not mistake idle time for wasted time. A day without scheduled activities from sunup to sundown does not

BOREDOM BUSTERS

OUTDOOR ACTIVITIES

Backyard scavenger hunt (by color, by theme, or random)

"Painting" the fence—bucket of water and real paintbrush

Boomerang in backyard

Water rockets

"Volcano" making (vinegar and baking soda)

Measuring the fence with a tape measure

INDOOR ACTIVITIES

Art cart

Woodworking caddy

Knitting needles and yarn

Sidewalk chalk

Window chalk

Modeling beeswax

Take apart an old radio or camera

Put together circuits

Fix something that's broken

Story rocks

Word search

Help Mama cook and clean

Create a new recipe

Listen to an audiobook

Water beads

Wood figures painting

Art kits from craft store

"Loose parts"

make an unproductive child but, rather, a happy one, a child who is capable of devising her own plan.

The thing about boredom is that from the outside, it looks exactly like inactivity. But inside, boredom is the incubator for every great idea, dream, and new creation. Boredom is the wardrobe through which every artist, inventor, and explorer must pass in order to enter new worlds. It is the toll that must be paid before children can flourish in their imaginations.

As parents, our challenge is to help our children walk through it rather than avoid it. Our temptation is to give them a screen, fill up their time, and scratch their shallow itch to save ourselves from their cries for relief. But that bypasses the deep soul work that fosters creativity and imagination in our kids. By stifling their complaints for something to do, we squelch their capacity to transform idle moments into valuable time. In effect, we stunt their creative growth.

"This savoring of life is no small thing. The element of wonder is almost lost today with the onslaught of the media and gadgets of our noisy world. To let a child lose it is to make him blind and deaf to the best of life."

—GLADYS M. HUNT

Currently, as I write these very words, my twelve-year-old is constructing a full-body bear costume out of cardboard, complete with moving joints, arm bands, and moving fingers. Why, you may ask? Who knows? But I recognize the work of boredom when I see it. The power of inspiration and the belief that he can bring it to life has him working around the clock.

But oh, my kitchen. The mess is of epic proportions. There are threads of hot glue strung from floor to ceiling. Cardboard cutouts and scrap paper are scattered all over the floor. Paint is splattered across every surface. And despite the cleanup he does every night before bed, I wake up to an entirely new construction zone the next morning.

I could choose to let practicality win, insist I'm not irrational for sequestering his creativity to another room, convince myself a kitchen is not for crafting, and declare that responsibility equals orderliness. But where, may I ask, is he to go? What is homeschooling if not art class as well as history class? What is self-directed learning if not an experiment in living?

What is this lifestyle if not an incubator for wonder?

Show me a child who knows how to fill an afternoon in spite of no organized activities at his disposal, and I'll show you a kid who won't have to worry about boredom for the rest of his life. Even more, I'll show you an individual who can create something remarkable out of nothing.

PRACTICAL WONDER

Wonder exists whether we foster it or not. It dwells in the depths of our souls, and if the embers haven't entirely been snuffed out, it doesn't take much to reawaken the flames. Spending time in nature is a sure way to foster wonder. Kids can't help but be drawn to the mysterious, from the mesmerizing flight of the hummingbird to the unusual identity of the assassin bug.

Education is not the opposite of wonder. When done right, education continually applies a child's natural sense of wonder to discover new things and, in turn, fills them with more wonder.

Robert Sapolsky, the author of *The Trouble with Testosterone*, wrote, "The purpose of science is not to cure us of our sense of mystery and wonder, but to constantly reinvent and reinvigorate it."[1]

Wonder spurs curiosity. Curiosity drives inquiry. And inquiry always leads to discovery. If you want to help your kids make great discoveries, expose them to a plethora of phenomena. From charting weather patterns and studying photosynthesis to experimenting with gravity, a deliberate dabbling with wonder will move children from curiosity to inquiry to knowledge.

Read books in the settings of their subjects. Enjoy *Black Beauty* at the equestrian center, *The Swiss Family Robinson* in the backyard tree house, and *Treasure Island* on the banks of your nearest body of water. Get lost in good books by first getting lost in the woods.

Take a nature walk to collect specimens, and then make handicrafts using only the items you found. Create a "nature nook" or "cabinet of curiosities" in your home, and save their sacred shelves for only the best finds. Devise scavenger hunts for items that can be found only during specific seasons, such as icicles in winter, cicada shells in summer, and pine cones in fall.

Take up the practice of nature journaling and teach your children that artistic skill doesn't matter as much as the experience. Practice painting mushrooms, honeycombs, and bird's nests until your children notice the difference in how they are made. Gather natural materials and attempt your own nests to get a greater appreciation for what our feathered friends require.

Skip the math workbook and take your numbers out into nature. Calculate gallons of milk and the length of fence per acre at the nearest farm. Watch how they churn butter for science and climb the hay bales for P.E. Study symmetry by finding leaves that mirror their other halves.

Keep your eye on the celestial calendar, and pull out the telescope or download a star-viewing app for sky-watching parties at night. Make the moon phases with cookies, or create the constellations with nails and string. Find out what it takes to become an apiarist, start keeping chickens, or visit the wild ponies at Chincoteague. Let learning come alive in your hands.

Play the music loud and host dance parties in your kitchen. Clear the closets of clutter and let them become secret play spaces. Build shelves around the front window, install a bench seat, and create a book nook where your kids can escape into literature. Learn how to make sourdough. Create your own ice cream, trail mix, pumpkin bread, or apple butter.

In the springtime, collect raindrops in a beaker and document each rainfall. Run outside to splash in puddles and save the worms that got stuck on the sidewalk. Come inside to watercolor the cloudy skies, green galoshes, and unwieldy umbrellas. Talk about where the animals go when it rains, and laugh about your drenched clothes.

Push back the living room furniture and pile blankets and pillows on the floor to turn your read-alouds into parties. Make the most of rainy days by going outside to feel the rain on your face. Install your own sundial, rain catcher, or wind turbine to take the elements into your control.

Visit the thrift store for fashion finds, and have your children craft their own line of clothing. Hang a hummingbird feeder, fill it with nectar, and wait for the miniature marvels to appear. Find out what sort of wildlife lives in your neighborhood, and go out on muddy days looking for footprints.

Visit the library, but refuse to be merely a patron. Learn how the Dewey decimal system works and help the librarian return the books to their rightful places. Learn from visiting authors, attend a workshop or two, or even lead your own class on an area of expertise.

Find the most remote place in nature within minutes of your house and howl like a wolf. Chase butterflies and pick wildflowers, but don't just pick them. Save them. Press them into books. Press them in picture frames. Learn all about them. Memorize their scientific names.

Grow the most exotic plant your climate can accommodate. Grow tomato plants from seeds on your windowsill, and then transplant them to your garden when they get too big for the pot.

Host an art show, a science fair, a maker market, or a nature festival. Take your best forest finds and exchange them with someone in a far-off place. Start a small business and give the proceeds to someone in need. Learn how to bind books, mount jewelry, or code a website.

Light candles or build a fire and read under the blankets for the whole day. Read poetry aloud for the sheer pleasure of it. Plan a backyard Shakespeare night with friends. Invite your neighbors and reenact your favorite stories by the beloved bard.

Lie down on the grass and feel the earth beneath you. Walk outside after dark and hold up your arms to a sky filled with stars. Drive to a clearing and watch the full moon rise over the horizon. Make snow angels in the fresh powder. Catch snowflakes on your tongue. Find shapes in the puffy clouds on an autumn day. Catch fireflies at dusk and the sunrise at dawn.

Become members of the local aquarium. Visit museums. Explore tidepools. Go whale-watching in winter. Look for owls at night. Become a tourist in your own hometown.

Follow your children's daydreams out the window, into the backyard, and down the road. Seize the opportunities when their imaginations are wandering, and give them the freedom to chase them. The books and projects are patient. The question is, are you?

The world is your classroom. Your curiosity is the course. Get a degree in the life lessons that intrigue you, and print out your own diploma acknowledging the work that you've done.

Wonder is waiting.

Afterword

WHEN I DECIDED TO HOMESCHOOL, THE FIRST BOOK
I read to my children was *The Call of the Wild* by Jack London.
I have no idea why I chose this for my three young boys,
only two, five, and seven at the time, but over the years it has
become an anthem of sorts for our homeschooling experience.

As you may know, it's the story of a dog named Buck who
lives a pampered life at a California homestead until he's
kidnapped from his home and shipped to Alaska, where he is
forced to pull a sled during the gold rush in the Klondike.

He has to fight for his life against another dog in a death
match to become the pack leader, and he's passed from master
to master, being mistreated, until he's finally adopted by a
caring owner who lets him be exactly who he was made to be.

"Love, genuine passionate love," London wrote, "was his for
the first time."

It is at this moment when Buck hears the call of the wild.

"Deep in the forest, a call was sounding," London wrote,
"and as often as he heard this call, mysteriously thrilling and
luring, he felt compelled to turn his back upon the fire and the
beaten earth around it, and to plunge into the forest, and on
and on, he knew not where or why; nor did he wonder where or
why, the call sounding imperiously, deep in the forest."

In the freedom of his newfound wildness, Buck discovers where he truly belongs. As he comes and goes from the homestead, he connects with the nearby wolves. He leaves for longer and longer periods at a time, and while he occasionally comes back to check on his beloved master, he eventually goes to live with the wolves, completely wild + free.

There are times when I look at my children and marvel that we're entering our ninth year of homeschooling. The way we live and learn is so vastly different from the ways of most other people that I used to have moments of panic that I was doing something wrong. But over the years, I've come to a perfect peace with the decision we made. Society may tell us it should be a certain way, but that doesn't mean it's right for our family.

I'm amazed at all the ways my children have grown over the past decade. It has been in the freedom and peace of our wildness that they have discovered who they truly are.

One day, my children will venture out of the house as they hear the faint cry of their own calling. They'll leave for longer and longer periods of time, gaining confidence in their abilities, independence, and experiences in the world, until they find their own way.

And while I trust that they will come home to visit their beloved mother as much as they can, they will eventually make their home away from mine and answer the call of their own . . .

The call of the Wild + Free.

WE
BELIEVE

WE BELIEVE that childhood is a time
to foster wonder, creativity, and discovery
through play and exploration.

WE BELIEVE that children learn because
they want to, not because they're forced to.

And **WE BELIEVE** in letting them learn at their own pace.

WE BELIEVE in giving children an abundance of
opportunities, time, and access to beauty—like art, music,
literature, nature, and their own imaginations.

WE BELIEVE this path isn't just for childhood but for a
lifetime of pursuing their own interests, responding to life and
not bells, and building a life based on purpose, not perfection.

We are the misfits, the renegades,
the square pegs in round holes.

But we are not alone. We have each other.

And we are in this
TOGETHER.

Further Reading

For the Children's Sake: Foundations of Education for Home and School by Susan Schaeffer Macaulay

The Brave Learner: Finding Everyday Magic in Homeschool, Learning, and Life by Julie Bogart

The Read-Aloud Family: Making Meaningful and Lasting Connections with Your Kids by Sarah Mackenzie

Rethinking School: How to Take Charge of Your Child's Education by Susan Wise Bauer

A Gracious Space: Daily Reflections to Sustain Your Homeschooling Commitment by Julie Bogart

Teaching from Rest: A Homeschooler's Guide to Unshakable Peace by Sarah Mackenzie

Free to Learn: Why Unleashing the Instinct to Play Will Make Our Children Happier, More Self-Reliant, and Better Students for Life by Peter Gray

Last Child in the Woods: Saving Our Children from Nature-Deficit Disorder by Richard Louv

How to Raise a Wild Child: The Art and Science of Falling in Love with Nature by Scott D. Sampson

Home Grown: Adventures in Parenting off the Beaten Path, Unschooling, and Reconnecting with the Natural World by Ben Hewitt

Project-Based Homeschooling: Mentoring Self-Directed Learners by Lori Pickert

Let's Play Math: How Families Can Learn Math Together— and Enjoy It by Denise Gaskins

The Art of Self-Directed Learning: 23 Tips for Giving Yourself an Unconventional Education by Blake Boles

Gifts Differing: Understanding Personality Type by Isabel Briggs Meyers and Peter B. Myers

Acknowledgments

I've heard it said that writing a book is a lonely endeavor. And while I know what they mean, I'm grateful to be surrounded by the most beautiful tribe of people.

My beloved Ben: You believe in me more than I believe in myself, and there are no words for that kind of love and support. You have championed this project like it was your own, and it simply would not exist without you. You are my favorite story and my forever love.

My children, Wyatt, Dylan, Cody, Annie, and Millie: You are my heart, my whole world, and my favorite people to be around. My deepest joy is being your mama, and my greatest privilege is watching you soar.

My Wild + Free community: The ones who have answered the call. I'm so grateful to link arms with you and reclaim the wonder of childhood together.

My agent, Alex Field: You took a chance on a homeschool mom with an idea for a book and helped bring it into existence. Your calm, steady guidance through it all was exactly what I needed.

Katy Hamilton: You believed in this book from the start. As an editor extraordinaire, your thoughtful consideration and skillful shaping of the content brought this beautiful book into existence.

Judith Curr, Laina Adler, and the entire HarperOne team: You managed to create a book that was better than I could have ever imagined.

Susan Schaeffer Macaulay: Your insightful books put words to my heart's desires when I was just at the beginning of my motherhood journey. On behalf of this generation of mothers, our children, and our children's children: thank you for answering the call in your life.

Dad: You shaped me more than you know by always valuing my thoughts and opinions when I was just a whippersnapper. You made me feel ten feet tall.

Mom: What more can I say? It was always you.

Jennifer Naraki: You often called me "Bold One," and I can't help but think you helped speak this book into being. You are deeply missed, my friend, but your beautiful spirit lives on.

Last but not least, my dear friends: You know who you are. Your encouragement, insight, and support this past year spurred me on to the finish line. My life is richer because of you.

Notes

Chapter 1: The Light Went Out in His Eyes

1. "Teens More Stressed-Out than Adults, Survey Shows," NBC News, February 11, 2014, https://www.nbcnews.com/health/kids-health/teens-more-stressed-out-adults-survey-shows-n26921.

2. John Holt, *Learning All the Time* (New York: Perseus Books, 1989), 110.

3. Susan Wise Bauer, *Rethinking School: How to Take Charge of Your Child's Education* (New York: W. W. Norton, 2018), 112.

Chapter 2: Reclaiming Motherhood

1. There is no right way to homeschool our children, and the main educator will vary from family to family. I know homeschooling mothers of all kinds—those who stay at home full-time, some who work from home, and others who work away from home. And I know wonderful fathers who do the same, joining the homeschooling efforts full-time, part-time, or not at all.

2. Penelope Trunk, "Moms Do Most of the Homeschooling Because Duh," *Penelope Trunk* (blog), September 27, 2016, http://education.penelopetrunk.com/2016/09/27/moms-do-most-of-the-homeschooling-because-duh.

3. Jeff Green, "Men Still Outnumber Women 2-to-1 as Speakers at Conferences," *Bloomberg News*, November 1, 2018, https://www .bloomberg.com/news/articles/2018–11–01/men-still -outnumber-women-2-to-1-as-speakers-at-conferences.

4. Wild + Free (@wildandfree.co), Instagram post, n.d., https:// www.instagram.com/p/BmBOX1zgdLQ/.

Chapter 3: The Call to Homeschooling

1. Ryan P. Denee, "Making the Most of Family Time," *Real Truth*, n.d., https://rcg.org/realtruth/articles/070629-001-mtmoft.html.

2. Ken Robinson, *The Element: How Finding Your Passion Changes Everything* (New York: Penguin Books, 2009), 238.

3. Jean Piaget and Peter H. Wolff, *Play and Development: A Symposium with Contributions by Jean Piaget, Peter H. Wolff, René A. Spitz, Konrad Lorenz, Lois Barclay Murphy, and Erik H. Erikson*, ed. Maria W. Piers et al. (New York: W. W. Norton, 1972), 27.

4. Piaget and Wolff, *Play and Development*, p. 27.

5. Peter Gray, "Kids Learn Math Easily When They Control Their Own Learning," *Psychology Today* (blog), April 15, 2010, https:// www.psychologytoday.com/us/blog/freedom-learn/201004 /kids-learn-math-easily-when-they-control-their-own-learning.

Chapter 4: Preparing for Your Journey

1. Mariam Issimdar, "Homeschooling in the UK Increases 40% over Three Years," BBC News, April 26, 2018, https://www.bbc .com/news/uk-england-42624220.

2. Nikki Moore (@moorelittlemen), Instagram post, n.d., https:// www.instagram.com/p/BsdnWjlFi4W/.

Chapter 5: Becoming Wild + Free

1. Peter Gray, *Free to Learn: Why Unleashing the Instinct to Play Will Make Our Children Happier, More Self-Reliant, and Better Students for Life* (New York: Basic Books, 2013), 5.

2. Susan Schaeffer Macaulay, *For the Children's Sake: Foundations of Education for Home and School* (Wheaton, IL: Crossway Books, 1984), 90.

3. A. C. H. Smith, *Jim Henson's Labyrinth: The Novelization* (Los Angeles: Archaia, 2014), 89.

Chapter 6: Objections to Homeschooling

1. Mahita Gajanan, "The Cost of Raising a Child Jumps to $233,610," *Money*, January 9, 2017, http://time.com/money /4629700/child-raising-cost-department-of-agriculture-report/.

2. Brian D. Ray, "Homeschooling Growing: Multiple Data Points Show Increase 2012 to 2016 and Later," NHERI (National Home Education Research Institute) (blog), April 20, 2018, https:// www.nheri.org/homeschool-population-size-growing/.

Chapter 7: The Socialization Myth

1. Elisa Meyer, "Homeschooling Parents Stop Teaching Because the Rapture Is Coming," World Religion News (blog), November 15, 2015, https://www.worldreligionnews.com /religion-news/christianity/homeschooling-parents-stop -teaching-because-the-rapture-is-coming.

2. Haley Potter, "Do Home-Schoolers Do Better in College than Traditional Students?," *USA Today*, February 18, 2012, http:// college.usatoday.com/2012/02/18/do-home-schoolers-do-better -in-college-than-traditional-students/.

3. Potter, "Do Home-Schoolers Do Better?"

4. Not the child's real name.

5. Isabel Shaw, "Social Skills and Homeschooling: Myths and Facts," FamilyEducation.com, n.d., https://www.familyeducation.com /school/homeschooling-socialization/social-skills-homeschooling -myths-facts.

6. Peter Gray, *Free to Learn: Why Unleashing the Instinct to Play Will Make Our Children Happier, More Self-Reliant, and Better Students for Life* (New York: Basic Books, 2013).

7. Gray, *Free to Learn*, 197.

8. Gray, *Free to Learn*, 197.

9. Gray, *Free to Learn*, 203.

10. Gray, *Free to Learn*, 203.

Chapter 8: The Qualification Myth

1. John Holt, *How Children Learn* (Boston: Da Capo Press, 1983), 105.

2. Susan Wise Bauer, "A Homeschooling Conversation with Susan Wise Bauer: Advice for Newbies, Curriculum, and Terrible, No-Good Days," *Keeper of the Home* (blog), May 14, 2012, https://

keeperofthehome.org/a-homeschooling-conversation-with-susan
-wise-bauer-advice-for-newbies-curriculum-and-terrible-no-good
-days/.

Chapter 9: The Learning Myth

1. William Torrey Harris, *The Philosophy of Education* (New York: D. Appleton, 1906).

2. Henry Beston, *The Best of Beston: A Selection from the Natural World of Henry Beston from Cape Cod to the St. Lawrence*, ed. Elizabeth Jane Coatsworth (New York: David R. Godine, 2001), 83.

3. Friedrich Froebel, *The Education of Man*, trans. W. N. Hailmann (New York: D. Appleton and Co., 1892), 1–2.

4. David Elkind, "The Price of Hurrying Children," *Psychology Today* (blog), June 27, 2008, https://www.psychologytoday.com /us/blog/digital-children/200806/the-price-hurrying-children.

5. John Holt, *How Children Learn* (Boston: Da Capo Press, 1983), 50.

6. Holt, *How Children Learn*, 50–51.

7. Susan Wise Bauer, *Rethinking School: How to Take Charge of Your Child's Education* (New York: W. W. Norton, 2018).

8. Marion Brady, "What Do Standardized Tests Actually Test?," *Washington Post*, August 1, 2014, https://www.washingtonpost.com /news/answer-sheet/wp/2014/08/01/what-do-standardized -tests-actually-test/?utm_term=.1cc60e87d618.

9. Julie Bogart, "It All Adds Up," Brave Writer, February 10, 2014, http://blog.bravewriter.com/2014/02/10/homeschool-advice-it -all-adds-up/.

10. Julie Bogart with Ainsley Arment, "Practical Tips for Natural Learning," *Wild + Free* podcast, Episode 33, April 8, 2018, https:// soundcloud.com/bewildandfree/episode33.

Chapter 10: The Rigor Myth

1. Joseph Mercola, "Hydrogen Peroxide or Soap and Water to Clean Your Wound?," Mercola.com, June 11, 2016, https:// articles.mercola.com/sites/articles/archive/2016/06/11 /hydrogen-peroxide-wound-cleaning.aspx.

2. Susan Schaeffer Macaulay, *For the Children's Sake: Foundations of Education for Home and School* (Wheaton, IL: Crossway Books, 1984), 89.

3. Lori McWilliam Pickert, *Project-Based Homeschooling: Mentoring Self-Directed Learners* (North Charleston, SC: CreateSpace, 2012), 11.

4. Sarah Mackenzie, *Teaching from Rest: A Homeschooler's Guide to Unshakable Peace* (Camp Hill, PA: Classical Academic Press, 2015), 4.

Chapter 11: The College Myth

1. Blake Boles, "11 Great Reasons to Skip College," *Blake Boles dot com* (blog), n.d., https://www.blakeboles.com/2011/05/11-great-reasons-to-skip-college/.

2. Kelsey Sheehy, "Home-Schooled Teens Ripe for College," *U.S. News & World Report*, June 1, 2012, https://www.usnews.com/education/high-schools/articles/2012/06/01/home-schooled-teens-ripe-for-college.

3. Sheehy, "Home-Schooled Teens Ripe for College."

4. Haley Potter, "Do Home-Schoolers Do Better in College than Traditional Students?," *USA Today*, February 18, 2012, http://college.usatoday.com/2012/02/18/do-home-schoolers-do-better-in-college-than-traditional-students/.

5. Princeton University Undergraduate Admission, n.d., https://admission.princeton.edu/how-apply/home-schooled-students.

6. Jennifer Gonzalez, "Three Reasons Students Don't Get into Top Colleges," *Cult of Pedagogy* podcast, Episode 69 transcript, n.d., https://www.cultofpedagogy.com/episode-69/.

7. Boles, "11 Great Reasons to Skip College."

Chapter 13: The Influences of Homeschooling

1. CiRCE Institute, "Definitions of Terms," n.d., https://www.circeinstitute.org/resources-what-classical-education/definitions-terms.

2. Susan Wise Bauer, "What Is Classical Education?," WellTrainedMind.com, last updated June 3, 2009, https://welltrainedmind.com/a/classical-education/.

3. CiRCE Institute, "Definitions of Terms."

4. "Fast Facts," Classical Conversations, n.d., https://members.classicalconversations.com/christian/about/fast-facts.

5. Leigh A. Bortins, *The Question: Teaching Your Child the Essentials of Classical Education* (Southern Pines, NC: Classical Conversations Books, 2013).

6. Dorothy Sayers, *The Lost Tools of Learning* (Louisville, KY: GLH, 2016), 23.

7. Andrew Kern, "Why Latin, Pars Quattuor: Civilization," CiRCE Institute, May 25, 2012, https://www.circeinstitute.org/2012/05/why-latin-pars-quinta-civilization.

8. Author interview with Elsie Iudicello, March 27–31, 2019.

9. "The Montessori Approach," Small World Montessori School, n.d., http://swmschool.org/programs/the-montessori-approach/.

10. Valeria Maltoni, "Women of Impact: Maria Montessori, Broke Gender Barriers," n.d., https://italianstyle.me/women-of-impact-maria-montessori-broke-gender-barriers/.

11. Susan Schaeffer Macaulay, *For the Children's Sake: Foundations of Education for Home and School* (Wheaton, IL: Crossway Books, 1984), 86.

12. "Waldorf 101: The Art of Waldorf Education," Whidbey Island Waldorf School, n.d., http://www.wiws.org/about-waldorf-education/waldorf-faq/.

13. Robert Mays and Sune Nordwall, "What Is Waldorf Education?," n.d., https://waldorfanswers.org/Waldorf.htm.

14. *Oxford English Dictionary*, s.v. "anthroposphy, noun [mass noun]," accessed May 1, 2019, https://en.oxforddictionaries.com/definition/anthroposophy.

15. LeadTogether, "Core Principles of Waldorf Education from the Pedagogical Section Council of North America," amended August 2014, http://leadtogether.org/core-principles-waldorf-education-psc-2014/.

16. Carolyn Edwards, Lella Gandini, and George Forman, eds., *The Hundred Languages of Children: The Reggio Emilia Approach to Early Childhood Education* (Norwood, NJ: Ablex, 1993), 79.

17. Louise Boyd Cadwell, *Bringing Reggio Emilia Home: An Innovative Approach to Early Childhood Education* (New York: Teachers College Press, 1997), 52.

18. Edwards et al., *Hundred Languages of Children*, 71.

19. Patrick Farenga, "The Foundations of Unschooling" (revised version of keynote speech to the Irish Unschooling Conference, May 2016), *John Holt GWS* (blog), https://www.johnholtgws.com/the-foundations-of-unschooling.

20. Paraphrased from Pam Sorooshian, "Principles of Unschooling," http://sandradodd.com/pam/principles.html.

21. Stephanie Hanes, "Free-Range Education: Why the Unschooling Movement Is Growing," *Christian Science Monitor*, February 14, 2016, https://www.csmonitor.com/USA/Education/2016/0214/Free-range-education-Why-the-unschooling-movement-is-growing.

22. Farenga, "Foundations of Unschooling."

23. Edwards et al., *Hundred Languages of Children*, xii.

Chapter 15: Creating a Family Culture

1. Lawrence J. Cohen, *Playful Parenting: An Exciting New Approach to Raising Children That Will Help You Nurture Close Connections, Solve Behavior Problems, and Encourage Confidence* (New York: Ballantine Books, 2001), 5.

2. Cohen, *Playful Parenting*, 142.

Chapter 17: The School of Nature

1. Scott D. Sampson, *How to Raise a Wild Child: The Art and Science of Falling in Love with Nature* (New York: Mariner Books, 2016), 14.

2. Susan Schaeffer Macaulay, *For the Children's Sake: Foundations of Education for Home and School* (Wheaton, IL: Crossway Books, 1984), 156.

3. Victoria L. Dunckley, "Nature's Rx: Green-Time's Effects on ADHD," *Psychology Today* (blog), June 20, 2013, https://www.psychologytoday.com/us/blog/mental-wealth/201306/natures-rx-green-times-effects-adhd.

4. Sampson, *How to Raise a Wild Child*, 37.

5. Richard Louv, *Last Child in the Woods: Saving Our Children from Nature-Deficit Disorder* (Chapel Hill, NC: Algonquin Books of Chapel Hill, 2008), 47–48.

6. Cecilie Cronwald, "Free Play More Important than Organised Sport," *ScienceNordic*, December 28, 2011, http://sciencenordic.com/free-play-more-important-organised-sport.

7. Linda Åkeson McGurk, *There's No Such Thing as Bad Weather: A Scandinavian Mom's Secrets for Raising Healthy, Resilient, and Confident Kids (from Friluftsliv to Hygge)* (New York: Touchstone, 2017).

8. Louv, *Last Child in the Woods*, 7.

9. Josée Bergeron, "Positive Ways to Talk to Kids About the Weather," *Backwoods Mama* (blog), January 13, 2019, https://www.backwoodsmama.com/2019/01/positive-ways-to-talk-to-kids-about-the-weather.html.

10. Bergeron, "Positive Ways to Talk to Kids."

11. David Sobel, *Nature Preschools and Forest Kindergartens: The Handbook for Outdoor Learning* (St. Paul, MN: Redleaf Press, 2016), 109.

12. Alison Flood, "Oxford Junior Dictionary's Replacement of 'Natural' Words with 21st-Century Terms Sparks Outcry," *The Guardian*, January 13, 2015, https://www.theguardian.com/books/2015/jan/13/oxford-junior-dictionary-replacement-natural-words.

13. Peter Gray, *Free to Learn: Why Unleashing the Instinct to Play Will Make Our Children Happier, More Self-Reliant, and Better Students for Life* (New York: Basic Books, 2013), 180.

14. Charlotte M. Mason, *Home Education*, Charlotte Mason Home Education Series, Bk. 1 (Jilliby, New South Wales: Living Book Press, 2017), 61.

15. Erica Beck Spencer, "Nature Journaling with Expert John Muir Laws: Not Just for Nature-Loving Teachers!," Delta Education, March 7, 2017, https://www.deltaeducation.com/resources/blog/mar-2017/nature-journaling-with-expert-john-muir-laws.

16. Anna Botsford Comstock, *Handbook of Nature Study* (Oxford: Benediction Classics, 2009), 2.

17. Louv, *Last Child in the Woods*, 226, 173.

Chapter 18: The Power of Story

1. Sarah Clarkson, *Caught Up in a Story: Fostering a Storyformed Life of Great Books and Imagination with Your Children* (Monument, CO: Storyformed Press, 2013), 25.

2. Sarah Mackenzie, *The Read-Aloud Family: Making Meaningful and Lasting Connections with Your Kids* (Grand Rapids, MI: Zondervan, 2018), 51.

3. Neil Postman, *The End of Education: Redefining the Value of School* (New York: Vintage Books, 1995), 116.

4. Jim Trelease, *The Read-Aloud Handbook* (New York: Penguin Books, 2013), 45.

5. Gladys M. Hunt, *Honey for a Child's Heart: The Imaginative Use of Books in Family Life* (Grand Rapids, MI: Zondervan, 2002), 27, 30.

6. Susan Schaeffer Macaulay, *For the Children's Sake: Foundations of Education for Home and School* (Wheaton, IL: Crossway Books, 1984), 115.

7. Trelease, *Read-Aloud Handbook*, 4.

8. Child Trends, "Reading to Young Children," updated February 2013, https://www.childtrends.org/wp-content/uploads/2015/06/indicator_1434077726.6918.html.

9. Harris Eisenberg, "Humans Process Visual Data Better," Thermopylae Sciences and Technology, September 15, 2014, http://www.t-sciences.com/news/humans-process-visual-data-better.

10. Erica Reischer, "Can Reading Logs Ruin Reading for Kids?," *The Atlantic*, June 3, 2016, https://www.theatlantic.com/education/archive/2016/06/are-reading-logs-ruining-reading/485372.

11. Reischer, "Can Reading Logs Ruin Reading for Kids?"

12. Christina Clark and Kate Rumbold, National Literacy Trust, "Reading for Pleasure: A Research Overview," November 2006, https://files.eric.ed.gov/fulltext/ED496343.pdf.

13. Stephen Krashen, "Free Voluntary Reading: New Research, Applications, and Controversies" (paper presented at RELC Conference, Singapore, April 2004), http://www.sdkrashen.com/content/articles/singapore.pdf.

14. Sarah Mackenzie, *The Read-Aloud Family: Making Meaningful and Lasting Connections with Your Kids* (Grand Rapids, MI: Zondervan, 2018), 93.

Chapter 19: The Pedagogy of Play

1. David Sobel, *Nature Preschools and Forest Kindergartens: The Handbook for Outdoor Learning* (St. Paul, MN: Redleaf Press, 2016), 63.

2. Victoria Clayton, "Should Preschools Teach All Work and No Play?," NBCNEWS.com, updated August 6, 2007, http://www.nbcnews.com/id/20056147/ns/health-childrens_health/t/should-preschools-teach-all-work-no-play/#.XF96HC2ZMnU.

3. Sobel, *Nature Preschools and Forest Kindergartens*, 41.

4. Vince Gowmon, "Inspiring Quotes on Child Learning and Development," VinceGowmon.com, https://www.vincegowmon .com/inspiring-quotes-on-child-learning-and-development/.

5. Peter Gray, *Free to Learn: Why Unleashing the Instinct to Play Will Make Our Children Happier, More Self-Reliant, and Better Students for Life* (New York: Basic Books, 2013), 175.

6. Valerie Strauss, "How 'Twisted' Early Childhood Education Has Become—from a Child Development Expert," *Washington Post*, November 24, 2015, https://www.washingtonpost.com /news/answer-sheet/wp/2015/11/24/how-twisted-early -childhood-education-has-become-from-a-child-development -expert/?noredirect=on&utm_term=.90b96c5f0af1.

7. Edward Miller and Joan Almon, *Crisis in the Kindergarten: Why Children Need to Play in School* (College Park, MD: Alliance for Childhood, 2009), 7.

8. Sobel, *Nature Preschools and Forest Kindergartens* (Saint Paul, MN: Redleaf Press, 2016), 84.

9. University of Otago, New Zealand, "Research Finds No Advantage in Learning to Read from Age Five," December 21, 2009, https://www.otago.ac.nz/news/news/otago006408.html.

10. David Whitebread and Sue Bingham, "Too Much, Too Young: Should Schooling Start at Age 7?," *New Scientist*, November 13, 2013, https://www.newscientist.com/article/mg22029435-000 -too-much-too-young-should-schooling-start-at-age-7.

11. Whitebread quoted in Priya Mahtani, "School Starting Age," http://www.stpaulssteinerschool.org/wp-content/uploads/2015 /12/school_strating_age.pdf.

12. Susan Schaeffer Macaulay, *For the Children's Sake: Foundations of Education for Home and School* (Wheaton, IL: Crossway Books, 1984), 126.

13. Helen Keller, *The Story of My Life* (New York: Dover, 1996), 22.

14. Lori McWilliam Pickert, *Project-Based Homeschooling: Mentoring Self-Directed Learners* (North Charleston, SC: CreateSpace, 2012), 131.

Chapter 20: The Curriculum of Curiosity

1. Lauren McGaughy, "Who's 'Essential'? See How Historical Figures Are Ranked as Texas Trims What It Teaches," *Dallas*

News, updated September 24, 2018, https://www.dallasnews
.com/news/education/2018/09/20/hillary-clinton-helen
-keller-could-cut-history-classes-texas-else-could-get-ax.

2. Juliet Robertson, "Simon Nicholson and the Theory of Loose
    Parts—1 Million Thanks," Creative Star Learning, December 8,
    2017, https://creativestarlearning.co.uk/early-years-outdoors
    /simon-nicholson-and-the-theory-of-loose-parts-1-million-thanks.

3. Simon Nicholson, "How NOT to Cheat Children: The Theory of
    Loose Parts," *Landscape Architecture* 62 (October 1971): 30–34,
    https://media.kaboom.org/docs/documents/pdf/ip/Imagination
    -Playground-Theory-of-Loose-Parts-Simon-Nicholson.pdf.

4. Lori McWilliam Pickert, *Project-Based Homeschooling: Mentoring
    Self-Directed Learners* (North Charleston, SC: CreateSpace,
    2012), 108.

5. Paul Tough, *How Children Succeed: Grit, Curiosity, and the Hidden
    Power of Character* (New York: Houghton Mifflin Harcourt, 2012),
    33–34.

6. Tough, *How Children Succeed,* xv.

7. Walter Isaacson, *Einstein: His Life and Universe* (New York: Simon
    & Schuster, 2007), 14–15.

8. George Lucas Educational Foundation, "Sir Ken Robinson on
    the Power of the Imaginative Mind (Part Two)," *Edutopia* (blog),
    October 15, 2008, https://www.edutopia.org/video/sir-ken
    -robinson-power-imaginative-mind-part-two.

Chapter 21: The Magic of Wonder

1. Maria Popova, "Robert Sapolsky on Science and Wonder," *Brain
    Pickings* (blog), n.d., https://www.brainpickings.org/2012/08
    /28/robert-sapolsky-on-science-and-wonder/.